eos

EOS Cycling Holidays

Published by EOS Cycling Holidays Ltd, Manchester, United Kingdom
ISBN: 978-0-95776617-4-5
Copyright © Eric van der Horst, 2022

Maps 1:25.000 and 1:50.000 scales are licensed under the Open Data Commons Open Database License (ODbL) by the OpenStreetMap Foundation (OSMF), openstreetmap.org and opendatacommons.org.
© OpenStreetMap contributors

Maps 1:1... ...nted by Philip's and ...ional. Based upon ...ap data with the ...Stationery Office. ...Licence Number ...d.

...nd author have ...accuracy of all ...book. However, ...le for any errors ...o responsibility ...ence sustained ...of information ...uidebook, via ...S tracks and/ ...esentation on ...r GPS tracks ...dence of the

...nd Oscar ...Kees C.

...nted by Latitude Press, Windermere, Cumbria, United Kingdom

C0000054134

England North-South Cycle Route

From Scotland to the Isle of Wight, with the best of the North Sea Cycle Route

Eric van der Horst

Contents

The table below shows how the route is divided into 20 sections. It includes a brief summary of the characteristics; traffic-free routes in bold.

Route	Route Section	Distance	🚲	🚶	🚌	🚗	Grading of terrain	Highlights	Page
1	Berwick upon Tweed - Alnwick	81 km	17%	68%	14%	1%	Generally easy, some short climbs	Berwick, Lindisfarne Holy Island, Bamburgh & Dunstanburgh Castles, Northumberland Coast	24
2	Alnwick - Newcastle	83 km	41%	54%	5%	-	Generally easy, one moderate climb	Alnwick, Warkworth & Tynemouth Castles, Woodhorn Museum, Northumberland Coast	30
3A	Newcastle - Heddon on the Wall	31 km	79%	18%	3%	-	Generally easy, one serious climb	*Hadrian's Cycle Way*, Tyne Estuary, Newcastle's Grainger Town & Castle	38
3B	Newcastle - Heddon on the Wall	44 km	68%	28%	4%	-	Moderate to hard, some serious climbing	Angel of the North, *Hadrian's Cycle Way*, Tyne Estuary, Newcastle's Grainger Town & Castle	38
4	Heddon on the Wall - Durham	53 km	89%	10%	1%	-	Generally easy, some moderate climbs	Hadrian's Wall at Heddon on the Wall, *Derwent Walk Country Park*, *Lanchester Way*	46
5	Durham - Middlesbrough	66 km	61%	32%	7%	-	Generally easy, some short climbs	Durham World Heritage, Hartlepool Headland and Museums, River Tees Transporter Bridge	52
6	Middlesbrough - Whitby	68 km	21%	70%	9%	-	Moderate to hard, some serious climbing	Captain Cook's School, North York Moors National Park, Commondale Moor, Esk Dale	60
7	Whitby - Scarborough	60 km	53%	24%	22%	1%	Moderate to hard, some serious climbing	Whitby Town & Abbey, *Cinder Track*, North Yorkshire Coast, Scarborough Castle & Beaches	66
8	Scarborough - York	63 km	-	100%	-	-	Moderate, some serious climbing	Yorkshire Wolds, Sledmere House, Wharram Percy deserted village, Stamford Bridge	74
9A	Scarborough - Hull	71 km	36%	59%	5%	-	Generally easy, some moderate climbs	Burton Agnes Hall, East Riding, Hornsea Coast, *Trans Pennine Trail*	78
9B	Scarborough - Hull	100 km	30%	59%	10%	1%	Moderate, some serious climbing, then easy	Flamborough Head, Bridlington Coast, East Riding, Hornsea Coast, *Trans Pennine Trail*	78
10	Hull - York	72 km	18%	73%	8%	1%	Generally easy, some short climbs	City of Hull, Beverley old town, lower Yorkshire Wolds, Pocklington, Stamford Bridge	84
11	York - Doncaster	88 km	48%	37%	14%	1%	Generally easy	York (cathedral, museums, walls), *Trans Pennine Trail*, Humberhead Levels, Selby Abbey	90
12	Doncaster - Oughtibridge	58km	61%	33%	5%	1%	Moderate, some serious climbing	Doncaster, Sprotbrough Falls, *Trans Pennine & Upper Don Trails*, Wharncliffe Woods	98
13	Oughtibridge - Ashbourne	100 km	44%	54%	1%	1%	Hard to strenuous, a lot of serious climbing	Peak District National Park, Stanage Edge, Castleton caves, Bakewell, *Monsal & Tissington Trails*	104
14	Ashbourne - Leicester	94 km	23%	60%	16%	1%	Generally easy, some short climbs	Derbyshire Dales, Burton-on-Trent brewery, National Forest, *Ivanhoe Trail*, Leicester attractions	112
15	Leicester - Stratford-upon-Avon	99 km	36%	48%	15%	1%	Generally easy, some short climbs	*Great Central Way*, Rugby's rugby site, Stockton Locks, Royal Leamington Spa, Warwick Castle	120
16	Stratford-upon-Avon - Oxford	100 km	20%	75%	4%	1%	Moderate, some serious climbing	Shakespeare's Stratford-upon-Avon, The Cotswolds, Roman Villa, Blenheim Palace, City of Oxford	126
17	Oxford - Alton Barnes	97 km	56%	41%	3%	-	Moderate to hard, some serious climbing	Didcot Railway Centre, Wantage, *The Ridgeway*, Uffington White Horse, Avebury stone circle	134
18	Alton Barnes - Salisbury	47 km	18%	74%	8%	-	Generally easy, some short climbs	Alton Barnes White Horse, Stonehenge stone circle, Old Sarum ruins, Salisbury Cathedral	140
19	Salisbury - Lymington	64 km	15%	76%	8%	1%	Generally easy, some short climbs	New Forest National Park, Bolderwood & Rhinefield Ornamental Drive, *forest trails*, Lymington ferry	144
20	Isle of Wight & Portsmouth	71 km	31%	57%	12%	-	Moderate to hard, some serious climbing	Isle of Wight, The Needles, Alum Bay, *Tennyson Trail*, Sandown beach, Hovertravel for Portsmouth	148

Typical itineraries:

Berwick-upon-Tweed - York - Portsmouth: 1323 km (816 miles)
Newcastle - York - Portsmouth: 1159 km (715 miles)
Berwick-upon-Tweed - York: 505 km (312 miles)
Berwick-upon-Tweed - Hull: 513 km (317 miles)
York - Portsmouth: 818 km (505 miles)
Hull - Portsmouth: 890 km (549 miles)
York - Alton Barnes (for London-Land's End): 636 km (393 miles)
Hull - Alton Barnes (for London-Land's End): 708 km (437 miles)

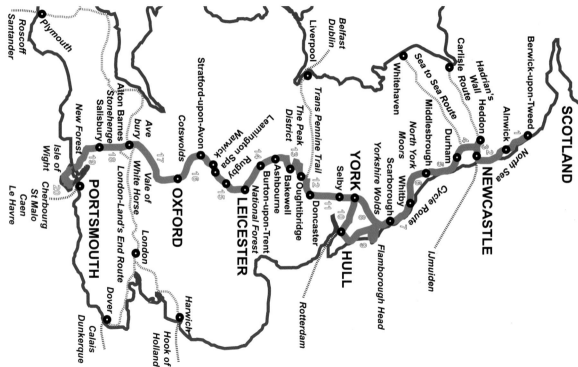

Route Summary

The routes in this book are designed for **touring cyclists** who enjoy **sightseeing** by bicycle, whilst not being hindered by motorised traffic. Our routes are definitely **not the fastest** routes. Instead, we guide you via highlights of outstanding **natural beauty**, **culture**, **architecture** and **history**, with as many **famous landmarks** as possible. Welcome to our **#realjourneys**!

At the Scotland-England border, our route starts by joining the **North Sea Cycle Route** in **Berwick-upon-Tweed**, following it to **Hull** via **Newcastle**, with a direct link to the international ferries in those cities. Our route continues inland to **York**, finding England's spine, southbound through the splendid **Pennines** and **Peak District**. The large industrial cities of the **Midlands** are avoided by meandering via the **National Forest**, historic **Leicester**, **Leamington Spa**, **Warwick** and **Stratford-upon-Avon**. The scenic **Cotswolds** take you to **Oxford**, from where the **Ridgeway** takes you deep south via **Salisbury** to the **New Forest**, the **Isle of Wight** and **Portsmouth**.

Whether you are cycling south from Scotland or taking the train up from Newcastle, the coast of **Northumberland** between **Berwick upon Tweed** and **Newcastle** will take your breath away. **Lindisfarne Holy Island** with its unique causeway and five historic remote castles are the main attractions. One of them is **Alnwick Castle**, famous for its Harry Potter film appearances.

Newcastle is the largest city on the route. With the estuary of the **River Tyne**, things never feel crowded. You cycle via the famous **Angel of the North**, **Millennium Bridge** and historic **Grainger Town** to remains of the Roman **Hadrian's Wall**.

Derwent Walk Country Park features a world class cycle path in a wooded valley, heading for the World Heritage site of **Durham**, with its historic city square, cathedral and castle. Returning to the North Sea Coast, **Hartlepool Headland** and the famous **River Tees Transporter Bridge** take you via industrial **Middlesbrough** into the **North York Moors National Park**.

After a demanding ride in beautiful countryside with moors and valleys, **Whitby** town and abbey are at the start of the coastal **Cinder Track** to the seaside resort **Scarborough**. Cycle to **York** via the Yorkshire Wolds or head for the **Hull** ferry.

From the Hull ferry, you can also join our route south via York. **York** is England's most popular tourist destination after London, famous for its cathedral, city walls and **National Railway** and **Jorvik Museums**. Via the low lying **Humberhead Levels**, **Selby Abbey** and **Doncaster**, the **Trans Pennine Trail** takes you to higher ground. The **Don Valley Trail** via the **Wharncliffe Woods** take you to the **Peak District National Park**.

Via the pretty **Derbyshire Dales**, **Burton on Trent** with its brewery museum and the **National Forest** you'll arrive in **Leicester**. The **National Space Centre** and **King Richard III Museum** can keep you occupied before heading further south to the orginal rugby grounds of **Rugby**, stylish **Royal Leamington Spa**, grand **Warwick Castle** and the hustle and bustle of Shakespeare's **Stratford-upon-Avon**.

The **Cotswolds** are remarkably quiet, featuring hilly countryside hardly affected by modern times. Its marvel is the **Blenheim Palace World Heritage** site, just before arriving in famous **Oxford**. Then you make your way into the **Wessex Downs** via the **Ridgeway**, taking you via **Uffington White Horse** to the World Heritage stone circles of **Avebury** and **Stonehenge**. **Salisbury** is famous for its beautiful cathedral.

At isolated **Stanage Edge** you'll find yourself on the top of the world. This spectacular vaultline of rock continues to **Castleton**, famous for its caves and castle. The **Monsal Trail** features spectacular tunnels and high bridges and takes you to bustling **Bakewell**. The scenic **Tissington Trail** will finally take you out of the hilly Pennines.

Deep south, forest tracks in the **New Forest National Park** take you to the **Isle of Wight** ferry. The cliffs of **The Needles** are your ultimate 'end of the land' finale of the ride. Via the spectacular **Tennyson Trail** you'll arrive at **Sandown Beach** before hovercrafting to bustling **Portsmouth** with its numerous railway and ferry connections.

How to get there: ferries, trains, planes and 'End-to-End'

If you are visiting from the European continent, the North Sea **ferry crossings** between **The Netherlands** and the United Kingdom are the obvious connections to get started on the route. Both **Newcastle** and **Hull** ferry ports are directly on the route, connecting respectively to Amsterdam IJmuiden (www.dfdsseaways.co.uk) and Rotterdam Europoort (www.poferries.com). Our guidebook 'Cycling in Amsterdam and The Netherlands' connects to both these continental ferry terminals, so you could make a full round trip when using both ferries! Sailing times are 11-15 hours, so night crossings are most convenient, as you travel while you sleep; book a cabin!

At the southern end of the route, there are various options to return to the continent, depending on your final destination. From **Portsmouth**, various ferries head for **France**; Cherbourg, Caen, Le Havre and St Malo (www.britanny-ferries.co.uk). French cyclists are recommended to use these ferry connections, travelling from Portsmouth north by train to their desired starting point (see next page) and cycling back south.

From Portsmouth, Dutch, Belgian and German riders could take the **train** to **Dover**, with only one required change in **Brighton** (see next page). From Dover, various ferry operators can take you to Calais or Dunkirk. Those keen on more cycling mileage could connect to our 'London-Land's End Cycle Route' at **Alton Barnes**, cycling east via London to either Dover or Harwich. Dutch-language riders can also consider cycling the coastal Portsmouth-Dover route via the south coast with a guidebook written by Dutch author Kees Swart ('Fietsen rond het Kanaal', ISBN 978-90-77056-33-2).

For mileage-makers who are cycling from **John 'o Groats** in Scotland to **Land's End** in Cornwall, it is possible to use this book in combination with our 'London-Land's End Cycle Route'. By using both books you would be served with a fully-described route for the English section of the journey between Berwick-upon-Tweed and Land's End in Cornwall. Once again, change books at Alton Barnes, where the two routes cross.

Monumental York Station with its famous curve

If you are traveling to the United Kingdom from overseas, it is important to know that European ID cards are no longer sufficient to enter the United Kingdom. You will need a passport, valid for at least six months from the date of arrival.

Those who wish to fly to the UK can best then travel by train to either York, Oxford or Brockenhurst and rent bikes from the rentals there. You'll then have to take bicycles on the train either at the start or end of your ride (or both). Note that bike rentals and bike repair shops on the way are both listed from page 154.

Typical bike space on Cross Country Trains

There are 49 **stations** where you can join or leave the route. Taking bicycles on trains is free but capacity is limited. Relevant is the **Cross Country Trains** service between **Edinburgh** and **Bournemouth** with a compulsory change at station **Birmingham New Street**. Major stations on this route are shown on the map on the right.

An example of bike spaces on these trains is in the picture on the left. You will have to hang your front wheel on a hook, taking off all your luggage. There are three such spaces available in a unit, with a regular train normally having two units on board. Travel between Berwick-upon-Tweed and Birmingham will take just over four hours, Birmingham-Portsmouth with a change at Southampton takes about three hours. Expect such long-distance connections to run about 4-5 times per day. It is practical to keep changes to a minimum, as changing trains with bikes is not the most relaxing thing to do. For longer journeys buy **tickets in advance** to keep the price acceptable (£230 pp for Berwick-Portsmouth at best) and to have a **reserved space** for your bike. Book online via www.crosscountrytrains.co.uk.

How you could do it: a sample itinerary

Here we have a sample itinerary, showing how you could cycle the full route in three to four weeks. Remember, any itinerary is possible as the accommodation listings cover the full route. Also, note the itinerary in this chapter does not match the route sections as shown on pages 2/3.

Day 1: Berwick-West Mains (35 km/22 miles)

Whether you opted to rent bikes from **York** bike rental, arrived by ferry in **Newcastle** (and cycled to Newcastle's station via our direct route on pages 39 and 43) or did any other 'bikes on the train' scenario; disembark in **Berwick** around lunch time. Have a browse around town, possibly with a visit to the local museums. Via **Spittal Promenade** you cycle the coast to the **tidal causeway** of **Lindisfarne**. Check you still have three hours for a safe crossing, so you can visit the Abbey and Castle on the island, making your way back to the mainland before high tide. The cosy bunkhouse, small campsite and B&B in **West Mains** and **Fenwick** are then nearby.

Day 2: West Mains-Alnwick (70 km/43 miles)

This is the ultimate day ride for castle fans, as the castles of **Bamburgh** and **Dunstanburgh**, dramatically located on the Northumberland coast, are both worth a visit in their own right. Mind you, **Alnwick Castle**, at the end of today's ride, has the boldest appearance, famous for the Harry Potter films. If you wish to visit all castles, consider splitting this stage into two days, for example with a stay at coastal **Seahouses**. If you limit yourself to one day, visit Alwick Castle in the afternoon, followed by a stay in town. Campers can stay in **Embleton** or **Creswell**.

Day 3: Alnwick-Newcastle (111 km/69 miles)

This is an exploring stage from the countryside into the 'big city', making it a long, rewarding day. A first serious climb takes you via **Warkworth Castle** back to Northumberland's coast. Its scenery up to **Lynemouth** is stunning, but then large industrial sites push us inland. The industrial heritage **Woodhorn Museum** could provide for an extended lunch. From **Blyth** the coastal route is once again at its best, all the way into **Newcastle**. Take our route via the Tyne Cycle Tunnel and **Angel of the North** statue before checking in at the central YHA or a hotel.

Day 4: Newcastle-Durham (73 km/45 miles)

Today's cycling distance allows you to browse Newcastle's **Grainger Town** in the morning, possibly with a visit to **Newcastle Castle**. Late morning, make your way to **Heddon on the Wall** to have a picnic in the field next to the remains of **Hadrian's Wall**. After lunch, there is plenty of time to ride the scenic **Derwent Walk Country Park** route via the high ground at **Consett**. Take in views from **Hownsgill Viaduct** just off the **Lanchester Way**. This route takes you all the way to **Durham**. Enjoy a B&B stay, with **Haswell** providing the first campsite since Creswell.

Day 5: Durham-Kildale (97 km/60 miles)

Durham with its World Heritage cathedral, castle and bridges is a lovely place, worthy of a two-night stay. This stage takes you to the **Hartlepool Headland**, **Hartlepool Harbour** as well as **Seaton Carew Beach**, which all have their own distinctive identities. Industrial **Middlesbrough** features the unique **Transporter Bridge**, allowing you to cross the **River Tees** in style. Keep on the move and climb steadily towards the **North York Moors**. Beyond lively **Great Ayton**, near **Kildale**, a bunkhouse, a campsite and B&B accommodation are all available.

Day 6: Kildale-Scarborough (78 km/48 miles)

Take the morning to enjoy the scenic dales of **North York Moors National Park**, making your way to tourist magnet **Whitby**. With its harbour, iconic **99 Steps**, **abbey ruins** and links with the famous **Dracula story** you may want to spend an extra day in this area. The YHA has two unique hostels here, right next to the abbey and at **Boggle Hole**, a remote coastal location. The scenery is king on the **Cinder Track**, taking you to the famous coastal resort of **Scarborough**. All accommodation types are available here, as are beaches, a harbour and a castle.

Day 7: Scarborough-York (94 km/58 miles)

This rural stage takes you via **Cayton Bay Beach** into the hills of the **Yorkshire Wolds**. Small attractions on the way are **Sledmere House**, the deserted village of **Wharram Percy**, the **Stamford Bridge** battlefield and **Murton Park**. Those who make use of the **Hull ferry** have their own day stages to/from Hull. Routes merge in **York** where all types of accommodation are available once again.

River Wear at World Heritage City Durham

Whitby Abbey and the famous 'Dracula' cemetery

Day 8: York-Wombwell (96 km/59 miles)

Let's first state that **York** is well worth a two night stay. You shouldn't miss out on the epic walks via **The Shambles** and the medieval city walls, the cathedral and top class museums. If there is a day to be added to your itinerary, it should be here. The following stage is as flat as a pancake across the **Humberhead Levels,** with **Selby Abbey**, **Doncaster** and **Conisbrough Castle** all worth a break on the way. Although accommodation is limited (no hostel or campsite options), **Wombwell** makes a good stage town. More B&Bs can be found in **Penistone.**

Day 9: Wombwell-Castleton (64 km/40 miles)

This is the stage of **the big rise**, taking you up to a height of 445m above sea level in the **Peak District National Park**. Via the **Trans Pennine Trail**, **Upper Don Trail** and **Wharncliffe Woods** you make your way to **Stanage Edge**, the most remote location on our route. This an exposed cliff face where the hard rock from the north touches the softer rock from the south. This all becomes clear in **Castleton** where you can see the old main road crumbling away under the force of nature. Various **caves** are in reach from the hostel and numerous B&Bs, a great afternoon!

Day 10: Castleton-Ashbourne (65 km/40 miles)

A serious climb takes you via the high **Peak Forest** to the world class **Monsal Trail**. Spectacular tunnels and bridges lead you to **Bakewell**. Located in a beautiful valley, this old scenic town is a tourists' favourite, ideal for lunch breaks. Another climb takes you to ancient **Arbor Low**, the 'Stonehenge of the peaks'. The scenic **Tissington Trail** with numerous campsites descends gradually to **Ashbourne**.

Day 11: Ashbourne-Leicester (92 km/57 miles)

The Derbyshire Dales make for a pleasant morning ride to **Burton-on-Trent**, famous for its beer brewing. The **National Brewery Centre** is good lunchtime entertainment. The afternoon brings a ride across the rural **National Forest** area. The **Ivanhoe Trail** takes you into the city of **Leicester**. Pick the **National Space Centre**, **King Richard III Museum**, the **abbey ruins** or remains of the **Roman wall**, depending upon your personal interests. Hostel accommodation is lacking in the area. Nice campsites can be found in **Rosliston**, **Ibstock** and **Ashby Magna**.

Day 12: Leicester-Stratford (95 km/59 miles)

A rural ride takes you via the **Rugby** area (alternative route to the world's first rugby ground available) to the 'triple tourist towns' of **Leamington Spa**, **Warwick** and **Stratford-upon-Avon**. These towns feature elegant buildings, a world class castle and Shakespeare's heritage respectively. It makes sense to split this stage into two, with a stay near Warwick, to see it all. Stratford hosts all types of accommodation.

Day 13: Stratford-Oxford (94 km/58 miles)

The **Stratford-on-Avon Greenway** is the last flat stretch before experiencing some climbing into the **Cotswolds**. This rural hilly area features various country gardens, a **Roman villa** and **Blenheim Palace World Heritage**. Except for **Moreton-in-Marsh** midway, there is not much accommodation available if you want to split this ride into two (recommended for a visit to Blenheim). There are no campsites in the area, except for near **Oxford**. This historic university city with its many attractions and museums is on par with York, well-worth a two night stay.

Day 14: Oxford-Letcombe (35 km/22 miles)

This itinerary caters for exploring Oxford, with the cycling starting from 2pm or so. Don't miss the **Radcliffe Camera**, **Bodleian Library**, **Bridge of Sighs** and **Christ Church Cathedral**. Alternatively, if you like trains, you could spend some serious time at the **Didcot Railway Centre**. Today's short ride leads us via pretty **Wantage** to the start of the **Ridgeway** at **Letcombe Regis**, with a rural bunkhouse, B&B or campsite stay.

Day 15: Letcombe-Salisbury (88 km/54 miles)

Start early today, as progress on the unsurfaced, historic high-land passage of the Ridgeway will be slow. The majestic **Uffington White Horse**, **Barbury Castle** and the stone circle of **Avebury** are all on this route. Only from Avebury, your journey on tarmac resumes. Via Wiltshire's highest hill, **Milk Hill** and the equally impressive **Alton Barnes White Horse** you'll arrive at world famous **Stonehenge**. From here it is a short ride to **Salisbury**. **Old Sarum** and England's highest cathedral spire are eye-catching attractions. Salisbury features a campsite and various B&Bs.

Day 16: Salisbury-Yarmouth (70 km/43 miles)

The **New Forest National Park** takes centre stage on today's ride. In this area of woods and heaths, wild ponies roam free, even in villages. **Bolderwood** makes the perfect spot for a picnic lunch. The **Ornamental Drive** is a scenic forest road. From **Brockenhurst** with its bustling bike rental, you cycle traffic-free on great gravel tracks. From **Lymington Pier**, a ferry brings you to **Yarmouth** on the **Isle of Wight**.

Day 17: Yarmouth-Portsmouth (71 km/44 miles)

The stage starts with a ride via the iconic **Needles**. There are few places in the world where the land ends so dramatically as here. The high **Tennyson Trail** provides more breathtaking views. **Sandown** has a great beach. You may want to spend the night here before taking the hovercraft to Portsmouth. Plan an 18th day for your journey home. (This would be the 24th day when using all 'extra day' options.)

How to use this guidebook

This guidebook contains over 1,300 km (just over 800 miles) of routes. All **route directions** are written in telegram style in such a way that you do not need a bike computer. Maps always match the directions on the same page, with visitor information scattered around it.

Due to space restrictions, the route directions of the book only allow you to cycle **from north to south**. If you wish to cycle in the opposite direction you can use the maps and/or our GPS tracks. To obtain the **GPS tracks** email *eoscyclingholidays@gmail.com* quoting '**GPS-NS-2022**'. We'll email the tracks to you within three working days. Upload the files onto your outdoor navigation device or phone with such an app.

The route is divided into **20 sections**. These are displayed on pages 2 and 3 showing characteristics of all route sections like highlights and grading of the terrain. **Pictorials** show the percentages of types of cycling conditions.

The ⬳ symbol means traffic-free cycling on a cycle path either adjacent to a road or completely separate like on a dismantled railway. The ⬩ symbol stands for quiet road, with only occasional motorised traffic. The ⬰ symbol symbolises a road with possibly fast moving traffic or regular traffic flow. The ⬰⬰ symbol represents a busy main road, where an adjacent footpath is always available.

Percentages of the route types are repeated at the start of every chapter, together with an overview of all **stations** on the way. This allows you to hop on/off trains with the bike and to cycle short route sections. We haven't included **car park** information but free parking is generally available on the outskirts of towns. You'll also find an **elevation chart** at the start of every route section. Note: these charts are generalised for clarity and only give a general idea about the climbing and descending of the stage. They don't show every ascent and descent of the route!

The scales and style of the **maps** do vary per page. Every map has the essential clarity to find your way around. The waypoints on the maps, matching the directions, ensure you are aware of the map scale. The route directions are written in such a way that you should never go wrong! For reasons of clarity we are using **kilometres** on the maps and in the directions of this book; divide by 1.6 to get miles!

On the maps you will also find letters, matching the **facility listings** from page 154. These allow you to quickly find accommodation and/or bike repair shops on or near the route. When a service provider is further away, a dotted line on the map will direct you there, in combination with directions in the listings.

Key to used symbols and abbreviations

→	turn right
←	turn left
↑	straight on
↗	smooth turn right
↖	smooth turn left
↘	sharp turn right
↙	sharp turn left
↱	first turn right, then immediately left
↰	first turn left, then immediately right
⚲	cycle path or cycle lane
↳	quiet road
🚗	road with possibly fast moving traffic or regular traffic flow
🚗🚗	busy main road; an adjacent footpath is always available!
⚜	tourist attraction, viewpoint or location of special interest
⚘	beach or seafront promenade
♨	shop(s)
☕	cafe/pub with light refreshments
🍴	pub/restaurant serving meals
⛱	picnic area or bench at prominent location
⌂	hotel, guesthouse or bed & breakfast
⛪	hostel or bunkhouse (YHA, YMCA or independent)
▲	campsite
⚒	bike repair shop

Newcastle	city, town, village, attraction or rural pub (note the name of a locality is in *italic* if there is a station!)
(1)	National Cycle Route number (signposted)
T-jct	T-junction at the end of a road; either turn left or right
jct	junction
give-way jct	junction where you have to give way to traffic on other roads
rndabt	roundabout
ep	at end of the path
1st rd	first road
2nd p	second path
lhts	traffic lights
ped lhts	pedestrian lights/pedestrian crossing
car pk	car park
imm	immediately
house no	house number

Br	Bridge	Mt	Mount/Market
Cl	Close	Pd	Parade
Cr	Crescent	Pk	Park
Ct	Court	Pl	Place
Dr	Drive	Rd	Road
Gdns	Gardens	Sq	Square
Gn	Green	St	Street
Gr	Grove	Tc	Terrace
Gt	Gate	Wk	Walk
Is	Island	Wy	Way
Ln	Lane		

Cycling culture in England

Cycling as a means of transport has been in decline in England since the 1950s. For more than five decades, **road layouts** have been designed with only motorised traffic in mind. Pedestrians have been pushed onto fenced pavements and cyclists have been largely forgotten. Privatisation of the railways, along with closure of about 15,000 km (9,000 miles) of the railway network, pushed even more people into cars. These policies created a **driving-addicted nation**. Many people think that roads are just made for cars and, sadly, poor role models continue to spread this mindset.

Author Eric van der Horst (middle) acted as 'Cycling Dutchman' ambassador in Devon from 2009 until 2017

However, **change** has been in the air since the 2000s. Congested roads, the environment and the growth of obesity among the population have brought cycling back in the spotlight. The **National Cycle Network** was created by the **Sustrans** charity and the success of **British racing cyclists** made cycling fashionable, with former racer **Chris Boardman** acting as ever-patient, myth-busting cycling-for-all ambassador.

The 2010s brought serious **public debate** about the need for proper cycling infrastructure. Particularly in the large cities, local campaigning groups have been successful getting the cycling message across to their local councils. City centres in London, Bristol and Manchester now feature 'Dutch-style' traffic-free cycle paths, proving to be hugely popular, pushing demand for more quality paths and different street design.

However, the reality is that, away from these hot spots, safe and enjoyable cycle routes for day to day use are still **out of reach** for many people. Most of the English road network remains hostile to cycling, with **continuity** and **quality** being major issues. Cycle paths often feature poor surfaces or can end suddenly. Routes are often poorly signposted and can even keep you deliberately away from an attraction or view.

This guidebook does everything feasible to **overcome** these problems. It principally avoids main roads and keeps away from the bad and ugly as much as possible, providing you with a **fully continuous enjoyable route**. Approximately 65% of our route is signposted with **National Cycle Network** signs (see below). This network, created by the Sustrans charity is a great resource for exploring by bike. However, to be able to create our continuous route north-south, we had to utilise some cycle routes with very poor surface. Walking your bike or avoiding these sections altogether may be necessary for you; see page 18 for more information.

Our England North-South Cycle Route uses large parts of routes 1, 5, 6, 14, 24, 41, 44, 45, 54, 62, 63, 65, 66, 68, 72, 165 and 166 , **celebrating the achievements** of the National Cycle Network (NCN). Our route is 35% traffic-free. The Hadrian's Cycle Way, Derwent Valley Country Park, Lanchester and Great Central Ways, Cinder Track, Trans Pennine, Upper Don, Monsal, Tissington, Ivanhoe and Tennyson Trails, the Ridgeway and forest tracks in the New Forest all provide amazing scenery. The connecting friendly lanes take you into rural England, with beautiful towns and villages to be discovered, not to mention all those famous landmarks; the ultimate mix!

Some "new cyclists" or "cyclists to be" might be put off by the fact that 65% of the routes in this book are indeed on-road. Be reassured that the vast majority of the journeys in this book are on **very quiet roads**. However, it helps a lot if you are able **to take control** over traffic situations as a cyclist and that you are aware of the main hazards and risks. Essential theory and helpful techniques can be found on pages 16 and 17.

International visitors need to be reminded that the British **keep to the left**, whether they travel on a road or a cycle path. If you are used to riding on the right, keeping left is a serious blow to all natural reflexes you normally use when participating in traffic. Be extremely cautious when taking junctions. Work out for yourself where you are supposed to be and look everywhere before making a move! Also, keep reminding each other to cycle on the left, especially on quiet roads and after a break. Most people quickly adapt to ride on the left, but remaining "aware" of riding on the left is essential!

Route types and your cycling style

Traffic-free cyclepaths 🚲 (35%):

English cycle paths are always **shared** with pedestrians, which sometimes causes conflicts. Cyclists should always **give way** to pedestrians, slowing down when approaching and ringing their bell. You will notice many pedestrians find it difficult to deal with cyclists. They tend to step out of the way in the direction you don't expect or can be very slow to react. Unfortunately, this means you often end up cycling dead-slow, especially if there are dogs and children around. Always try to pass as wide as possible. On narrow canal paths ("tow paths") cyclists are also expected to give way to fishermen and boaters. On cycle paths running parallel to a main road, you are generally expected to give way to traffic moving in and out of side roads and driveways. Occasionally, this book takes you onto a **footpath** or pedestrian street where cycling is forbidden. Please obey the "dismount" notes in the directions and walk bikes on these sections to avoid issues.

Quiet roads 🚶 (58%):

On (very) quiet roads, the biggest risk for a cyclist is being hit by cars moving in and out of **driveways** and **side roads**. These turning drivers look for other cars, so be where drivers look! **Be visible** and try to cycle in the **middle of your side of the road** passing side roads.

Be **always on your guard** for traffic joining the road you are on and be sure to make **eye contact** with any turning drivers to check they've seen you. As a general rule, you should keep **at least one metre** away from the road side.

Another risk for cyclists on quiet roads is **hazardous overtaking** by traffic from behind. You should play an active role to ensure that overtaking takes place safely. If you hear a car approaching from behind, try to move out to the middle of your side of the road before the vehicle gets close. This will **force** traffic to **slow down**!

Looking over your shoulder also helps, as it makes you a person, rather than being an object "in the way". Meanwhile, keep going; it is your right to do so. It is essential to maintain your "middle in the lane position" until you feel it is safe for drivers to overtake you. To show you are happy to be overtaken, pull back to your "normal metre from the roadside" position and temporarily stop pedaling, looking again over your shoulder as necessary. If drivers still hesitate you could wave them through! On narrow roads, you might want to pull in and stop to let traffic through.

Avoid cycling through narrow gaps with moving traffic around you. Also, stay well away from **parked cars**, **buses** and **lorries**. When overtaking these, wait until it is clear before moving to the opposite side of the road and keep ample space; don't get hit by an opening door, or worse, a vehicle pulling out! Also, **adjust your own speed** to factors such as visibility, surface and weather conditions; know your own brakes!

Roads with regular flow 🚗 (6%):

Unfortunately, we haven't been able to create a route just via cycle paths or quiet roads. You will occasionally be exposed to some fast moving traffic or, in towns, to reasonably regular flows of motorised traffic. **Assertive road positioning** is essential to keep safe here. As soon as you start cycling close to the roadside, drivers will try to overtake you "in the same lane". You might think this is OK, but the margin of error is large and if something goes wrong, **you** end up in hospital or worse! Also, you expose yourself once again to being **overlooked** and being hit by traffic coming out of driveways and side roads. So, you want to **force** drivers to overtake on the other side of the road. This is only possible by cycling **in the middle of your side of the road**. Adopt this position if you feel it is essential for your safety, especially in blind bends and when turning at junctions. For a turn, look behind before pulling out and signal. Then, make **eye contact** with drivers around you just before making a turn!

Busy main roads 🚗🚗 (1%):

The cycling style explained on these pages is **officially adopted** by the British government (Bikeability). The principles generally work, but on busy roads, where you can't keep up with the speed and the intensive flow of the traffic, it is very hard to enforce these principles. Drivers can get quite hostile, so why bother? Very occasionally, we have no choice other than taking you via this type of road, but we have ensured you can always cycle or **walk** your bikes on pavements.

Your author providing adult Bikeability training (2015)

Cyclists from continental Europe must further know that a general priority for traffic from the right doesn't exist in the UK. At most junctions, clear road markings will show the priorities.

Cycling with children:

Always keep to cycle paths until children have achieved **full control** of their bikes. To protect a child on quiet roads, you cycle either **two abreast** (child on the inside, you on the outside) or **behind** him/her. Ensure they listen to your instructions and only move in front of them if you need to show them where to go. If you have multiple children, put the most confident child at the front and ensure he/she keeps the same speed as the weakest child in your party.

Children should only cycle on roads with a regular flow or fast moving traffic (🚗) if parent and child are both happy and confident to do so. Cycling on main roads (🚗🚗) is only recommended for confident parents and teenagers. You decide on your own limits; there is no shame in walking!

Gear, equipment, barriers and rough stretches

65% of our route is on roads, but the remaining 35% is off-road. Many cycle paths have a **tarmac surface**, but there are stretches with a **gravel** surface. Most of this gravel will be **smooth**, but some stretches also consist of **rough** gravel, **scree and stone** or even **open ground**, often combined with steep gradients. Trouble stretches are summarised in the table on this page. Remember, mostly, the **stunning scenery** is why we take you to these places. That is why we still prefer the discomfort over the alternatives as shown in the table. Remember you will still be able to ride some of the distances shown, just walk bikes where you truly cannot ride; take your time!

This is why **road racing bikes** are **not suitable**, as their slick tyres will truly struggle. A **touring/hybrid bike** with semi-slick tyres will get you a long way. **Mountain bikes** with fat tyres and suspension will ease some pain. **E-bikes** will also have to slow down; think of 11 km/h (7 mp/h) or less. Expect to walk E-bikes as well!

Examples of off-road sections; tarmac, smooth gravel, rough gravel, scree and stone and open ground

Route	Pages	Stretch	Length	Issue	Alternative
3	40-41	Bowes Railway Museum - Angel of the North	3.5 km	rough gravel on steep gradients	direct riverside route, no Angel of the North
6	64	Commondale - Castleton (North York Moors)	2.8 km	rough gravel on steep gradients	via Sandhill Bank and Langburn's Bank roads
6	65	Aislaby - Briggswath	1.6 km	rough gravel on steep gradients	via Aislaby Lane, A171 and A169
7	69	Robin Hood's Bay - Ravenscar	7.6 km	rough gravel, scree and stone	via A171, train Middlesbrough-Scarborough (!)
7	69	Ravenscar - Hayburn Wyke Waterfall	4.9 km	scree and stone, mud after rain	via Scarborough Road and Hodgson Hill roads
10	86	Cottingham - Beverley	2.8 km	rough gravel	via A164, train Cottingham-Beverley
12	102	Willow Bridge beauty spot	1.0 km	open ground, gravel, gradient	via Bower Hill and Roughbirchworth Ln roads
12	103	Wharncliffe Woods - Oughtibridge	0.6 km	rough scree and stone, gradient	via route 627, Stephen Ln and Oughtibridge Ln
13	105	Ronksley Hall Farm & Ravelin Reservoir	3.0 km	rough gravel, scree and stone	via Woodbank Rd, Rails Rd and Lodge Ln
13	106	Long Causeway - Stanage Edge	3.9 km	rough gravel, scree and stone	via Soughley Ln, Fulwood Ln, Ringinglow Rd
15	121-122	A5 crossing - Houlton Estate (near Rugby)	1.5 km	rough gravel, mud after rain	via Lilbourne Rd, Hillmorton Ln and Houlton Wy
17	137	Ridgeway Letcombe Regis - Charlbury Hill	16 km	open ground, gravel, mud after rain	via B4507, train Didcot-Salisbury (!)
17	138	Ridgeway Chiseldon - Avebury	13 km	open ground, gravel, mud after rain	via 🚲 & Rockley route, train Didcot-Salisbury (!)
18	142-143	Little Durnford - Old Sarum	2.1 km	open ground, gravel, mud after rain	tarmac route on pages 142-143
20	149	Tennyson Trail	4.6 km	rough gravel on steep gradients	via 3055

*The stretches in the table above are marked with a **red line** on our maps rather than the regular blue*

Wouldn't it be fantastic if **recumbent bikes**, **tandems**, **trailers** or even **cargo bikes** could use our route? Sadly, this is not possible. Despite smooth terrain as shown in the left picture above, there is the challenging terrain as outlined on the previous page. On the next picture, some Dutch friends of the author are also kindly displaying another issue; **barriers** at the start and end of cycle paths. As the pictures show, these come in all sorts and sizes, designed to stop motorbikes. Unfortunately, this makes it virtually impossible to use anything else than a regular bicycle. You will encounter barriers like these on a daily basis.

In some places, the barriers even nearly stop regular bikes getting through. You may have to briefly turn your handlebars, roll your bike on the back wheel with the front wheel up or lift the entire bicycle. Very rarely, there is even a short flight of steps; some strength is required!

Additionally, it is recommended to use a bicycle with a rack on the back to carry pannier bags. Whatever the type of bike you choose; have **at least 18 gears** to be able to take in any serious climb. This is also why **BMX-bikes** for children are not ideal (no gears).

A set of two **pannier bags** will enable you to carry luggage for a cycling holiday of up to two weeks, providing you stay at indoor accommodation and can do some laundry midway. Outdoor panniers are the best and German manufacturer Ortlieb sets the standard for this type of bag. It is worth shopping around, but bear in mind that the cheaper you go, the more likely it is the bags will get damaged with regular intense use.

A **map holder** for on the bike's handlebars is advised, as this guide is designed to fit in such holders! A cheap **bike computer** (set on kilometres) is not essential, but makes it even easier to use this guide book's directions; ideal!

On a cycling holiday with **indoor accommodation** only, you should be able to fit the following in two panniers:

- 2 sets of clothes to be used for cycling during the day, including shirt, jumper and trousers/shorts
- 1 easy set of clothes to wear at night (pyamas)
- 1 nice set of clothes (for non-cycling related travelling and going out; don't use this set for sweaty walking or cycling!)
- plenty of socks and underwear
- proper waterproofs (coat and trousers), able to withstand cold winds and with a breathable inside layer
- light outfit for hot weather, including sun cap/shades
- small bag for toiletries
- small bicycle repair kit for emergency repairs
- small rucksack for valuable items
(you can bring this with you whilst you leave the pannier bags on the bike during lunch stops, attraction visits or for a short walk)
- passport, phone, reading book, travel insurance

Camping by bike is fun, but physically more demanding than Bed & Breakfast/hostel touring. You may need **pannier bags** on the **front wheel** (with an additional rack) to be able to carry a tent, inflatable mattress and sleeping bag on your bike as well. Don't cut down on quality. Good, light-weight materials are essential for happy camping tours by bike! If you have never done any cycle touring before, you should get some experience with a B&B/hostel tour first.

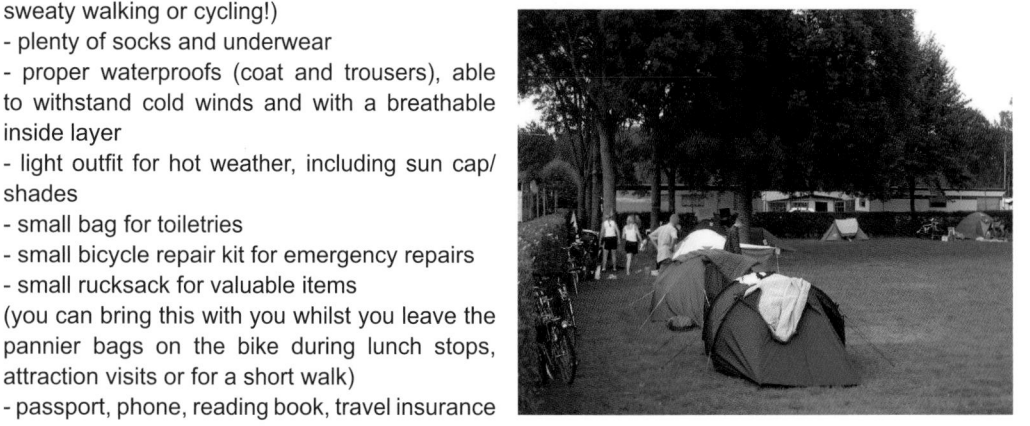

A **repair kit** (see picture) should at least contain:
- combi tool with spanners and screwdrivers
- spanner allowing you to take off wheels
- pump, spare tube, patches and tyre levers
(note 'Super Patch' kits don't need glue and are adequate for 99% of punctures!)

Ensure your bike is in a good state by taking it to a repair shop for a check-up before departure. If you run into serious trouble on the way you can use our bike repair shops listings from page 154.

Additionally, bring a good **bike lock**, allowing you to lock frame and wheels to a secure object. Many service providers are still getting used to cycling tourists and will require you to lock up bike(s) outside overnight.

Wear **bright clothes** when cycling on-road. High visibility vests are very popular. It is not legally required to wear **helmets** in the United Kingdom. Many people do, but also many people don't. Whatever your choice is; it is your **cycling style** which will really keep you safe, see page 16.

On long-distance journeys, it is inevitable that you will encounter **road works** somewhere. Cyclists will mostly be able to pass through, but when you can't, check out **OpenStreetMap** (www.openstreetmap.org). These great maps show all roads, cycle paths and footpaths worldwide! When looking for alternatives for problem stretches (see page 18) you may need this resource too. Please report serious closures to *eoscyclingholidays@gmail.com*. We endeavour to include your findings in our **route updates**, regularly published on **www.eoscycling.com**.

'On the road': accommodation, food and more

International visitors should visit from **May to September** to get the best of the weather. The negative image of British weather might do justice to wet weather in Scotland and Northwest England, but the east and south is generally dryer, with the south particularly milder. May and June are generally best, with fair weather in September too. Always be ready for rain though!

English **school holidays** usually start in the last week of July and last for six weeks. Also, be aware of the **bank holiday weekends** in May and August, dates varying per year. Always make **reservations** in advance for stays on these special weekends. In busy places like York, Oxford and the Peak District you should make reservations all year round. Coastal towns will get booked up during the summer holidays. In other areas you should be fine with making bookings on the day itself. Since the era of Covid-19 started, it is wise to call at least a few hours ahead, so you can check availability and arrangements of the venue prior to your arrival.

Bed & Breakfasts are part of England's heritage. There are many B&Bs (or guesthouses) around. You may end up in someone's private home with only some rooms open for guests. At the other end of the spectrum, there are large hotels offering "B&B". Note: pub accommodation can be noisy. Most B&Bs offer "full English breakfast" with traditional bacon, eggs, baked beans and sausages on toast. "Continental breakfast" (cereal, croissants, etc.) is generally available too. Hosts of smaller and/or rural places often go out of their way to ensure a pleasant stay.

Hostels allow you to sleep in shared dormitory rooms, but Covid-19 has troubled this type of accommodation. Private rooms are normally available. Hostels of the international hostelling organisation YHA are of a high standard and membership is not compulsory. Independent hostels and bunkhouses (for example at rural campsites) are also available. Standards vary; check out the reviews!

Campsites are generally available, except on the routes in and out of Newcastle and Hull. It is vital for campers to plan ahead, as distances between campsites can be substantial. Most campsites have good amenities, like modern shower/toilet blocks, but don't expect a swimming pool! Most campsites don't have shops, so make arrangements for your meals before heading for the campsite. Note "rough" roadside camping is not permitted in England. Landowners don't like trespassing by strangers, but a smile with a story about your odyssey may open hearts. Whatever happens; ask first before pitching your tent!

The **facility listings** from page 154 feature a mix of accommodation options available relevant for a particular route section. It is by no means a full overview of what is available. Generally, in busy cities and towns, we have only listed venues directly on the route. Nevertheless, hostels and campsites are always listed, even if these are a bit further away from the route. In rural places, most options are generally listed.

We haven't included details of chain hotels such as **Premier Inn** and **Travelodge**, as these companies only offer good value when booking well in advance. When making a booking on the arrival day, prices can be extortionate. Also, these companies may undercut local independent providers, slowly putting these out of business. This is a reason also **not** to book via **booking. com** or **airbnb**, as these make independent hoteliers pay commission fees, while they may already operate fine booking system themselves. By booking with a professional provider, you are avoiding 'cowboys' and you are supporting professional standards (hygiene, insurance, etc).

Pricing indication for one night of accommodation:
♠ B&Bs, guesthouses and hotels:
£40-£80 for a single room for one person
£70-£100 for a shared room with two people
£80-£140 for a family room up to four people
🏠 hostels/bunkhouses:
£15-£25 for a bunk bed in a shared dormitory
£50-£70 for a basic room with two people
£80-£100 for a basic family room up to four people
⛺ campsites:
Prices are either around £10 per person or around £20 per pitch. If you travel on your own, it is worth to select campsites charging per person.
Indication of location of venue:
🏃 reasonably quiet and peaceful surroundings
📶 located near noisy traffic or street noise (people)

Also important: we have omitted venues requiring a minimum stay of two nights from our listings. 'Caravan and motor-home campsites' (not permitting tents) are not listed either. Of course, long term cottage lets and venues requiring a membership have been ignored too. These places will all show on a Google Search though; go by our listings for a convenience experience!

For **day-time travel** (always avoid cycling in the dark!) free public toilets and **pubs** are great facilities for cyclists. Pubs generally open from 11 am or at noon and offer affordable lunches. Just going to the toilet without purchasing any food or drinks is fine. Common lunches are a "Ploughmans" (fresh bread with cheese, pickles and salad) or a jacket/baked potato. Cornish pasties filled with vegetables and meat are also popular. At most pubs, you have to order your food at the bar and immediate payment will be required. **Take aways** like fish and chips, Chinese or Indian make easy evening meals.

Very rural pubs are listed by their full names in the route directions. **Facilities** in towns and villages are indicated by symbols only (see page 13). This allows you to **see at a glance** how far it is to the next en-route facility. Shops are generally open Mon-Sun, banks and post offices Mon-Sat noon. The British Pound is the only accepted currency. Credit card payments are widely accepted, even for small amounts. ATMs (cash machines) are available in most towns.

Route 1: Berwick-upon-Tweed - Alnwick (Denwick)

81 km / 50 miles: 🚲 17%, 🚶 68%, 🚗 14%, 🚗🚗 1%
Stations: Berwick-upon-Tweed, Chathill

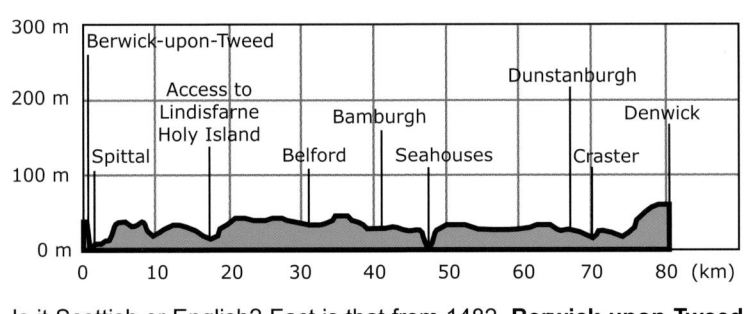

Looking out over the River Tweed and its many bridges at Berwick-upon-Tweed

Is it Scottish or English? Fact is that from 1482, **Berwick-upon-Tweed** has been officially part of England, after it had been switching sides numerous times. The castle ruins, despite being partly built-over by the railway station, still look out impressively over the tidal River Tweed and remind us of a battled past. From the station there is no other route than a busy main road, leading you under the historic city gate. The ramparts extend around the old scenic town centre. Berwick's history is told in the **Barracks and Main Guard Museum** (£6 pp) and **Berwick Museum and Art Gallery** (free with Barracks Museum ticket). Leaving town, you'll be cycling the **Old Bridge**, built in 1624, taking you to Tweedmouth.

Lindisfarne Holy Island with its castle and abbey ruins

Cycling the Scotland link

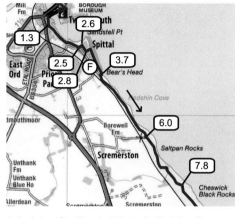

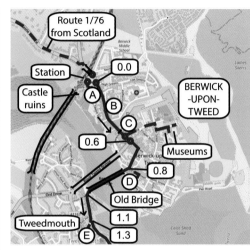

Our route starts at Berwick's railway station. If you are cycling from Scotland to Berwick, do so with the signposted cycle route. You'll cycle via the station when heading into town (note the last section into town is signposted as route 1/76). If you make your way to/from Berwick by train and can't resist taking a selfie with a Scotland sign, there is one on the A6105, 8 kms (5 miles) west via routes 1/76; note it is uphill! Follow North Rd, Castle Terrace and Paxton Rd from the station.

0.0 At end of station access rd, at rndabt, go south → (Castlegate, to Town Centre, **1**) 🚗🚗 *(walk on footpaths as needed)*

0.6 At 2nd rndabt ↑ into town centre of ⬅🏠🏨🚉🚌🍴 **Berwick-upon-Tweed**, then imm 1st cobbled rd → (West St)

0.8 At end of rd ↑ onto bridge 🚗 *(for 🏨 ←)*

1.1 At end bridge, keep ↖ (Main St, **1**)

1.3 1st rd ↖ (Dock Rd, to Spittal Pr, **1**)

2.5 At give-way jct ← (Sandstell Rd) *(**ignore** signs route 1!)*

2.6 1st rd → (at small green, no signs)

2.8 1st rd ← (see signs 'dead end rd'), at end → via ⬅🏛 **Spittal Promenade**

3.7 At very last house ↗ via narrow path, ep ↙ onto rd uphill (**1**), at end of rd ↑ via gravel path (**1**), becomes grass path

6.0 At ep ↖ via rd (**1**)

Route 1: Berwick-upon-Tweed - Alnwick (Denwick)

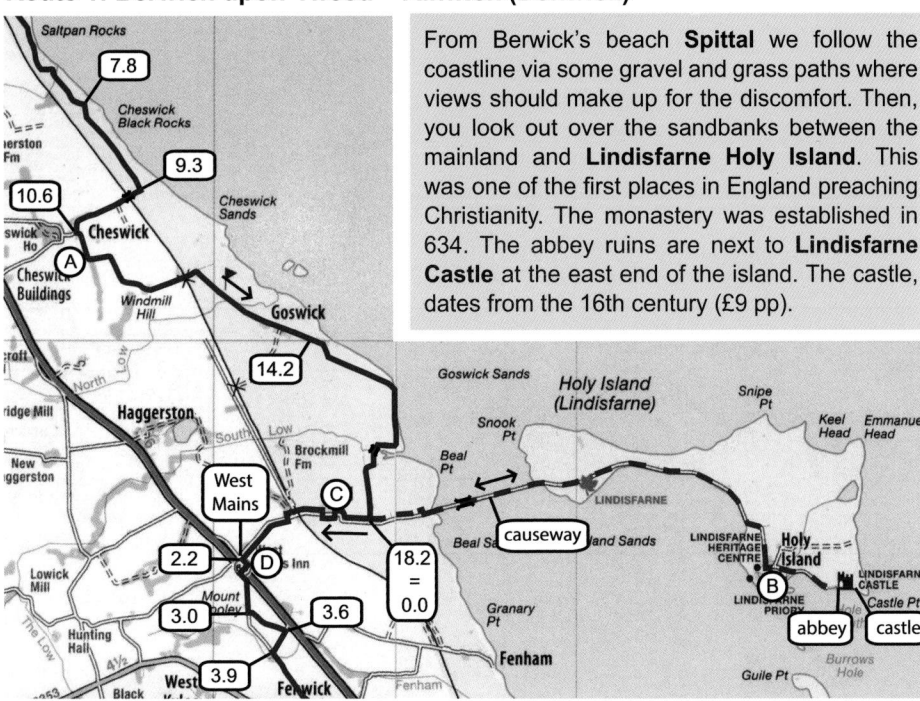

From Berwick's beach **Spittal** we follow the coastline via some gravel and grass paths where views should make up for the discomfort. Then, you look out over the sandbanks between the mainland and **Lindisfarne Holy Island**. This was one of the first places in England preaching Christianity. The monastery was established in 634. The abbey ruins are next to **Lindisfarne Castle** at the east end of the island. The castle, dates from the 16th century (£9 pp).

7.8 At end of rd, just before bunker on hill, ↗ via gravel path (to Lindesfarne Causeway, **1**)

9.3 1st gravel rd → (**1**), cross railway via bridge, ↑

10.6 At T-jct ← via tarmac rd (**1**)

14.2 At end of rd ↑ through gate onto private rd (**1**), at private gate ↗ via gravel path (**1**), becomes grass, then gravel again, with bridge over stream

18.2 At end of gravel path *reset mileage:*
For ⊁ 🏠 🥄 🍴 **Lindisfarne Holy Island** ← *via path*

The unique **causeway road** to Lindisfarne Holy Island gets flooded during high tide. Allow 3-4 hours for a full visit to the island. It is a 16 km (10 miles) return ride to the abbey ruins and castle. For crossing times check **https://holyislandcrossingtimes.northumberland.gov.uk**.

0.0 *(18.2)* For continued route → via gravel path on right side of rd (**1**), ⚙️ jumps from one side of the rd to the other side of the rd multiple times, keep ↑

2.2 At main rd ← via lay-by ⛺ 🏨 🚻 🍴 🍴 **West Mains** (**1**), at end use ⚙️ crossing ↑, then 1st rd ↗ (**1**)

3.0 1st rd ↖ (**1**)

3.6 At T-jct → (**1**)

3.9 At T-jct ← (**1**)

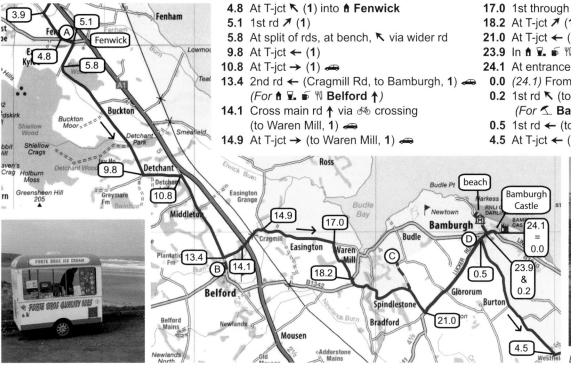

4.8 At T-jct ↖ (**1**) into ⌂ **Fenwick**
5.1 1st rd ↗ (**1**)
5.8 At split of rds, at bench, ↖ via wider rd
9.8 At T-jct ← (**1**)
10.8 At T-jct → (**1**) 🚗
13.4 2nd rd ← (Cragmill Rd, to Bamburgh, **1**) 🚗
　　(For ⌂ 🍺 🛒 🍴 **Belford** ↑)
14.1 Cross main rd ↑ via 🚲 crossing
　　(to Waren Mill, **1**) 🚗
14.9 At T-jct → (to Waren Mill, **1**) 🚗

17.0 1st through rd → (to Chester Hill, **1**)
18.2 At T-jct ↗ (**1**) 🚗, 1st rd ↖ (**1**)
21.0 At T-jct ← (**1**) 🚗
23.9 In ⌂ 🛒 🍴 **Bamburgh** at T-jct ↗ (to Castle) 🚗
24.1 At entrance ⇐ **Bamburgh Castle** *reset mileage:*
0.0 *(24.1)* From castle entrance, rejoin rd ↗ 🚗
0.2 1st rd ↖ (to South, **1**) 🚗
　　(For ⌂ **Bamburgh** → *via rd 'The Wynding'*)
0.5 1st rd ← (to Seahouses, **1**)
4.5 At T-jct ← (to Seahouses, **1**)

Bamburgh Castle

Route 1: Berwick-upon-Tweed - Alnwick (Denwick)

You have now truly arrived in castle country and you may find **Bamburgh Castle** its crown jewel. Overlooking a stunning beach, its size is truly mind-boggling (£12 pp). **Dunstanburgh Castle** further south (£6 pp) has an equally striking location, but is smaller; the last mile has to be travelled on foot and the castle is in a less good state than Bamburgh's. Also in Bamburgh, the **Grace Darling Museum** tells the story of a brave young lady who braced the waves to save lives (free). The small town of **Seahouses** features scenic **North Sunderland Harbour**, with boat tours to nearby **Farne Islands**. A similar harbour can be found in small and pretty **Craster**, which is more quiet. **Howick Hall** was once home to former prime minister **Earl Grey** and the tea named after him can naturally be consumed at its cafe and **Gardens** (£9 pp).

5.6 At T-jct ↑ via 🚲 (to Seahouses, **1**), ep ↑ across car pk (**1**)

6.7 At give-way jct ← (to Bamburgh) 🚗, then 1st rd → (⟵**North Sunderland Harbour**), follow quay rd ↗

6.9 At 'Harbour Office', dismount and walk → uphill, after climb, resume cycling ↑ into 🏠 🛒 🛍 🍴 **Seahouses**

7.0 At rndabt ↑ (to Beadnell) 🚗, at next rndabt ↑ (to Ind Est), ↑ (to Embleton, **1**)

13.6 At T-jct → (**1**), keep ↑

20.8 At T-jct ← (to Embleton, **1**)

21.3 1st rd → (to Embleton, **1**)

North Sunderland Harbour in Seahouses and the ruins of remote Dunstanburgh Castle

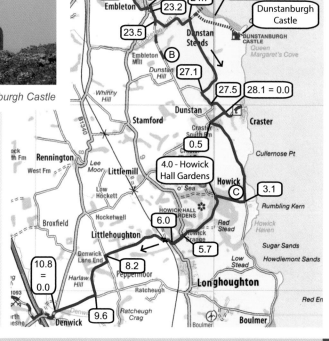

23.0 At give way-jct 🏠 🛏 🍴 **Embleton** ↑, at hill top, 1st rd → (Mount Pleasant, to Craster, **1**)

23.2 At T-jct ↑ (to Craster, **1**)

23.5 1st rd ↖ (to Craster, **1**) *(for ⛺ ↑)*

24.7 In hamlet 'Dunstan Steads' → via private gate (to Craster, **1**), ↑ across private grounds onto path (**1**) *(For ⚷ Dunstanburgh Castle and ⚓ Embleton Beach ↑ via rd)*

27.1 At T-jct ← (to Craster, **1**)

27.5 At T-jct ↖ (to Craster, **1**)

28.1 At next jct *reset mileage:* *(For ⚷ 🛏 🍴 Craster ↑ via rd)*

0.0 *(28.1)* For continued route go east → (to Alnmouth, **1**)

0.5 At give-way jct ← (to Alnmouth, **1**)

3.1 Follow sharp bend to the right → (to Alnmouth via rd, **1**)

4.0 At ⚷ 🛏 **Howick Hall Gardens**, follow sharp bend to the left ←

5.7 At give-way jct ↑ (Coastal Route)

6.0 1st rd ↗ (to Howick Quarry) (***ignore** signs route 1!*)

8.2 At T-jct ← (to Alnwick), 1st rd → (see sign 'no lorries over 7.5t')

9.6 At T-jct → 🚗

10.8 At T-jct *reset mileage*

Route 2: Alnwick (Denwick) - Newcastle Ferry

83 km / 51 miles: 🚲 41%, 🚶 54%, 🚐 5%, 🚗🚗 0%
Stations: None

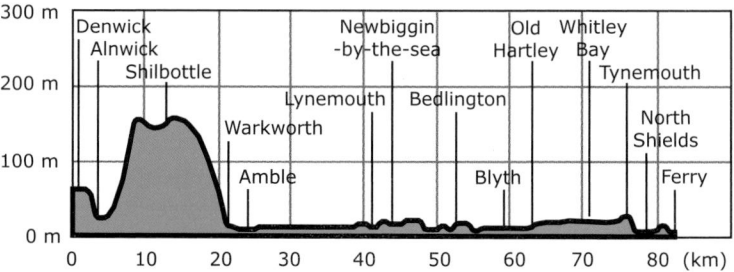

We are temporarily heading inland away from coastal Route 1, mainly to allow a visit to iconic **Alnwick Castle**. Many films and TV programmes have used this castle as a backdrop, from Ivanhoe to Black Adder. It most famously starred as Hogwarts School of Witchcraft and Wizardry in **Harry Potter**. With parts of the castle dating from 1096, it played its part in history too, most notably during the War of the Roses. Allow a full morning or afternoon for a visit (£13 pp). Our approach from the north provides fine views of the castle; slow down to take in its majestic presence! In the town of **Alnwick** itself, the **Bailiffgate Museum** features local social history and art (£4 pp). Don't miss the scenic Market Place!

Alnwick Castle features broomstick training 'Harry Potter-style' and archery sessions

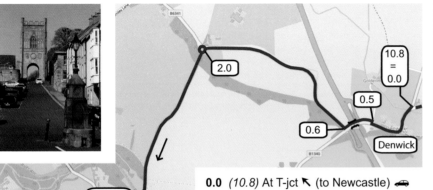

The hills south of Alnwick allow you to experience your first considerable climb on the route. A country lane route takes you to the compact town of **Warkworth**. Its castle is still an impressive sight despite its ruined state (£8 pp). From Warkworth, the route rejoins official coastal route 1. Between harbour town **Amble** and **Lynemouth** the coast line remains rural, with **Druridge Bay Beach** stretching for miles. The visitor centre with cafe at **Ladyburn Lake**, just behind the sand dunes, could be a nice lunch break and provides shelter should the weather turn nasty on this exposed stretch.

0.0 *(10.8)* At T-jct ↖ (to Newcastle) 🚗
0.5 Just after large white route sign (for crossing A1) cross rd ↑ onto pavement on right side of rd
0.6 After bridge over A1, 1st rd → (to Eglingham)
2.0 At rndabt ← (to Almwick)
3.5 In ⛲🏠🏨🏪🛒🍴 **Alnwick** at 2nd junction, *reset mileage:*
0.0 *(3.5)* 2nd rd → (to St James Church Centre), see gate at hill top
0.1 After town gate, at give way jct ↑ (see signs 20 mph zone)
0.4 At bend to the right, go visually ↑ (Howling Ln)
0.9 At T-jct (end of 'Beech Gr') ←
1.1 At T-jct (see sign 'St Thomas Close Workshops') → via pavement on right side of rd
1.3 1st rd ← (Battlements), keep ↑ via tarmac rd

Market Place, Alnwick

Route 2: Alnwick (Denwick) - Newcastle Ferry

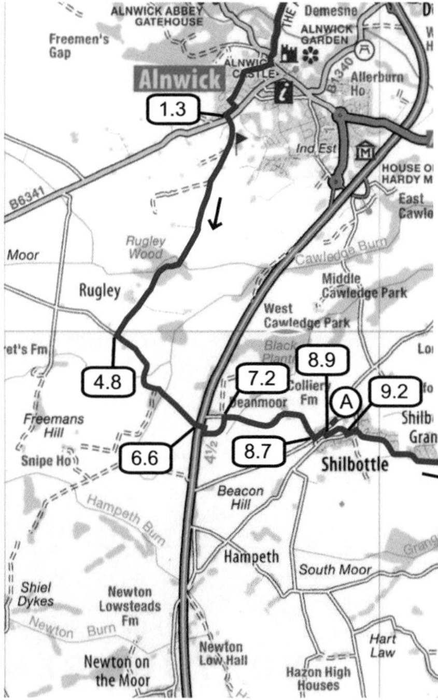

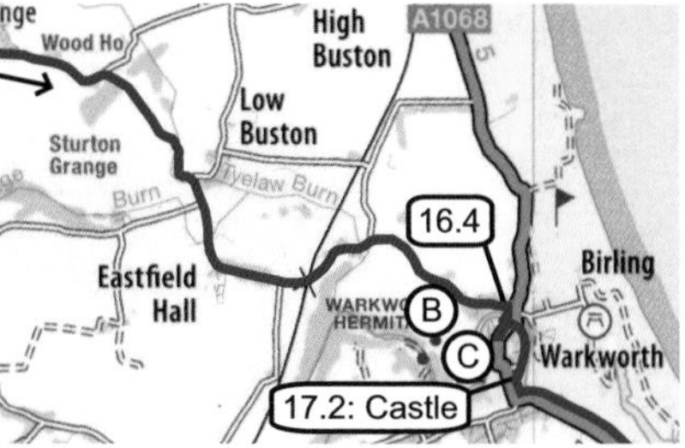

4.8 At T-jct (end of 'Rugley Rd') ←
6.6 At T-jct → (to Mopeth, A1) (🚗🚗!), then 1st rd ← (to Deanmoor)
7.2 At T-jct → (no signs)
8.7 At give-way jct ← (to Alnwick), then 1st rd → (to Village Farm)
8.9 1st rd ← (to Village Farm)
9.2 At T-jct ←, at next T-jct ↗ (see War Memorial on left side of rd), at 🚩 **Shilbottle** *(shop)* keep ↑ via tarmac through rd
16.4 At T-jct → via pavement on right side of rd (to Amble), after 50m ↗ onto historic bridge, after bridge imm ← and cross main rd ↑ (The Butts) *(**ignore** signs route 1!)*
(for 🏠 🚩 📷 🍴 *Warkworth use main rd ↗ for 200m, then 1st rd ↘)*
17.2 At T-jct ↖ via pavement on left side of rd
*(for ⚜ **Warkworth Castle** cross rd into driveway)*

Warkworth Castle

Beyond Lynemouth, a power station and dormant aluminium smelter pushes the route inland into an industrial landscape. The **Woodhorn Museum** is built on the site of a former coal mine, marking Northumberland's mining heritage (£7 pp). **Newbiggin by the Sea** has a pretty beach, overlooked by a couple worryingly close to the sea, see page 35. Cycling in a predominantly urban industrial landscape around **Ashington** and **Bedlington** cannot be avoided. Once you have crossed the River Blyth, a riverside path takes you to **Blyth** and its docks, with a superstore directly on our route.

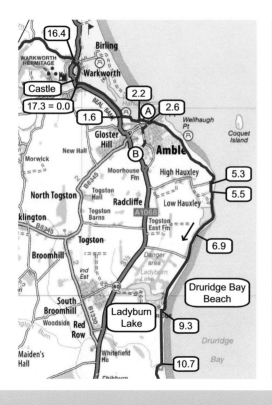

17.3 At next jct *reset mileage:*

0.0 *(17.3)* 1st rd ← via narrow pavement on left side of rd (to Amble, **1**), becomes 🚲

1.6 Go ← into driveway 'Amble Marina' (**1**), at split of rds ↗, at entrance marina, follow grass path ↗ around fence of marina

2.2 Ep ↗ across car pk 🏠 🅿 📷 🍴 **Amble**, then ← onto rd, at T-jct ← (one-way rd, to Harbour Village, **1**), keep ↑

2.6 At T-jct ↖ (**1**), keep ↑ (**1**)

5.3 Out of town, after beach bungalow with no 6, 1st rd ↖ (to Low Hauxley, **1**)

5.5 At end of tarmac rd ↖ onto gravel rd (one-way rd with no entry sign, **1**), gravel rd becomes gravel path, keep ↑

6.9 Ep ↑ via rd (**1**) (⌒ **Druridge Bay** *on left*)

9.3 At end of tarmac rd, after gate ← via path (**1**) *(for* 🚻 📷 🍴 **Ladyburn Lake** →*)*

10.7 Keep to main path ↗ across stream

11.8 Just before bend to right of wide path, go ↖ via narrow path (**1**), ep ↑ via rd (**1**)

13.2 At T-jct ↑ via through rd (to Ashington, **1**)

16.3 In ⌒ 📷 ⛺ **Cresswell** ↑ (to Lynemouth, **1**)

20.6 At rndabt 🅿 📷 **Lynemouth** ← (**1**)

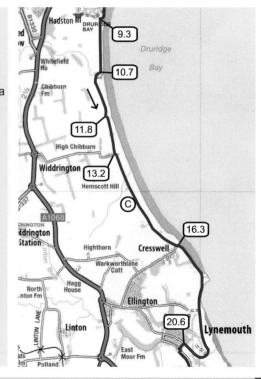

Route 2: Alnwick (Denwick) - Newcastle Ferry

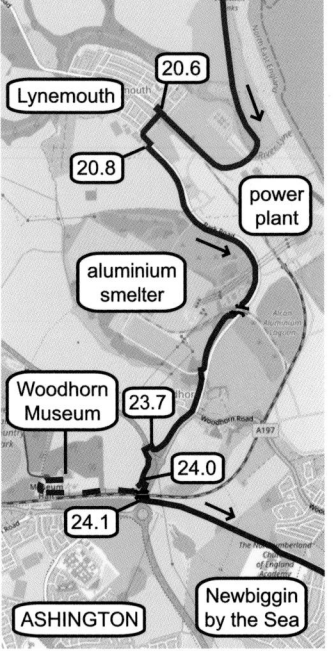

20.8 At sign 'Cemetery' ⬆ onto 🚲 on right side of rd, keep ⬆

23.7 Ep cross rd, then ⬅ via 🚲 on right side of rd, after large sign 'Woodhorn' 1st rd ↗ (to Ashington, **1**)

24.0 1st 🚲 ⬅ (**1**) *(for ⚘ 🍴 **Woodhorn Museum** ⬆ via rd)*

24.1 After bridge over rd, just before large rndabt, cross main rd ⬅ onto 🚲 (**155**), becomes 🚲 on right side of rd

25.8 At T-jct (to North Seaton, **1**) ➡ 🚗 *(for 🚻 ⬅)*

26.1 3rd rd ⬅ (at shops ⚓ 🏧 🍴 **Newbiggin by the Sea**, Sidney Cr), then after house no 3, 2nd rd ➡

26.2 At end, dismount and go ⬅, resume cycling on coast rd

26.5 At end of rd ⬆ via 🚲

26.7 After courts ➡ via path, ⬆ onto rd (see 'Spital Pt' car pk)

27.4 At T-jct ⬅ via 🚲 on left side of rd (to Ashington, **155**), after 100m, cross rd at lhts ⬆ onto 🚲 on right side of rd, then follow 🚲 ↗ away from main rd (**155**)

27.9 Imm after tunnel, 1st 🚲 ⬅ (to Cambois, **1**)

28.3 At large rndabt, cross 2x side rds at crossings ↙, then onto 🚲 ↗ on right side of main rd (to Chambois, **1**)

30.2 After bridge, at split of paths ↖ *(ignore signs route* **1***!)*

30.5 After bridge, go down zigzag ↘, at ep ⬅ via rd (to East Sleekburn) 🚗

31.2 At T-jct ⬅ (to East Sleekburn) 🚗

32.5 After bridge with ramps, 1st rd ➡ (to East Sleekburn, **1**)

Woodhorn Museum and Sean Henry's famous statue 'Couple' at New Biggin

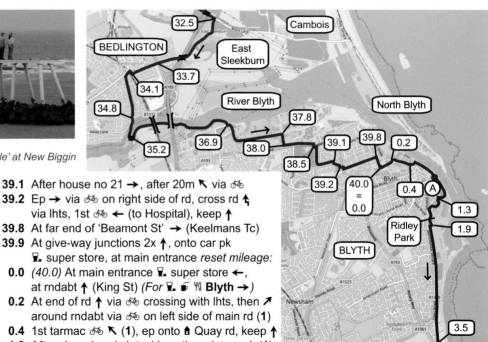

33.7 At jct with lhts ↑ (Thompson St, **1**) 🚗

34.1 At sharp bend to the right → via 🚲 on left side of the rd (to Town Centre) (*ignore signs route* **1**), ← cross railway via path on left side of rd (🚉 🚲 **Bedlington**), then imm 1st rd ←

34.8 At pub 🍺 🍽 **The Bank Top** ↑, go down-hill

35.2 Imm after river bridge 1st 🚲 ← (**1**), keep ↑

36.9 Ep ← via rd (to Tynemouth, **1**), keep on this road (*ignore signs route* **1***!*)

37.8 At T-jct (end of 'Coniston Rd') →

38.0 At T-jct ← via 🚲 on left side of main rd, after petrol station, cross ↟ to path on other side

38.5 1st rd → (Temple Av)

39.1 After house no 21 →, after 20m ↖ via 🚲

39.2 Ep → via 🚲 on right side of rd, cross rd ↟ via lhts, 1st 🚲 ← (to Hospital), keep ↑

39.8 At far end of 'Beamont St' → (Keelmans Tc)

39.9 At give-way junctions 2x ↑, onto car pk 🚉 super store, at main entrance *reset mileage:*

0.0 *(40.0)* At main entrance 🚉 super store ←, at rndabt ↑ (King St) (*For* 🚉 🍺 🍽 **Blyth** →)

0.2 At end of rd ↑ via 🚲 crossing with lhts, then ↗ around rndabt via 🚲 on left side of main rd (**1**)

0.4 1st tarmac 🚲 ↖ (**1**), ep onto ⚓ Quay rd, keep ↑

1.3 After sharp bend, 1st wide path ← into park (**1**)

1.9 At far end of park ← via 🚲 on left side of rd (**1**)

Route 2: Alnwick (Denwick) - Newcastle Ferry

Ridley Park in Blyth, Seaton Sluice at Old Hartley and the stunning coast towards Whitley Bay

From Blyth, you follow the coast via a cycle path busy with pedestrians on sunny days. Via **Old Hartley** you arrive in Newcastle's urban sprawl with **Whitley Bay** and **Tynemouth**. The coastal route makes it worthwhile. At **CBK Kayak Hire** you can do sea kayakking (from £15 pp). The **Tynemouth Aquarium** (£13 pp) is just a bit further down the road. The **Tynemouth Castle and Priory** (£7 pp) stands on a headland at the mouth of the River Tyne. The **North Shields Heritage Center** shows local maritime heritage.

3.5 Follow 🚴 ↑ to far end of car pk, there ↖ via 🚴, (entrance ⚓ **South Beach, 1**), then 1st tarmac path ↗ into sand dunes (**1**), keep ↑ via tarmac 🚴
6.6 At ep ↖ via 🚴 on left side of main rd (**1**)
6.9 After bridge over 〰 **Seaton Sluice**, 1st rd ↖ (Collywell Bay Rd, **1**) into 〰 🏠 📷 🍴 **Old Hartley**
7.8 At T-jct ↖ via 🚴 on left side of main rd (**1**)
8.1 At rndabt ← via narrow rd (to Forth on Sea), ↑ (**1**)
8.3 At end of rd at car pk ↑ via gravel 🚴 (**1**)
9.6 Ep → via rd (to Tynemouth, **1**)

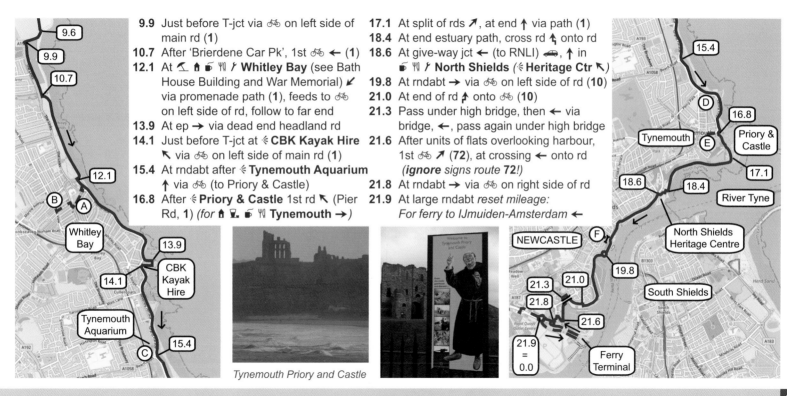

9.9 Just before T-jct via 🚲 on left side of main rd (**1**)

10.7 After 'Brierdene Car Pk', 1st 🚲 ← (**1**)

12.1 At 🛥 🏠 ⓘ 🍴 **Whitley Bay** (see Bath House Building and War Memorial) ↙ via promenade path (**1**), feeds to 🚲 on left side of rd, follow to far end

13.9 At ep → via dead end headland rd

14.1 Just before T-jct at ⓘ **CBK Kayak Hire** ↖ via 🚲 on left side of main rd (**1**)

15.4 At rndabt after ⓘ **Tynemouth Aquarium** ↑ via 🚲 (to Priory & Castle)

16.8 After ⓘ **Priory & Castle** 1st rd ↖ (Pier Rd, **1**) (for 🏠 🚉 ⓘ 🍴 **Tynemouth →**)

17.1 At split of rds ↗, at end ↑ via path (**1**)

18.4 At end estuary path, cross rd ↑ onto rd

18.6 At give-way jct ← (to RNLI) 🚗, ↑ in ⓘ 🍴 ⓘ **North Shields** (ⓘ**Heritage Ctr** ↖)

19.8 At rndabt → via 🚲 on left side of rd (**10**)

21.0 At end of rd ↑ onto 🚲 (**10**)

21.3 Pass under high bridge, then ← via bridge, ←, pass again under high bridge

21.6 After units of flats overlooking harbour, 1st 🚲 ↗ (**72**), at crossing ← onto rd (*ignore* signs route 72!)

21.8 At rndabt → via 🚲 on right side of rd

21.9 At large rndabt *reset mileage:* For ferry to IJmuiden-Amsterdam ←

Tynemouth Priory and Castle

Route 3: Newcastle Ferry - Heddon on the Wall

Direct route:
31 km / 19 miles: 🚲 79%, 🚶 18%, 🚐 3%, 🚗🚗 0%
Route via Angel of the North:
44 km / 27 miles: 🚲 68%, 🚶 28%, 🚐 4%, 🚗🚗 0%
Stations: Newcastle Central

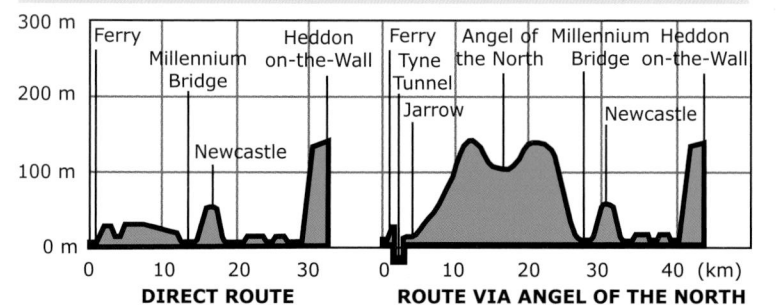

The urban area of **Newcastle upon Tyne** is home to more than 800,000 people, who are also known as 'Geordies'. Newcastle is the largest built-up area on our North-South route, but thanks to the presence of the River Tyne and various greenways on former railway lines, you will still be able to take in plenty of fresh air. From the international ferry terminal (linking with Amsterdam's seaport, IJmuiden) a direct route heads via the river valley towards Newcastle's City Centre, but there is also our alternative, challenging route available via the **Angel of the North**. To pose with your bike at this iconic landmark you have to face multiple steep climbs, tricky barriers and some paths with rough surface (see page 18). Whatever your choice, both route options meet at the equally famous **Millennium Bridge**.

Newcastle's compact City Centre consists of a maze of railways and main roads all leading to a series of landmark bridges across the gorge of the River Tyne. In between all this infrastructure, **Grainger Town** features some scenic avenues with a lot of buildings in classical style dating from the period 1835-1842, the heyday of Newcastle's industrial boom.

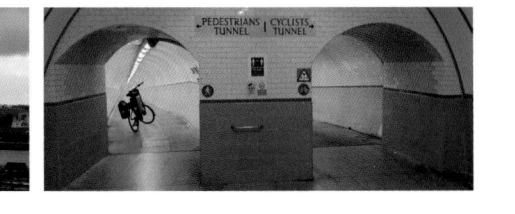

(Ferry Arrivals: At rndabt ← via 🚲 on right side of rd)

0.0 *(21.9)* At large rndabt with entrance to International Passenger Terminal (see large sign) ↑ via 🚲 on right side of rd (see slides swimming pool on yr right)

0.3 At next rndabt ↑, before bus stop ↟ via crossing with lhts onto 🚲 on left side of rd (to Wallsend, **72**)

0.5 At next rndabt ↑ via 🚲 on left side of rd (**72 W**), ↑

1.4 🚲 leads onto quiet dead end rd (**14**), keep ↑ via this rd *(ignore signs route* **72***!)*

1.9 Just before bus stops, join 🚲 on left side of rd ↑ (**14**)

2.0 After rd crossing, follow 🚲 with bend →, keep to 🚲 on left side of rd

2.4 *At entrance rd ⟨ **Tyne Cycle Tunnel***, reset mileage: For* **Angel of the North Route** *continue on page 40. For direct route to* **Newcastle City** *continue on right.*

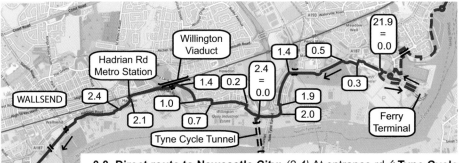

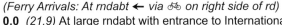

0.0 **Direct route to Newcastle City:** *(2.4)* At entrance rd ⟨ **Tyne Cycle Tunnel** ↑ via 🚲 (at back side of bus stop, to Quay Side, **72**)

0.2 Ep cross rd ↟, continue on right side of rd, at rndabt 1st rd ↗ (**72**)

0.7 After house no 177 → (Bewicke Rd, **72 W**), at end of rd ← via 🚲

1.0 Ep → via rd (see sign 'humps for 688 yds', **72 W**)

1.4 Just before ⟨ **Willington Viaduct** ← via 🚲 (to Hadrian Rd, **72 W**)

2.1 After station ↟ via crossing with lhts onto 🚲 on left side of rd (**72**)

2.4 At rndabt ↑ via 🚲, after 100m ↖ via gate onto ⟨ **Hadrian's Cycle Way (HCW)** (**72 W**), keep ↑ via 🚲 at various rd crossings

6.2 Where residential rd runs parallel to the path, at house no 45 keep ↖, then after 100m at split of paths, keep ↗ (**72 W**), keep ↑

8.8 1st 🚲 ← (HCW, **72 W**), imm → (see 'Foundry Ct), at rndabt ↑ (**72**)

10.0 After river bridge and mini rndabt, 1st 🚲 ← (HCW, **72 W**)

10.8 At ⟨ **Millennium Bridge** *reset mileage, continue on page 43*

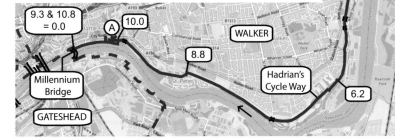

Route 3: Newcastle Ferry - Heddon on the Wall

2.4 = 0.0

direct route to City

Tyne Cycle Tunnel

0.7

JARROW

1.9

1.1

2.2

1.5

2.4

HEBBURN

3.9

3.7

4.2

MONKTON

Bowes Railway

4.9

FELLGATE

HEYWORTH

6.8

Bowes Railway

7.7

8.4

WREKENTON

10.3

Bowes Railway Museum

11.0

CONCORD

11.6

Angel of the North Route to Newcastle City:

0.0 *(2.4)* Go ← into ⛟ **Tyne Cycle Tunnel** building

0.7 Out of tunnel building ← via rd, 1st 🚲 → (**14**)

1.1 At 2nd rd crossing (with zebra) → via rd (*ignore signs route* **14**), then at T-jct ↰ (Grange Rd), at '🍴 **Viking Centre**' keep ↑

1.5 After 🍴 🛒 🍴 **Jarrow**, ↑ at jct (Grange Rd West)

1.9 At T-jct ← 🚗, after tunnel 1st rd → (Beech St)

2.2 At bend to the left, go ↑ onto 🚲, 1st 🚲 ← (**11**)

2.4 Cross rd ↑ onto 🚲 (to Monkton Village, **11**)

3.7 Ep → via rd (to Monkton Business Park, **11**)

3.9 2nd rd ← (Cheviot Rd) (*ignore signs route* **11**)

4.2 At T-jct ←, at end of rd ↗ via 🚲 (**11**), keep ↑

4.9 Cross rd onto 🚲 (**11**), keep ↑

6.8 Cross rd ↰ onto 🚲 (to Kibblesworth, **11**), keep ↑

7.7 Cross rd ↰ onto 🚲 (to Kibblesworth, **11**), keep ↑

8.4 Cross rd ↰ and ↖ via 🚲 (to Kibblesworth, **11**)

10.3 At ep, at ⛟ 🛒 **Bowes Railway Museum** ← via rd, 1st gravel path → (Bridleway to Eighton Banks)

11.0 At jct of paths ← via gravel path (no signs), after 200m, cross railway ↱ and keep ↑ via through path

11.6 At pub 🛒 🍴 **The Engine Room**, cross rd ↗ (**11**)

Angel of the North

12.1 1st path ←, leading under bridge of former railway (no signs)
12.2 Ep → via rd ('Winchester Lodge' on left side of rd), then 1st wide gravel path → (Bridleway), then 1st wide gravel path ← (no signs)
13.0 Before tunnel under main rd, 1st gravel path →, keep ↗ onto tarmac
13.5 At T-jct ← via path on right side of rd, keep on this path ↗ at rndabt
14.4 At ⚲ lhts, cross main rd ← (to ⮜ **Angel of the North**), *reset mileage*
0.0 *(14.4)* From bike bike parking rack at Angel of the North, head north via layby car pk, then ↑ via ⚲ on left side of main rd (to Wrekenton)
0.4 At bus stop ↗ via ramp, up bridge, cross main rd via high ⚲ bridge
0.6 Ep ← via rd (see 'Richmond Cl' opposite)
1.1 At T-jct →, 1st rd ← (Flexbury Grnds)
1.4 At T-jct → (Beechwood Av)
1.7 At T-jct →, at T-jct ← (Brampton Grdns), 1st rd → (Grisdale Grdns)
2.4 At T-jct ←, imm 1st rd → (Lorton Rd) *(for ⸙ ↑ via rd)*

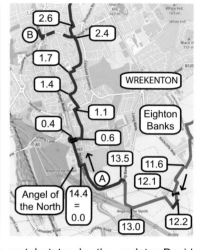

The alternative route via the **Angel of the North** takes you to the southern suburbs via the **Tyne Cycle Tunnel**, 12m under the river bed. The cycle tunnel was the first of its kind in Britain. After its opening in 1951 it attracted up to 20,000 people per day. A full refurbishment was completed in 2019, including the restoration of two original wooden escalators. From **Jarrow**'s High Street, the route is mostly rural via the former **Bowes Railway** which used to transport coal from pits near Durham. The **Bowes Railway Museum** features various original locomotives and rolling stock (£3 pp).

The **Angel of the North** is a large metal statue by the sculptor David Gormley. It was constructed in 1998 and quickly became an icon for northern England. Its location next to the main road, A1, has contributed to the statue's fame, welcoming motorists from the south arriving in the north and acting as a guardian angel for those driving south. The surrounding park makes for a perfect picnic spot. To get there by bike is a bit of a jigsaw puzzle, but we prove it is possible! Some very hilly residential streets, with many left and right turns, take you north to Newcastle's City Centre.

Route 3: Newcastle Ferry - Heddon on the Wall

Angel of the North Route (continued):

Tyne Bridge

2.6 2nd ← (Wynbury Rd)

3.0 At T-jct → (Church Rd)

3.5 At give-way jct ← (Sheriffs Hwy) 🚗, 1st rd → (Blue Quarries Rd)

3.9 1st rd ← (Causeway)

4.3 At T-jct ←, at give-way jct →, then 2nd rd ↖ onto 'half-circle', then after house no 73 on left side of rd, ↖

4.7 After house no 24 on right side of rd, at jct ↑ via path (note ''Brownsea Pl' on left)

4.9 1st rd → (Warburton Cr)

5.0 At T-jct →, imm 1st rd ←, at T-jct ← (Kingston Rd)

5.5 At give-way jct (end of Deckham Tc) ↑ (Fife St), 1st rd → (Ellison Villas), 1st rd ← (Cromwell St)

5.8 At give-way jct →, 1st rd ← (Herbert St)

6.3 At T-jct *dismount*, ↑ via path (walk bike on grass verge at steps)

6.4 At station ↑, resume cycling on 🚲 on right side of rd, imm after bridge → via wide shared 🚲, keep ↑

6.9 At 2nd rd crossing ↖ onto rd, at lhts ↑ (Neilson Rd)

7.4 At T-jct → (Saltmeadows Rd) 🚗, imm 1st rd ↙

7.6 1st 🚲 ← (just before car pk), ep ↑ via rd (to Newcastle, **14**)

8.2 At T-jct → (**14**), then follow sharp bend ← (**14**)

8.9 1st 🚲 → (to Millennium Bridge, **14**)

9.2 1st 🚲 → onto ⟨ **Millennium Bridge**

9.3 At end of ⟨ **Millennium Bridge** *reset mileage, continue on page 43*

Map labels:
9.3 & 10.8 = 0.0 — 8.9 — 9.2 — 8.2 — 7.6 — Millennium Bridge — 7.4 — 6.4 — 7.6 — GATESHEAD — 6.9 — 6.3 — Gateshead Stadium Metro Station — 5.8 — 5.5 — 5.0 — 4.9 — 4.7 — 4.3 — DECKHAM — 3.9 — 3.0 — 3.5 — 2.6 — 2.4

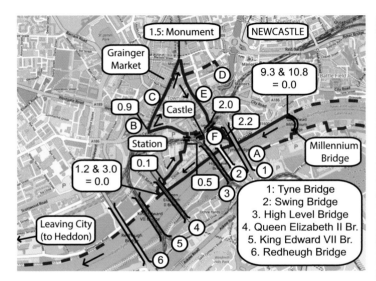

Use our City Centre route in the given direction. It uses handy cycle lanes and one-way routes. It also provides a great view of the Tyne Bridge!

0.0 *(9.3 & 10.8)* At north side of ⫷ **Millennium Bridge** go west via riverside pavement (**HCW**, **72 W**); shared path, walk bikes as needed!

1.2 Imm after high bridge 4 (see map), at info sign 'Quay Side', *reset mileage* *To skip our City Centre circular route, continue on page 44.*

City Centre circular route:

0.0 *(1.2)* At info sign 'Quay Side' → (to City Centre), then join rd →, at T-jct → (Forth Banks) (*ignore* signs 🚲 route to City Centre)

0.1 Imm after passing again under 'high bridge 4', 1st rd ↖ (Hanover St)

0.5 At end of cobbled rd ↗ via rd under railway, at end ← via 🚲 lane, 🚗 *(for* ⫷ **Castle** →*)*, keep ↑, follow 🚲 lane, then ↖ into station lay-by 🚗

0.9 At end of taxi rank **dismount** as needed, just before entrance station, cross main rd → into pedestrianised Grainger St (cycling permitted), keep ↑ at jcts with lhts 🚗, keep visually ↑ to large obelisk at very end

1.5 At ⫷ **Greys Monument** (central square ⫷ 🏠 🏛 🛋 📷 🍽 🍴 🄷 **Newcastle**), go ↘ (Grey St), keep ↑ at jcts 🚗 *(for* 🏛 ← *into Market St, 2nd rd* →*)*

2.0 At mini rndabt under high railway viaduct ↖ (to Quay Side), keep ↗

2.2 At jct with lhts ↖ 🚗, dismount at ⫷ **Tyne Bridge** and use lhts → to return to riverside pavement, there → go west via riverside pavement

3.0 Imm after high bridge 4 (see map), at info sign, *reset mileage*

Newcastle is famous for its bridges across the River Tyne. The **Millennium Bridge** with its modern steel arch has served cyclists since its opening in 2001. When it opens, it does so with an unusual tilt mechanism. The **Tyne Bridge** with its high steel arch dates from 1928. It may look familiar to you; its design was also used in Australia for Sydney's famous Harbour Bridge.

Historic **Grainger Town** features Newcastle's bustling central station, the covered **Grainger Market** and the landmark obelisk **Grey's monument** on the city's Central Square. It is named after a former British prime minister. His administration carried out electoral reforms and abolished slavery. **The Castle** deserves a special mention with its great medieval keep (£9 pp).

Route 3: Newcastle Ferry - Heddon on the Wall

The **River Tyne** is 118 kilometers (73 miles) long when measured from the source of the North Tyne near the Scottish border. To provide access for large cargo ships, parts of the tidal stretch up to near Heddon on the Wall have been dredged to a depth of nine meters. The riverside route heading west is part of the **Hadrian's Cycle Way** heading for Carlisle on the west coast, which endeavours to keep in the vicinity of Hadrian's Wall. For this book, we just visit Heddon on the Wall to see some wall remains (see page 47). If you wish to skip this sight (and a very steep climb), use the shortcut for Durham, saving you the 19 kilometer (12 mile) return trip to Heddon.

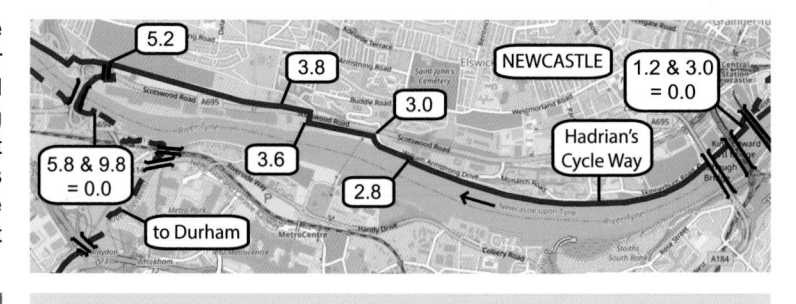

Grey's Monument

Grainger Market

0.0 *(1.2 & 3.0)*: At info sign 'Quay Side', head west via riverside pavement 🚲 (**Hadrian's Cycle Way (HCW)**, **72 W**); keep ↑
2.8 Join 🚲 ↑ on pavement on left side of rd (**72 W**)
3.0 At jct with lhts ↖ (to Scotswood), ↑ via 🚲 on left side of main rd
3.6 At next jct with lhts cross main rd ⤴ via crossing onto 🚲 on right side of rd (**HCW**, **72**)
3.8 1st 🚲 ↗ (to Newburn, **72**)
5.2 At jct of various cycle paths amidst trees, *choose your route:*
For our main route to **Heddon on the Wall***, continue on page 45.*
For a **shortcut to Durham** ← *via* 🚲 *(to Gateshead* **14***),*
leading to footbridge over main rd. After this bridge, go via 🚲 *on left side of rd onto river bridge. At end of the ramp down, reset your mileage after* **5.8** *km and use the last direction of page 48.*

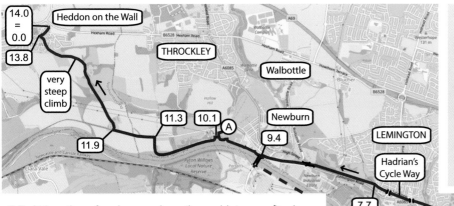

5.2 For route to **Heddon on the Wall** at jct of various cycle paths amidst trees, 2nd 🚲 ↖ (to Lemington, **72**)

5.4 Keep ↑ via 🚲 onto 🚲 on right side of main rd, at lhts cross rd ↑ via 🚲 crossing onto 🚲 on left side of rd (to Newburn, **HCW, 72**)

6.1 From riverside, follow ramp up ↗, then cross rd ↑ via 🚲 crossing with lhts (to Newburn, **HCW, 72**)

6.4 2nd rd → via 🚲 on right side of rd (to Newburn, **HCW, 72**)

6.6 Cross rd ← onto 🚲 (to Newburn, **HCW, 72**), this 🚲 is initially on left side of rd, but moves away onto course of former railway, keep ↑ via 🚲

7.7 At junction of various cycle paths amidst grass ↖ via 🚲 (**HCW, 72**)

9.4 Ep, cross rd at lhts ↑ (**HCW, 72**), at 🚣 **Tyne Rowing Club** ↑, keep to riverside route

10.1 At 🚣 **Hedley Riverside Coffee Shop** keep to riverside route, but after 1km, follow bend of wide gravel path, away from the river, ↗ through gate

11.3 At jct ← onto tarmac 🚲 (to Wylam, **HCW, 72**)

11.9 At rd with gates → via rd, leading across farm yard

13.8 At T-jct ↘ (see 'Heddon Methodist Church')

14.0 Car pk/information sign ⬅ **Hadrian's Wall**, *reset mileage*

Hadrian's Cycle Way, Newcastle

Route 4: Heddon on the Wall - Durham

53 km / 33 miles: 🚲 89%, 🚶 10%, 🚗 1%, 🚗🚗 0%
Stations: Blaydon

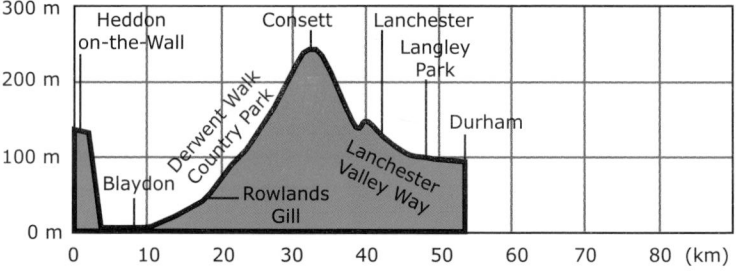

Heddon on the Wall is the closest town near Newcastle where you can take in an original section of **Hadrian's Wall** (see next page). The **Hedley Riverside Coffee Shop** and **Tyne Rowing Club** are the last facilities on the north bank of the River Tyne before finally crossing it to the south proper. Things are pretty industrial here, but with a sudden turn south into the narrow valley of the River Derwent things change rapidly. The **Derwent Walk Country Park** is a heaven of green amid the Newcastle suburbs, popular with locals. At **Nine Arches Viaduct** you will have left the city behind you, continuing your route on the course of a dismantled railway. It has a reasonable surface all the way to **Consett**. On the way, you will climb steadily towards the heights of the northern Pennines, providing stunning scenery. There are some shops off the path in **Rowlands Gill**. The **Derwent Walk Inn** is the only pub situated directly near the trail.

Hadrian's Wall World Heritage

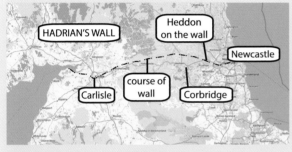

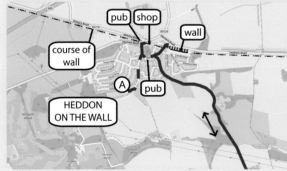

Hadrian's Wall was a Roman wall of defence to protect Roman Britain from unconquered tribes to the north. Emperor Hadrian commissioned the works in 122 AD. It took six years to complete the wall, which was 118 km long (73 miles). Nearly 1900 years later, most of the wall has vanished in urban areas, as stone works were used for building materials in medieval days. Only on the central rural section in the higher hills, long sections of wall remain. Hadrian's Wall got UNESCO World Heritage status in 1987.

You may be disappointed when visiting the 200 metres of wall remains at **Heddon on the Wall**, but this is truly all that is left of it in the Newcastle area. A car parking bay and information sign lead to the path next to it. Two pubs, a B&B and a shop in a petrol station (right on where the wall used to be!) allow a pleasant (overnight) break. Those who wish to experience more can follow the **Hadrian's Cycle Way** to **Corbridge Roman Town** (£9 pp). This site was not on the wall's route, but has some fine Roman remains and displays. It is directly on cycle route 72, 12 kms (8 miles) west, see next page for best access.

Route 4: Heddon on the Wall - Durham

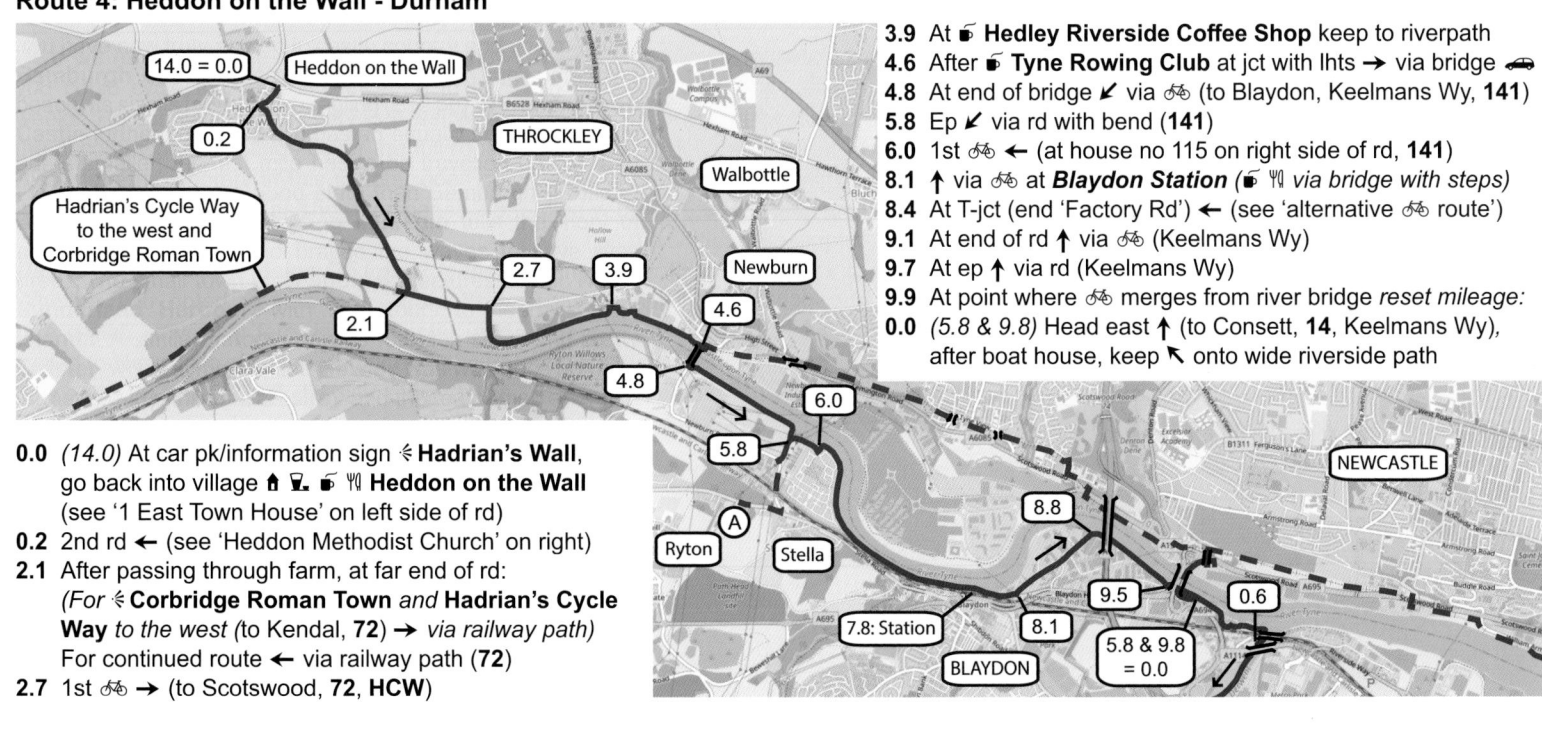

3.9 At ☞ **Hedley Riverside Coffee Shop** keep to riverpath
4.6 After ☞ **Tyne Rowing Club** at jct with lhts → via bridge 🚗
4.8 At end of bridge ↙ via 🚲 (to Blaydon, Keelmans Wy, **141**)
5.8 Ep ↙ via rd with bend (**141**)
6.0 1st 🚲 ← (at house no 115 on right side of rd, **141**)
8.1 ↑ via 🚲 at *Blaydon Station* (☞ 🍴 *via bridge with steps*)
8.4 At T-jct (end 'Factory Rd') ← (see 'alternative 🚲 route')
9.1 At end of rd ↑ via 🚲 (Keelmans Wy)
9.7 At ep ↑ via rd (Keelmans Wy)
9.9 At point where 🚲 merges from river bridge *reset mileage:*
0.0 *(5.8 & 9.8)* Head east ↑ (to Consett, **14**, Keelmans Wy), after boat house, keep ↖ onto wide riverside path

0.0 *(14.0)* At car pk/information sign 🚶 **Hadrian's Wall**, go back into village 🏠 🚉 ☞ 🍴 **Heddon on the Wall** (see '1 East Town House' on left side of rd)
0.2 2nd rd ← (see 'Heddon Methodist Church' on right)
2.1 After passing through farm, at far end of rd: *(For 🚶 **Corbridge Roman Town** and **Hadrian's Cycle Way** to the west (to Kendal, **72**) → via railway path)* For continued route ← via railway path (**72**)
2.7 1st 🚲 → (to Scotswood, **72**, **HCW**)

Terris Novalis sculpture by Tony Cragg

0.6 After passing under railway bridge ↑ via 🚲 (to Consett, **14**)
1.4 1st tarmac 🚲 → (**14**), 1st tarmac rd ← (**14**), ↑ under viaduct
1.7 After high viaduct ↗ onto 🚲 on left side of main rd (**14**), then
↖ into ⬖ **Derwent Walk Country Park**, keep ↑ via 🚲 (**14**)
2.8 Cross rd ↑ via 🚲 (**14**), keep following main tarmac path ↑
5.2 After bridge River Derwent imm → via tarmac path (**14**)
6.2 Ep → via railway path (**14**) onto ⬖ **Nine Arches Viaduct**
8.1 Ep ↖ via 🚲 on left side of rd (**14**), at next jct ↖ via 🚲 on left
side of rd (to Burnopfield, B6314) (🍺 ☕ 🍴 **Rowlands Gill** ↗)
8.8 Cross rd ↟ onto 🚲 on right side of rd (**14**),
then cross side rd 'Stirling Ln' ↗ onto 🚲 (to Consett, **14**)
12.3 Cross rd ↑ via 🚲 (to Consett, **14**)

Consett is a former mining town. The presence of coking coal and iron ore, in combination with the geographical vicinity to Newcastle's port, set the area on an industrial pathway in the 17th century, which continued until 1980, when the town's massive steelworks closed. The large slag heaps on the west end of town have been turned into a country park and most railways that carried the town's heavy goods have been turned into cycle ways. The **Terris Novalis sculpture** on the cycle trail symbolises the former importance of metal to Consett. Our route provides direct access to the shops and a superstore before briefly hitting the **Sea-to-Sea National Cycle Route 7**. It is worth cycling briefly onto its **Hownsgill Viaduct** as this has panoramic views towards the northern Pennines. Our route continues via the **Lanchester Valley Way**, mostly via an old railway line with a gravel surface. **Lanchester** has some pubs. In **Langley Park** you can visit **Diggerland** with entertainment for all ages (prices vary).

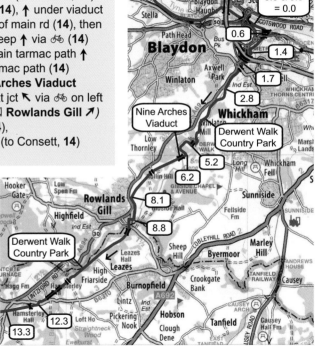

Route 4: Heddon on the Wall - Durham

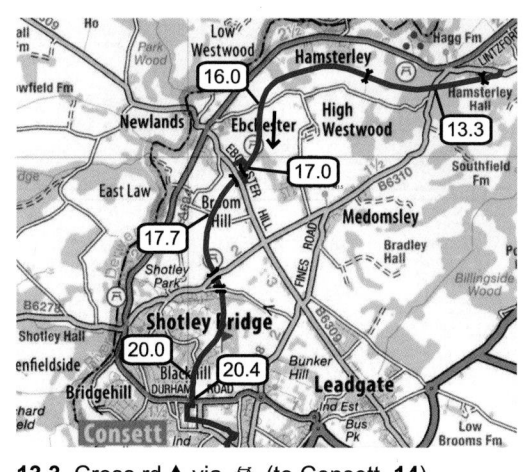

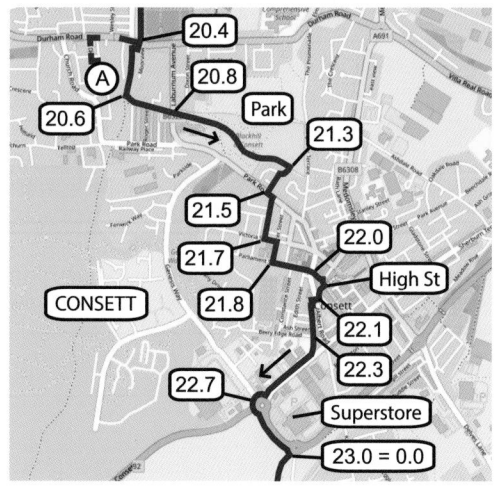

Lanchester Valley Way to Durham

13.3 Cross rd ↑ via ᗧ (to Consett, **14**)

16.0 Cross rd ↑ via ᗧ (to Consett, **14**)

17.0 *(For* 🍴 **Derwent Walk Inn** ↗ *via car pk)*

17.7 Cross rd ↑ via ᗧ (**14**)

20.0 Cross rd ↑ via ᗧ (no signs)

20.4 Cross rd via lhts, ⬆ via ᗧ (to Consett, **14**)

20.6 1st tarmac path ↖ onto tarmac rd (St Aidams St, **14**), keep ↑

20.8 Cross rd ↑ into ⬱ **Blackhill & Consett Park** (**14**), keep ↑

21.3 In steep climb, 1st rd → (house no 42 on left), 1st rd ← (house no 12 on right)

21.5 At T-jct (end 'Queens Gt') ←, 1st rd →

21.7 At end of rd ←, then after house no 17 on left side of rd, 1st rd → (no signs)

21.8 At T-jct ← (house "East Bank' on right)

22.0 At give-way jct ↑ (Middle St), at bend ↑ to shops of 🏧 🍴 ℉ **Consett**, after 20m →

22.1 At end of alley ↖, ↑ onto ᗧ, then cross main rd ⬆ onto pavement on right side of rd, 1st alley →, then ← (to Stanhope, **7**)

22.3 At T-jct ↑ via ᗧ (to Stanhope, **7**), keep ↗

22.7 At rndabt ← via 🚲 crossings onto ᗧ on right side (Rotary Wy, to Stanhope, **7**)

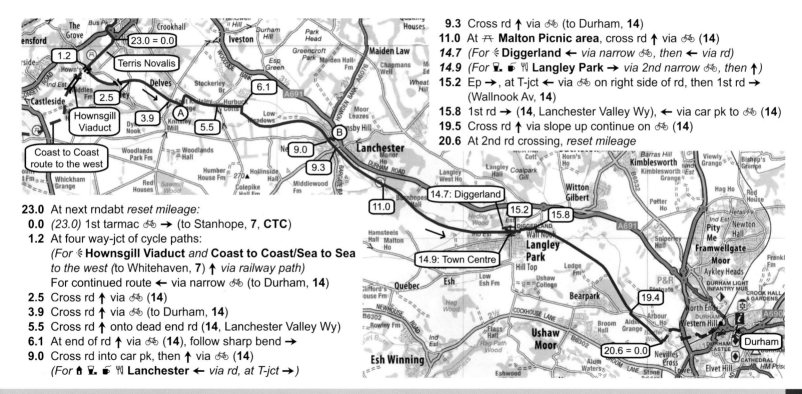

9.3 Cross rd ↑ via 🚲 (to Durham, **14**)

11.0 At 🏞 **Malton Picnic area**, cross rd ↑ via 🚲 (**14**)

14.7 *(For ⛴ **Diggerland** ← via narrow 🚲, then ← via rd)*

14.9 *(For 🏠 🚻 ⛽ 🍽 **Langley Park** → via 2nd narrow 🚲, then ↑)*

15.2 Ep →, at T-jct ← via 🚲 on right side of rd, then 1st rd → (Wallnook Av, **14**)

15.8 1st rd → (**14**, Lanchester Valley Wy), ← via car pk to 🚲 (**14**)

19.5 Cross rd ↑ via slope up continue on 🚲 (**14**)

20.6 At 2nd rd crossing, *reset mileage*

23.0 At next rndabt *reset mileage:*

0.0 *(23.0)* 1st tarmac 🚲 → (to Stanhope, **7**, **CTC**)

1.2 At four way-jct of cycle paths:
*(For ⛴**Hownsgill Viaduct** and **Coast to Coast/Sea to Sea**
to the west (to Whitehaven, **7**) ↑ via railway path)*
For continued route ← via narrow 🚲 (to Durham, **14**)

2.5 Cross rd ↑ via 🚲 (**14**)

3.9 Cross rd ↑ via 🚲 (to Durham, **14**)

5.5 Cross rd ↑ onto dead end rd (**14**, Lanchester Valley Wy)

6.1 At end of rd ↑ via 🚲 (**14**), follow sharp bend →

9.0 Cross rd into car pk, then ↑ via 🚲 (**14**)
*(For 🏠 🚻 ⛽ 🍽 **Lanchester** ← via rd, at T-jct →)*

Route 5: Durham - Middlesbrough

66 km / 41 miles: 🚲 61%, 🚶 32%, 🚗 7%, 🚗🚗 0%
Stations: Durham, Hartlepool, Seaton Carew, Billingham

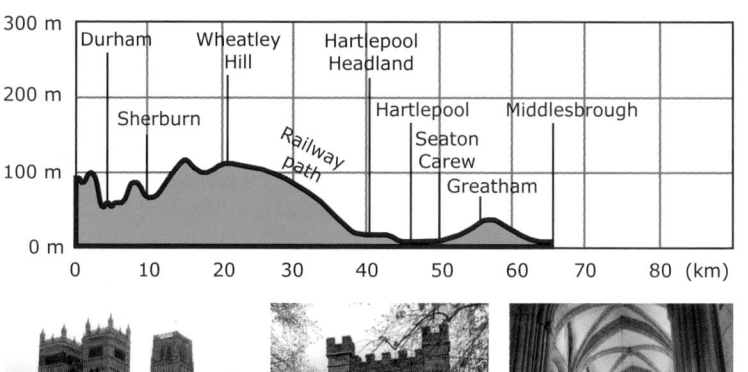

Built on a striking peninsula on the winding river Wear, historic **Durham** is one of England's finest compact conserved cities. It features the UNESCO World Heritage sites of **Durham Castle** and **Durham Cathedral**. The oldest buildings date from 1072. The site was a defensive stronghold of strategic importance to defend the troublesome border with Scotland and to control local English rebellions. Today, the castle is in use by **Durham University**, which welcomes visitors on guided tours across the site (£5 pp). The cathedral can be visited daily for a stroll around, spiritual reflection or to attend a service. The beautiful **Palace Green** connects the two sites. Just east from here, the **Durham Museum** presents the history of this Norman stronghold from medieval times to the present day (£3 pp).

To enjoy the best of the historic city centre, we leave official cycle route 14 to travel via the famous **Framwellgate Bridge** to the scenic **Market Place**. Take some time to take to enjoy both the Market Place and the Palace Green before continuing onto the equally beautiful **Elvet Bridge**. At the east end of town we rejoin cycle route 14, taking us to **Old Durham Gardens**, now restored to their former glory. Before doing so, you may wish to do a circular city walk; see the dotted line on the map on page 53.

From Durham, the route to the North Sea coast is reliant on a railway path that is not in great condition. We opted to avoid drainage issues at **Shotton Colliery** by travelling via **Wheatley Hill**. Our route is not perfect, but will keep you at speed, whereas on route 14 you may end up in mud!

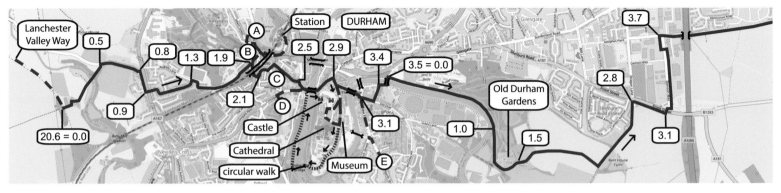

0.0 *(20.6)* Take tarmac rd ← (to Durham **14**), pass through farm (**14**)

0.5 At end of rd → via narrow 🚲 lane on left side of rd (**14**) 🚗

0.8 At T-jct with lhts → via 🚲 on right side of rd (to Durham, **14**)

0.9 After bus stops, cross rd ← onto 'St Monica Gr' (to City Centre, **14**)

1.3 At T-jct → (to City Centre, **14**), from sharp bend, use narrow 🚲 lane

1.9 At end of rd → (to City Centre, **14**) *(for **station** ↑)*, after high viaduct, at T-jct, use crossings ↑, at other side of rd ↖ via tarmac path (**14**)

2.1 At ep ↖ via rd, after bend to right imm ← via pavement (to City Centre, **14**), cross next rd ↑ onto pavement, then at rndabt 1st rd → *(note: **ignore** signs route **14!**, North Rd Methodist Church on corner)*

2.5 At sharp bend to the left, ***dismount***, go ↗, walk on pavement, after 50m, walk ↖ via cobbled rd onto ⛵ **Framwellgate Bridge**

2.9 At central square ⛵ 🏠 🚏 ☞ 🍴 ℹ️ ⌐ ***Durham***, walk →, at split of rds walk ↖ via cobbled rd downhill onto ⛵ **Elvet Bridge** *(for ⛵ **Durham Castle**, **Cathedral** and **Museum** walk ↗ uphill)*

3.1 At end of cobbled rd, use crossing of lhts to go ↑, resume cycling on rd (Old Elvet) 🚗, then 1st rd ← (Territorial Ln)

3.4 At T-jct → (Elvet Waterside), after 50m ← via river bridge

3.5 At end of river bridge *reset mileage:*

0.0 *(3.5)* Go east → via tarmac river path (to Sunderland, **14**)

1.0 After bend in river ↖ via wide path going away from the river (**14**)

1.5 Ep ↑ via rd *(⛵ **Old Durham Gardens** on your left)*, at next jct ← (**14**)

2.8 At jct with lhts → via path on right side of rd, becomes wide 🚲 (**14**)

3.1 At jct with lhts via 🚲 crossings ← onto 🚲 on right side of rd (**14**)

Route 5: Durham - Middlesbrough

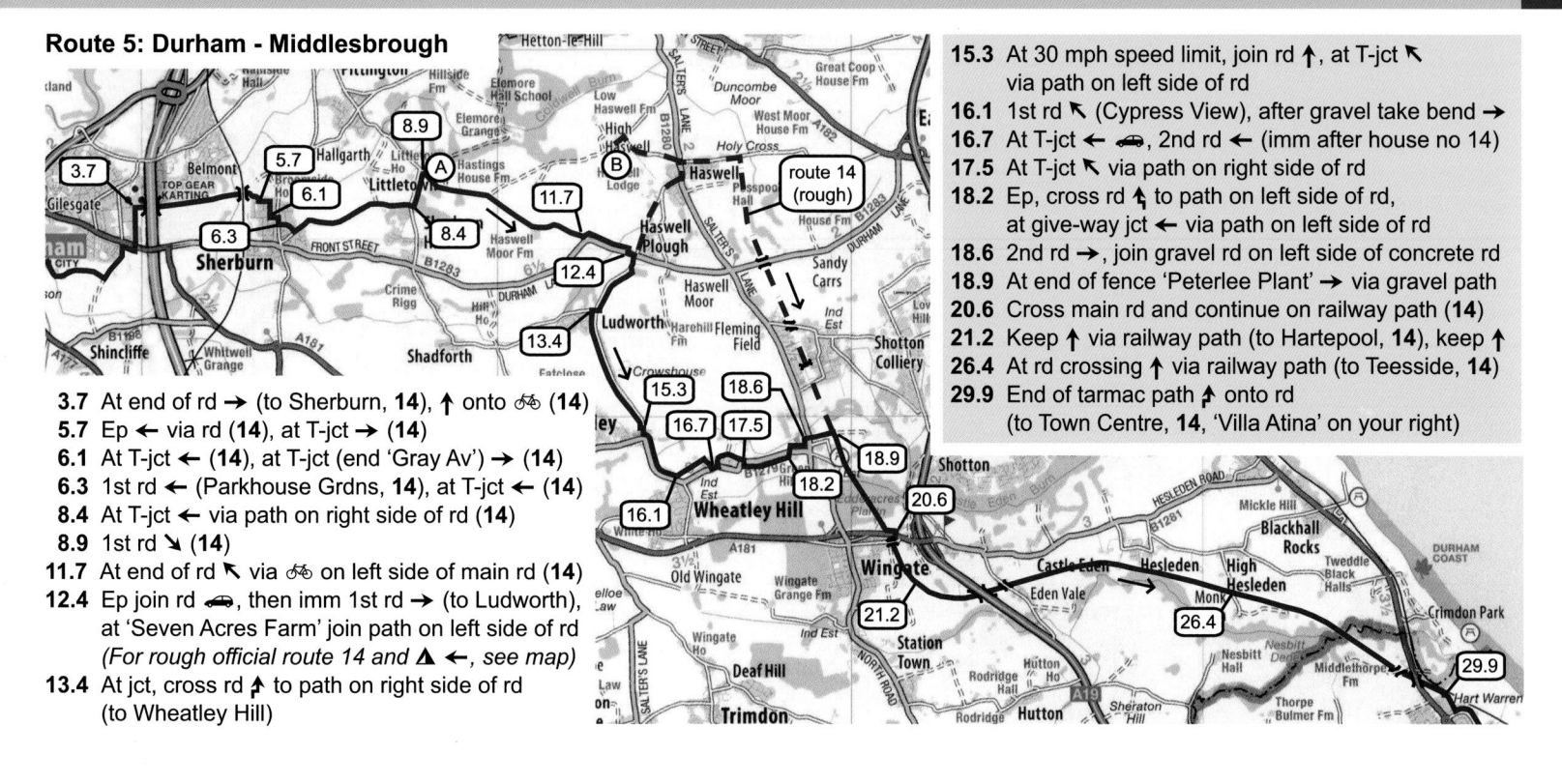

15.3 At 30 mph speed limit, join rd ↑, at T-jct ↖ via path on left side of rd

16.1 1st rd ↖ (Cypress View), after gravel take bend →

16.7 At T-jct ← 🚗, 2nd rd ← (imm after house no 14)

17.5 At T-jct ↖ via path on right side of rd

18.2 Ep, cross rd ↑ to path on left side of rd, at give-way jct ← via path on left side of rd

18.6 2nd rd →, join gravel rd on left side of concrete rd

18.9 At end of fence 'Peterlee Plant' → via gravel path

20.6 Cross main rd and continue on railway path (**14**)

21.2 Keep ↑ via railway path (to Hartepool, **14**), keep ↑

26.4 At rd crossing ↑ via railway path (to Teesside, **14**)

29.9 End of tarmac path ↟ onto rd (to Town Centre, **14**, 'Villa Atina' on your right)

3.7 At end of rd → (to Sherburn, **14**), ↑ onto 🚲 (**14**)

5.7 Ep ← via rd (**14**), at T-jct → (**14**)

6.1 At T-jct ← (**14**), at T-jct (end 'Gray Av') → (**14**)

6.3 1st rd ← (Parkhouse Grdns, **14**), at T-jct ← (**14**)

8.4 At T-jct ← via path on right side of rd (**14**)

8.9 1st rd ↘ (**14**)

11.7 At end of rd ↖ via 🚲 on left side of main rd (**14**)

12.4 Ep join rd 🚗, then imm 1st rd → (to Ludworth), at 'Seven Acres Farm' join path on left side of rd *(For rough official route 14 and ▲ ←, see map)*

13.4 At jct, cross rd ↟ to path on right side of rd (to Wheatley Hill)

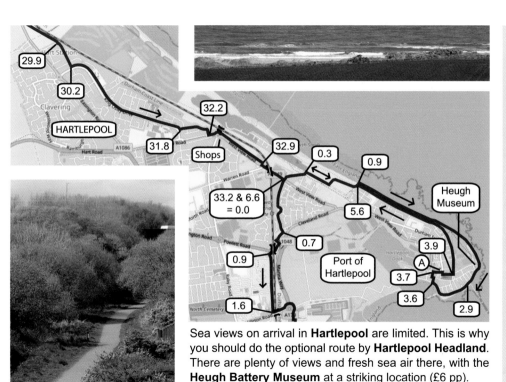

Sea views on arrival in **Hartlepool** are limited. This is why you should do the optional route by **Hartlepool Headland**. There are plenty of views and fresh sea air there, with the **Heugh Battery Museum** at a striking location (£6 pp).

30.2 At give-way jct ← via 🚲 on left side of rd (King Oswy Dr, to Town Centre, **14**)
31.8 After church bldng, 1st rd ← (Bruntoft Av, to Town Centre, **14**)
32.2 At T-jct ← via 🚲 (to Town Centre, **14**), follow 🚲 on left side of rndabt, ↑ via 🚲 on left side of rd (🚩 on right of rd)
32.9 Ep ↑ via rd 🚗 ('Warren rd' on right)
33.2 At 🚲 on left side of rd *reset mileage:*
Start Circular ⛵🏠 Headland Route:
0.0 *(33.2)* Go ← via 🚲 (to Headland)
0.3 Ep ↗ via rd, after rd into housing estate on the left, at the end of wall, 1st tarmac path ←
0.9 Ep ←, keep ← down onto coastal path, →
2.9 At ⛵ **Heugh Battery Museum** keep ↑
3.6 After lighthouse, at park →, 🔼 onto square
3.7 🔼 into ⛵ **park**, ep →, at bend → (Durham St)
3.9 After church, 1st rd ← (Friarage Grdns), ↑
5.6 End of rd ↖ via path, same route back to:
Start continued route:
0.0 *(6.6 & 33.2)* Join 🚲 → (to Town Centre, **14**)
0.7 Ep → via rd (**14**), at end of rd 🔼 via crossing onto 🚲 on left side of rd (**14**)
0.9 1st rd ↖ (Lancaster Rd, to Town Centre, **14**)

Route 5: Durham - Middlesbrough

The Heugh Battery and Royal Navy Museums

1.6 At jct with lhts ← via path on left side of rd (*ignore* signs route **14***!*)

1.8 Follow paths around rndabt for 3rd exit (→), keep to path on left side of rd (to Museums)

2.0 1st rd ← (The Highlight), at rndabt →, ↑ via gate, after ⛴ **Royal Navy Museum** ←, at ⛴ **Hartlepool Museum** again ← via path

2.4 At start of path next to docks, join rd ↗

2.7 At side rd 'Victoria Terrace' *reset mileage:* (For 🛏 ☕ 🍴 ⚓ **Hartlepool** (station and town centre) → via Victoria Tc, see map)

0.0 (2.7) For continued route ↑ via dead end rd (Maritime Av, to Yacht Club, **14**)

0.2 At rndabt ↑ (Maritime Av, to Greatham, **14**)

0.4 2nd rd ← (to Greatham, **14**) , at rndabt via 🚲 ramp onto coastal path, go → (**14**)

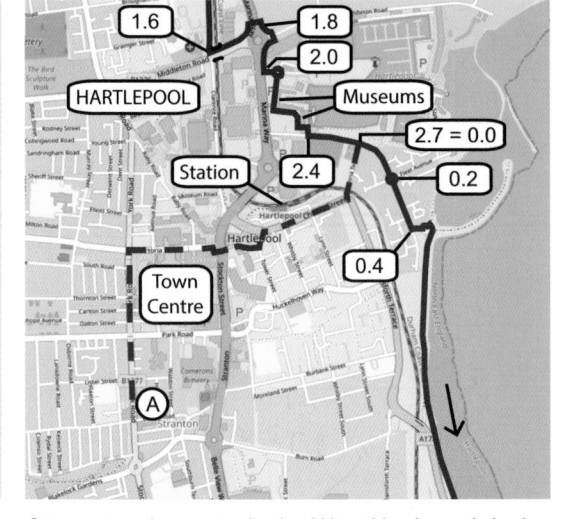

On the headland, you can't miss the nice park square with the **Hartlepool Borough Hall** (after 3.7 km on the previous page). This was Hartlepool's town centre until the construction of the railway and West Hartlepool docks in the 1840s. This caused a new town to grow on the mainland, taking over in importance. This is where the town centre is now.

Our route takes you via the West Hartlepool docks, with its **National Museum of the Royal Navy** (£8 pp) and the **Museum of Hartlepool** (free). Both museums feature historical ships. The Royal Navy museum features the HMS Trincomalee, Europe's oldest floating war ship. The Hartlepool Museum features paddle steamer PS Wingfield Castle.

3.5 At rd ramp onto ⬧ *Seaton Carew Beach*, go → and cross rd ↑ (Station Rd, to Grantham, **14**) 🚗

4.7 Cross rd ↑ from narrow 🚲 lane onto traffic-free 🚲 on right side of rd

5.1 Cross 'Brenda Rd' at 🚲 crossing, continue ↑ via lay-by rd on right side of main rd (to Grantham, **14**)

5.9 At rndabt, follow bend to the right, then ↟ via 🚲 crossing to left side of rd, then ↖ (to Grantham, **14**)

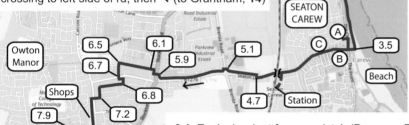

Hartlepool - Seaton Carew coastal cycle path

6.1 Ep ↑ via rd, at four-way jct ↑ (Benmore Rd, **14**)

6.5 At T-jct ← (**14**, 'Callander Rd' on your right)

6.7 At T-jct ← via 🚲 on right side of rd (**14**), then 1st rd → (Claymore Rd, to Grantham, **14**)

6.8 1st rd → (Caithness Rd, to Grantham, **14**)

7.2 At T-jct → (**14**), at next T-jct ← via 🚲 on right side of rd (Catcote Rd, to Grantham, **14**)

7.6 After shops 🚲 **Owton Manor**, 1st through rd → (Mowbray Rd, to Grantham, **14**)

7.9 1st rd ← (Holland Rd, to Greatham, **14**)

8.1 2nd rd → (Thetford Rd, to Greatham, **14**)

8.3 At bend to the right, 1st 🚲 ← (to Greatham, **14**)

8.5 Cross rd ↑, continue on 🚲 (to Greatham, **14**)

8.8 At jct with traffic lhts ↑ via rd (to Greatham, **14**) 🚗

9.4 In 🚲 🍴 **Greatham** *(pubs)* follow sharp bend → (to Billingham, **14**) 🚗

10.0 1st rd ← (dead end, to Billingham, **14**), narrows to gravel path, then tarmac rd again, keep ↑ (**14**)

Route 5: Durham - Middlesbrough

Approaching Teesside at Middlesbrough

12.9 At give-way jct, cross rd ↑ (🚗🚗!), then imm ↖ via gravel path (to Billingham, **14**) , ep ↖ via rd
13.5 At give-way jct ← (*ignore* signs route **14**) 🚗
13.8 After railway crossing, at T-jct
☞ 🍴 **Cowpen Bewley** (*pub*) ↘
15.5 After start 30 mph speed limit, 1st rd ← (Greenwoord Rd) 🚗
(*For station* **Billingham** ↑, *at lhts* → *via pavement on right side of rd*)

Seaton Carew is also known for the mysterious disappearance of sea kayaker John Darwin in 2002 during very calm sea conditions. He was announced dead, with his wife claiming a life insurance pay out, but he was found to be alive in 2007. Despite having been hidden by his wife for five years, there had been sightings of Darwin. Both served six years in prison.

Heading south from Hartlepool's docks, a cycle path right on the coast takes you to **Seaton Carew**, from where a sandy beach stretches towards the mouth of the Tees Estuary. This beach makes a great 2-3 hour return walk to the North Gare breakwater of the Tees. From there, the Tees riverbanks are completely taken over by the industrial complexes of Middlesbrough and Stockton-on-Tees. This pushes us back inland, initially via the **Owton Manor** housing estate, with a modest shopping arcade directly on the route. From there, we make our way to the edge of the vast housing and industrial estates of **Billingham**. With the official cycle routes embarking on even longer detours via Stockton-on-Tees, we guide you as comfortably as possible to our next landmark; Middlesbrough's **River Tees Transporter Bridge**. Check page 60 for information on whether you can choose our direct route to this bridge or to use the longer alternative route.

A1185

Stockton Road

Seal Sands Road

12.9

Cowpen Bewley

Cowpen Bewley

13.5

13.8

BILLINGHAM

Station

15.5

River Brook Tees

16.2 At side rd 'Byland Wy' ↑ via path on left side of rd

16.5 At rndabt take 2nd exit (↖), path on left side of rd (Belasis Av)

17.8 Ep, join rd ↑ 🚗, after 100m at T-jct → (Hope St) 🚗

18.0 At T-jct with lhts *reset mileage and choose your route:*

Direct route via River Tees Transporter Bridge (see page 60):

0.0 *(18.0)* At T-jct with lhts ← via narrow 🚲 on right side of rd (Clarence St)

1.5 At official end of 🚲 (shown by give way-marking on tarmac), continue ↑ on pavement for 5m, then → via tunnel under railway

1.7 Ep ↗ via main rd, after crossing with ⛴ **Transporter Bridge** *reset mileage* at jct with lhts, continue on page 61

Alternative route for River Tees Transporter Bridge:

0.0 *(18.0)* At T-jct with lhts → via narrow path on left side of rd (Clarence St), after tunnel under railway ↑ via 🚲 on left side of rd

0.8 Ep (see 🚲 sign 'Tees Bridges' beyond rndabt) cross rd ↑ onto 🚲 on right side of rd (🚗🚗!), keep ↑ via this 🚲

3.1 Just after high power lines across rd and before large rd junction, cross rd ← via 🚲 crossing with lhts, at other side ↗ via 🚲 on left side of rd (to Middlesbrough), keep ↑ via this 🚲

4.4 Whilst you are still on historic bridge, imm after crossing River Tees, ← via 🚲 ramp (1), leading down onto riverside 🚲, ↑ (1)

7.0 At sign ⛴ **'Teessaurus Park'** → via path (leaving riverside)

7.2 Ep ← via 🚲 on left side of rd, keep ↑ via this 🚲

8.6 At jct with lhts *reset mileage (for* ⛴ **Transporter Bridge** ←*)*

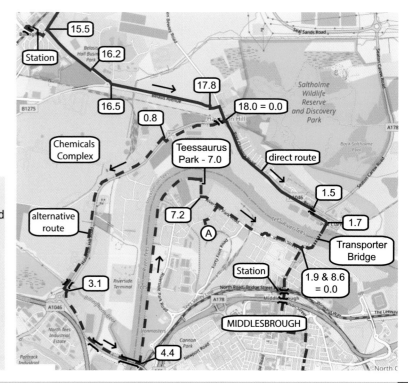

Route 6: Middlesbrough - Whitby (Ruswarp)

68 km / 42 miles: 🚲 21%, 🚶 70%, 🚗 9%, 🚗🚗 0%
Stations: *Middlesbrough, Great Ayton, Kildale, Commondale, Castleton Moor, Glaisdale, Sleight*

After having your share of cycling in industrial wasteland, things are literally on the up. Your arrival in **Middlesbrough** couldn't be more spectacular with the crossing of the monumental **River Tees Transporter Bridge**. The city centre with its imposing **Town Hall** breathes the pride of an industrial town which was incorporated in 1853, only 24 years after the conversion of a local riverside farm into a coal port. The wealth of the town and its rapid expansion with its iron and steelworks can still be felt. The new industries attracted workers from as far as Wales. Today, Middlesbrough is still known for its community choirs, originating from Welsh church choirs.

The **River Tees Transporter Bridge** is an industrial heritage structure dating from 1911. It allows a travelling 'gondola' road deck suspended from the bridge to travel across the river in 90 seconds. The structure provides shipping a clearance of 49 metres and allows up to 200 people and nine cars per crossing (£1 per cyclist). The visitor experience gives access to the glass lift to the top (£6 pp, pre-bookings essential). The bridge's opening times are 7am - 6pm on weekdays, 9am - 3pm on Saturdays, no crossings on Sundays. High winds and maintenance can result in extra closures. See page 59 for an alternative route.

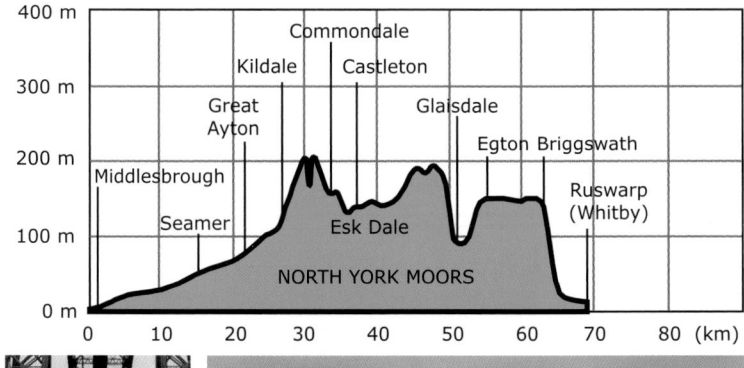

Downtown Middlesbrough

Cook monument near Great Ayton on the hilltop

Middlesbrough has a soft spot for the famous explorer **James Cook**. Cook grew up in nearby **Great Ayton** and found his sea legs in **Whitby**. He became well-known for his maps of North America's east coast and was sent into the unknown Pacific by the Royal Navy in 1768. His most famous achievements are the discovery of Australia's east coast, the circumnavigation of New Zealand and venturing deep into the Arctic circle. In Middlesbrough, a hospital and station bear his name. Great Ayton features the **Captain Cook Schoolroom Museum** (free) and an obelisk in the hills, visible from the road.

0.0 *(1.9 & 8.6)* At jct with lhts, head south (to York, **65**) 🚌, keep ↑ at jcts with lhts into ≼ ♠ 🛒 ☕ ▮ℱ ▮ *Middlesbrough*

1.0 Imm after ≼ **Town Hall** ← onto pedestrian promenade, with park ≼ **Centre Square** on right side (**65**)

1.3 At near end of promenade → via 🚲 (**65**), at rd crossing ↑ via 🚲 (**65**)

1.6 Ep cross rd ↑ via lhts onto Palm St (**65**)

1.8 At T-jct ← (**65**)

1.9 At T-jct (end of Clarendon Rd) → (**65**)

2.0 At T-jct ↗ via 🚲 onto Abingdon Rd (**65**)

Leaving Middlesbrough, you will do a slightly tiresome survey of over 100 years of English suburban development, each era with its own architecture. Green fields await you at the end!

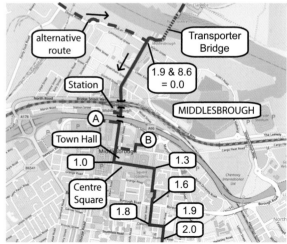

alternative route

Transporter Bridge

1.9 & 8.6 = 0.0

Station

MIDLESBROUGH

A

Town Hall

B

1.0

1.3

1.6

Centre Square

1.8

1.9

2.0

Route 6: Middlesbrough - Whitby (Ruswarp)

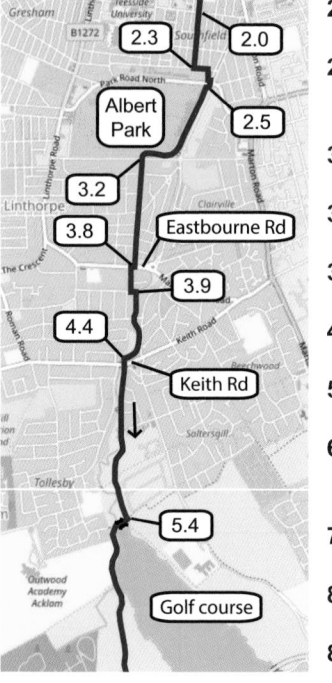

2.3 At T-jct ← (**65**), just before petrol station 1st rd → (Falmouth St, **65**)

2.5 At bend to the left, go ↑ via 🚲 crossing with lhts, then ↗ via 🚲 (to York, **65**), with 🚶 **Albert Park** on right hand side

3.2 Cross rd ↑ via 🚲 onto Southwell Rd (to Hemlington, **65**)

3.8 At T-jct with lhts 🚏 🚶 **Eastbourne Rd** ↗ onto 🚲 (**65**)

3.9 Ep ← via rd, then imm → via 🚲 (**65**), then cross quiet rd ↑

4.4 Go ↖ to crossing 'Keith Rd' with lhts, cross ↑ and continue via 🚲 (**65**)

5.4 At jct of paths → via old bridge across stream, then imm ↖ via 🚲 (**65**)

6.9 Ep ↖ via 🚲 on left side of 'Ladgate Ln', then ↗ onto 🚲 on right side of rd (to Hemlington, **65**), leading into tunnel, after tunnel ↖ via 🚲 (**65**)

7.7 At rd crossing with lhts ↑ via 🚲 (to Hemlington, **65**), keep following 🚲 ↗ around school

8.0 At rd crossing ↑ via 🚲 (to Hemlington, **65**), then cross quiet rd ↑, then keep ↖ via 🚲 (**65**)

8.2 At 🚲 T-jct → via 🚲 (to Hemlington, **65**)

8.4 After tunnel, follow bends, ep cross rd ← onto 🚲 (to Hemlington Lake, **65**)

8.8 After sharp bend to the left, 1st 🚲 → (to Hemlington Lake, **65**)

9.5 After tunnel, at split of paths, keep 'half ↗' via middle 🚲 (**65**)

10.0 At end of lakeside imm → via 🚲 (**65**), follow this 🚲, bending ↖, then crossing quiet rd and school entrance

10.7 Ep ← via rd, 1st rd → (Quarry Dr, **65**)

11.0 At T-jct 🚶 **Stainton** (pub) ← (**65**), ↑ follow rd with bends (to Yarm, **65**) 🚗

From Middlesbrough it is tempting to continue on the North Sea Cycle route, but this 'route 1' has a dead end beyond the town of Redcar, with no other route options available than a narrow winding main road. Our inland route via **North York Moors National Park**, however, treats you to very pleasant country lane cycling in stunning countryside.

The fun starts with a steady climb into the beautiful **Cleveland Hills** from **Great Ayton**. On your left you can't miss the half-coned **Roseberry Topping**, the most distinctive hill in the area. Also, on your left you will see the obelisk of **Captain Cook's Monument** on a hilltop.

At **Kildale**, the highlands truly begin. You will be climbing steeply now onto **Commondale Moor**. A rough gravel track to **Castleton** will slow you down (see page 18), but then it is all tarmac again into the quiet **Esk Dale**. Small railway stations keep popping up every few miles or so. Just beyond **Danby**, it is worth having a break at the modest **The Moors National Park Centre** before continuing to **Glaisdale**. There are no shops here, but a visit to the tiny **Museum of Victorian Science** could be a memorable moment. Book yourself a tour in this otherwise private home; call 01947 897440 during evening hours for a reservation.

A few miles from our route at high-up **Egton**, deep in the valley, **Grosmont** is the gateway to the **North Yorkshire Moors Steam Railway**. From here you can travel by steam to the market town of **Pickering** and back. With nearly 30 km (18 miles) of track, this is one of Britain's longest heritage lines (from £35 pp). Cycling on, a pleasant lane heads for **Aislaby**, from where a steep descent on rough gravel awaits you; be safe and walk it!

Crossing the Commondale Moor and the steam railway at Grosmont station

Route 6: Middlesbrough - Whitby (Ruswarp)

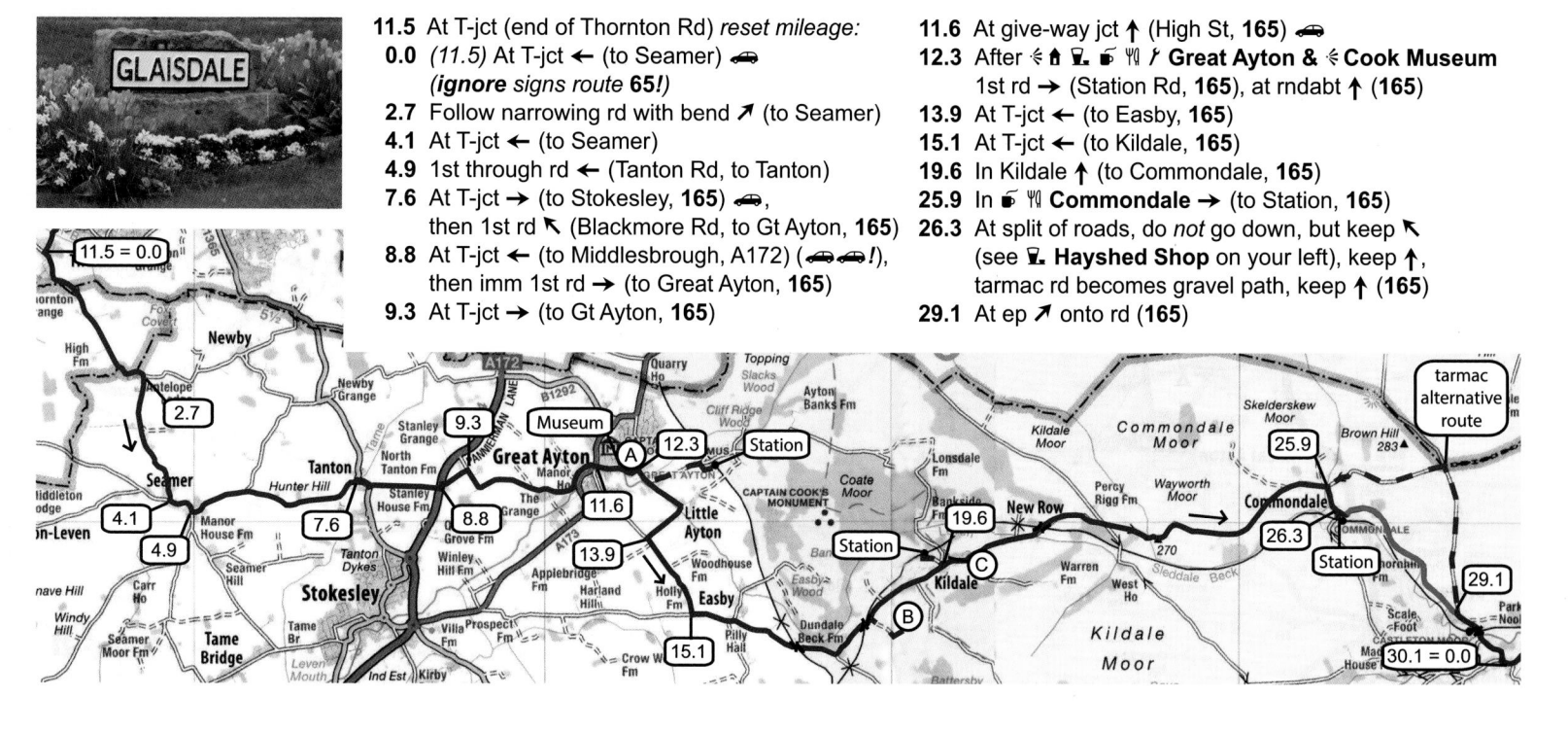

11.5 At T-jct (end of Thornton Rd) *reset mileage:*

0.0 *(11.5)* At T-jct ← (to Seamer) 🚗
   (ignore signs route 65!)

2.7 Follow narrowing rd with bend ↗ (to Seamer)

4.1 At T-jct ← (to Seamer)

4.9 1st through rd ← (Tanton Rd, to Tanton)

7.6 At T-jct → (to Stokesley, **165**) 🚗,
   then 1st rd ↖ (Blackmore Rd, to Gt Ayton, **165**)

8.8 At T-jct ← (to Middlesbrough, A172) (🚗🚗!),
   then imm 1st rd → (to Great Ayton, **165**)

9.3 At T-jct → (to Gt Ayton, **165**)

11.6 At give-way jct ↑ (High St, **165**) 🚗

12.3 After ⚞🏠🏛🛒🍴♪ **Great Ayton & ⚞ Cook Museum**
   1st rd → (Station Rd, **165**), at rndabt ↑ (**165**)

13.9 At T-jct ← (to Easby, **165**)

15.1 At T-jct ← (to Kildale, **165**)

19.6 In Kildale ↑ (to Commondale, **165**)

25.9 In 🛒🍴 **Commondale** → (to Station, **165**)

26.3 At split of roads, do *not* go down, but keep ↖
   (see 🏛 **Hayshed Shop** on your left), keep ↑,
   tarmac rd becomes gravel path, keep ↑ (**165**)

29.1 At ep ↗ onto rd (**165**)

30.1 At T-jct ⟨symbols⟩ **Castleton** *reset mileage:*
0.0 *(30.1)* At T-jct ← (to Danby, **165**)
0.6 Keep ↑ (to Danby)
(*ignore signs route* **165**!)
2.4 At give-way-jct ⟨symbols⟩ **Danby** ⤴
(Brier Hill, to Lealholm, **165**)
3.3 Follow sharp bend to → (to Lealholm)
(*ignore signs route* **165**!)
(⟨symbol⟩ **The Moors National Park Centre** →)

4.2 After tunnel under railway ↖ (no signs)
5.6 1st through rd ↗ (to Fryup)
6.8 At T-jct ← (to Lealholm)
10.0 At T-jct ↗ (to Glaisdale), keep ↑
12.6 At ⟨symbols⟩ **Glaisdale** *(pub)* ↑, keep ↑
(⟨symbol⟩ **Museum of Victorian Science** *after 50m on left side of the road in house*)
16.2 At T-jct ⟨symbols⟩ **Egton** *(pub)* → (to Egton Bridge), then 1st rd ↖ (to Grosmont, **165**)

16.7 1st rd ← (**165**, see sign 25% descent)
(*for* ⟨symbol⟩ **Moors Steam Railway** ↑)
17.5 At T-jct ↗ (**165**), keep ↑
22.4 At give way-jct ↑ (**165**), then imm after house no 27 → via wide gravel path (to Ruswarp **165**), pass through gate
24.1 Cross main rd ↑ (⟨car symbols⟩!) onto rd into ⟨symbol⟩ **Briggswath** (to Ruswarp, **165**) ⟨car⟩
26.7 *Reset mileage at T-jct* ⟨symbols⟩ **Ruswarp**

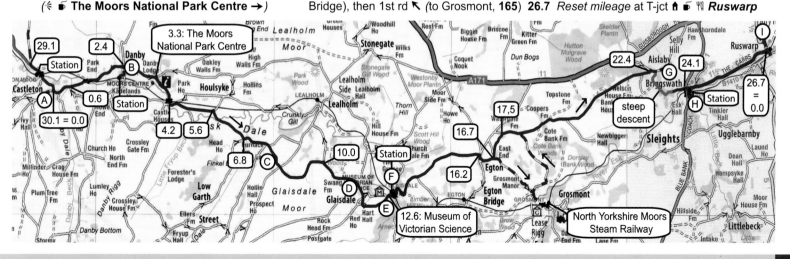

3.3: The Moors National Park Centre

12.6: Museum of Victorian Science

North Yorkshire Moors Steam Railway

Route 7: Whitby (Ruswarp) - Scarborough (Hunmanby)

60 km / 37 miles: 🚲 53%, 🚶 24%, 🚌 22%, 🚘 1%
Stations: Ruswarp, Whitby, Scarborough, Hunmanby

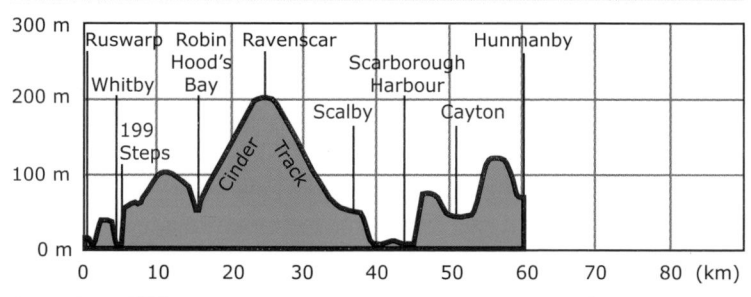

Whitby Abbey features an excellent YHA immediately next to the site.

England's North Sea coast is nowhere more spectacular then between Whitby and Scarborough. The North York Moors drop steeply down to sea level providing a rich array of cliffs, coves and bays, with the occasional pretty beach. Hugging the coastline here is the **Cinder Track**, a cycle path on a former railway, which (it has to be said) needs lots of improvements to truly become the very best section of the North Sea Cycle Route. In its current state, the stunning landscape has to work hard to make up for its rough and muddy stretches. Expect to do plenty of walking, especially between Robin Hood's Bay and Hayburn Wyke, see also page 18.

Pretty **Whitby** is the smaller of the two famous North Yorkshire seaside towns, but it has plenty to offer for a two-night break. Whitby is famous for its abandoned **Whitby Abbey**. Its ruins stand on a high cliff looking out over town and sea (£8 pp). **199 steps** are required to climb up the hill. This book invites you to push your bike up via the steep alley right next to these famous steps, immortilised by the famous 1897 Gothic horror novel **Dracula** by Bram Stoker. Opportunities to relive the story are provided at the **Dracula Experience** (£3 pp) and through **guided walks** via www.whitbystoryteller.co.uk. Whitby's scenic medieval fishing port also has plenty of smuggling stories, so select your preferred themed walk online (prices vary). The **Captain Cook Memorial Museum** could be your 'final intake' on England most famous explorer. The museum features a full overview of Cook's life and journeys (£7 pp). The **Whitby Museum** displays more maritime heritage of the area (£6 pp).

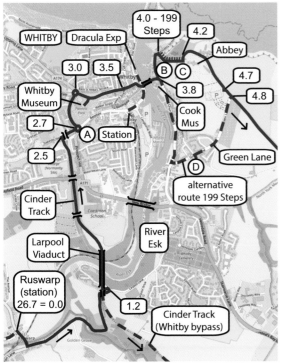

199 steps with the 'bike push-up' to Whitby Abbey; avoid the climb via Green Lane, see the map

0.0 *(26.7)* At T-jct 🏠 🛒 🍴 ***Ruswarp →*** (to Whitby, **165**) 🚗, after station and river bridge imm ← (to Whitby, **165**)

1.2 After climb and passing under viaduct, 1st rd ← (Private Rd to 'Riverside View'), imm ← up via tarmac path, at jct of paths ***choose your route:*** *(For Cinder Track, bypassing Whitby:* ← *(to Scarborough,* **1***), see maps)* **For main route via Whitby:** → (to Whitby, **1**) to ⛰ **Larpool Viaduct**

2.5 Follow tarmac path down ramp, at ep → via rd through narrow tunnel

2.7 At rndabt ← 🚗 *(**ignore** signs route* **1***!)*

3.0 At rndabt, furthest rd → (to Town Centre) *(For* ⛰ **Whitby Museum** → *into park)*

3.5 At side rd 'Brunswick St' ***dismount***, walk ↑ via pavements, keep walking ↑ into ⛰ 🏠 🅿 🛒 🍴 ℹ️ *Whitby*, at river resume cycling across bridge ↑ 🚗

3.8 After river bridge, in bend to right ← (to Whitby Abbey), walk as needed *(to avoid 199 Steps go → via alt. route)*

4.0 After sharp bend to the right ↗, using cobbled rd on right side of ⛰ **199 Steps**

4.2 Ep ↖ via rd *(For* ⛰ **Abbey** *and* 🏛 →*)*

4.7 At give-way markings, keep ↑ via rd

4.8 At 'Green Ln' ↑ (to Hawsker) *(For △ →)*

Route 7: Whitby (Ruswarp) - Scarborough (Hunmanby)

The **Cinder Track** starts with the impressive crossing of the River Esk via the **Larpool Viaduct**, which this book utilises on arrival in Whitby. The trail also allows you to bypass Whitby, see the map. Whatever you route choice, from **Hawsker** and its bike rental you are on the course of the old Whitby-Scarborough railway which closed in 1965.

At pretty **Robin Hood's Bay** the Cinder Track hits the coastal cliffs. If you like to experience driving off-road, the **North Yorkshire Off Road Centre** may be something for you; the campsite next-doors is bound to be noisy. If you want to stay overnight right on a truly unspoiled coastline, the YHA near **Fylingthorpe** is your first choice. The pub with campsite at **Hayburn Wyke** makes a good alternative option. Do not miss the walk to the coastal waterfalls here! More striking coastal views can be enjoyed at **Blea Wyke Point**. You also find tearooms in the old **Ravenscar** station here; it is a favourite with local cyclists and the only trail cafe en-route.

Views from the Cinder Track near Robin Hood's Bay

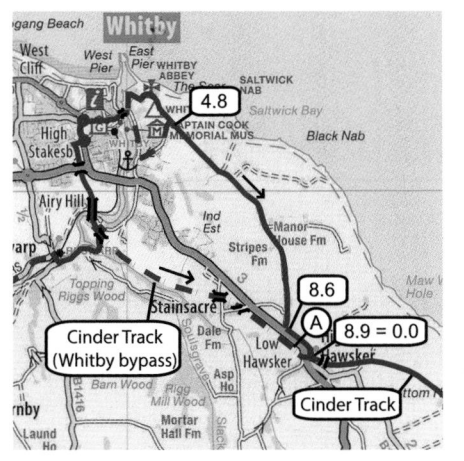

8.6 At T-jct ← via 🚲 on left side of rd (A171, to Scarborough)
8.9 At rd crossing with lhts, *reset mileage (Whitby bypass route merging):*
0.0 (8.9) Go east ↖ onto 🚲 (Cinder Track, to Scarborough, **1**)

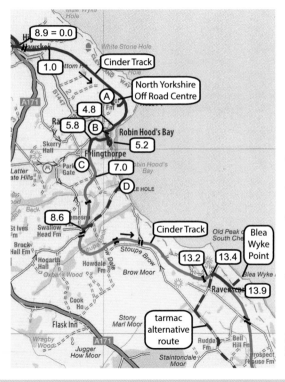

1.0 Cross rd ↑ (Cinder Track, **1**)

4.8 Ep ← onto tarmac rd (**1**), at T-jct ← 🚗, keep ↑ *(ignore signs route 1!)*

5.2 At rndabt ⛲🏠🚻🍴 **Robin Hood's Bay**, after visit, turn around (go back) 🚗, then 1st rd ← (Thorpe Ln, to Fylingthorpe)

5.8 In bendy section, 1st 🚲 ↖ (Cinder Track, **1**), keep ↑ via 🚲

7.0 At rd crossing ↑ via 🚲 (**1**)

8.6 Ep ↙ via rd, then imm ↗ onto 🚲 (**1**)

13.2 Ep ↗ onto cobbled path with tarmac strip on right hand side (**1**), becomes concrete

13.4 At end of concrete path ↖ onto rd, imm sharp bend to → (Station Rd, **1**)

13.9 At 🍴 **Ravenscar** *(tearooms)* ↑ via narrow tarmac path onto railway path *(For short walk to ⛲ **Blea Wyke Point** ← via grass path, park bikes at road side)*

19.8 Cross wide gravel path ↑ via 🚲 (**1**) *(For short walk to ⛲ **Hayburn Wyke Waterfall** ←, park bikes at small car pk, use public footpath ↗ via ▲)*

23.0 Ep cross rd ↑ via car pk ↑ via 🚲 (**1**)

24.6 Ep cross rd via lhts, then ← via 🚲 on right side of rd (**1**), 1st narrow 🚲 ↗ (**1**)

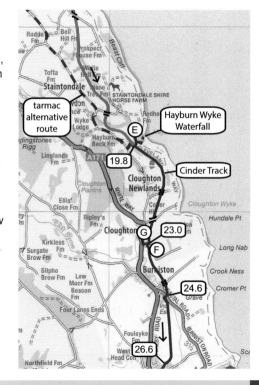

Route 7: Whitby (Ruswarp) - Scarborough (Hunmanby)

Scarborough has attracted holidaymakers since the 1660s with its spa and can therefore be regarded as Britain's first seaside resort. We leave the Cinder Track in the northern suburbs, which allows you to enjoy all coastal cycling Scarborough has available. There are two sandy beaches, separated by a headland where the **Scarborough Castle** ruins provide great views. Its 12th century great tower is the centrepiece of a royal palace begun by Henry II (£9 pp).

Before arriving at **North Bay Beach** you will pass the entrances of **Peasholm Park** and the **North Bay Railway**. The park opened in 1912 and is well known for its Japan-inspired features and Asian vegetation. You may hear the sounds of nearby steam locomotives embarking on their 1.4 km journey to the far end of the bay (£5 pp). As this is a miniature railway, different scales and the enthusiastic staff will make short journeys feel like an adventure. If you like quiet beaches, North Bay is the one.

South Bay Beach is naturally more crowded with the town centre and the old harbour on its doorstep. Beyond this, the **Rotunda Museum** on top of the cliff is one of the oldest purpose-built museums in the world, dating from 1829. It features fossils and minerals, an art gallery and of course the fine building itself (£3 pp). The former **Spa** building is at the southern end of the seafront and is now a theatre venue. The **Spa Cliff Lift** is a fine piece of Victorian engineering. A return up and down the cliff costs £2 pp.

North Bay Railway

North Bay Beach

Toll Gate

Scarborough Castle

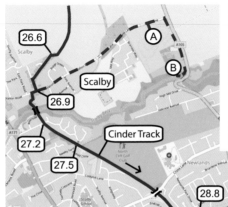

26.6 Ep ← via rd, at T-jct ← (**1**)
26.9 At T-jct → *(for ▲ ⛺ ←)*, 1st rd ← (Chichester Cl, **1**), after house no 23 ↗ to continued 🚲 Cinder Track (**1**)
27.2 At rd crossing ↑ via 🚲
27.5 At rd crossing ↑ via 🚲
28.6 After passing under rd viaduct, at four-way 🚲 jct, at sign 'Gallows Field' (see ball court/cycle cross track) 1st 🚲 ← *(ignore signs route 1!)*
28.8 Ep, join rd → via lhts, 1st rd ← (Givendale Rd)
29.2 At T-jct →, 1st rd ↖ (Ryndle Cr)

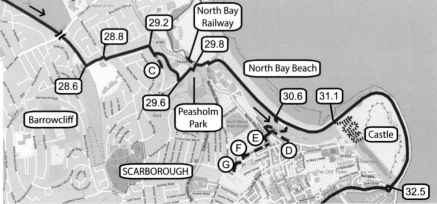

29.6 At T-jct ← (see building Manor Heath on corner), at next T-jct → via pavement on right side of main rd, dismount *(entrance ⛬ **Peasholm Park** →)*
29.8 Cross main rd ⬆ via lhts *(for ⛬ **North Bay Railway** ←)*, continue ↑ on pavement, after rndabt, join rd ↑ (⛬ **Royal Albert Drive** and ⛱ **North Bay Beach**) 🚗
30.6 Keep ↑ (to South Bay, ⛬ **Marine Drive**) 🚗 *(for ⤵ ↗)*
31.1 *(For ⛬ **Scarborough Castle** → via footpath uphill)*
32.5 At rndabt ↑ (harbour on left side of rd) 🚗

Route 7: Whitby (Ruswarp) - Scarborough (Hunmanby)

South Bay Beach

Our route hugs the scenic bottom of the cliffs, but walking your bike may be required during busy hours. Beyond the Spa, the route drops briefly onto a beach, only accessible during low tide. When you are at the Rotonda Museum turn off, look up website **www. tidetimes.org.uk** and choose for the route on top of the cliffs as needed. Under no circumstances you should attempt to cycle across crashing waves! Both routes merge at the end of town. We head inland to **Hunmanby**. Avoid the steep and winding **White Gate Hill** during rush hours, as traffic will be busy. Unfortunately, there is no alternative; take care!

32.9 At jct with lhts ↑ 🚗🚗
(For 🏠 🛏 📷 🍴 ℹ️ *Scarborough*)
33.5 *Reset mileage* at rndabt:
For ⛵ **Rotunda Museum**, **station** and *alternative route* → (see map)

Note: **Tidal section ahead!** If you are at this point within 90 minutes before or 90 minutes after high tide, use the alternative route!

0.0 *(33.5)* At rnabt ↑, head south via sea front (⛵ **South Bay Beach**), keep ↑
0.5 At end of rd dismount, walk ↑ via path under ⛵ **Spa Theatre**, at ⛵ **Spa's Cliff Lift** ↑, only resume cycling when not too busy, keep ↑
1.4 After tidal beach section, follow wide bendy gravel path ↑ up the cliffs
1.8 At end ← via tarmac path with benches, dismount as needed, ep → onto rd
2.1 At give-way jct ↑ (Wheatcroft Av)
2.2 At jct with lhts ← via 🚲 at left side of main rd (**1**), at ep *reset mileage*

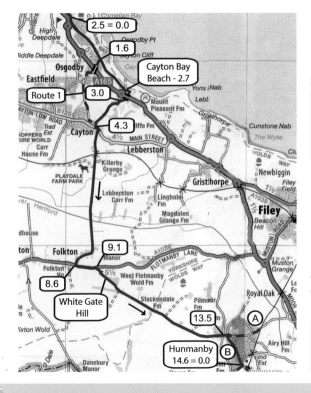

0.0 *(2.5)* At ep (see sign 'St Michael's Ln) join rd ⬆, then at bottom of hill, at T-jct ↖ (Filey Rd, **1**) 🚗
1.6 At jct for 'Osgodby Ln', keep ⬆ (see sign 'dead end rd except 🚲') (**ignore** signs route **1!**)

> The road ahead is closed for motorised traffic due to coastal erosion. At the time of publication of this book, the road was still open for cycling. This policy may change in the future. Alternative route 1 to Cayton is marked on the map. For now, enjoy the quiet coastal scenic route!

2.7 Just before rndabt ↖ via dead end rd, after entrance ⬅ ⛱ **Cayton Bay Beach** 1st 🚲 → into tunnel
3.0 Ep, join rd ↖ 🚗 (☕ 🍴 **The Tow Bar** after 50m)
4.3 At T-jct ← 🚗, then after 100m at 🚉 **Cayton** 1st rd → (Station Rd, to Playdale Farm, **1**)
8.6 At T-jct ← (**1**) 🚗 *(tricky right turn ahead!)*
9.1 1st rd ⬈ (to Hunmanby, **1**) 🚗 *(hazardous climb!)*
13.5 At mini rndabt ⬆ (to Bridlington, **1**) 🚗
14.6 After town centre 🏠 🚉 ☕ 🍴 *Hunmanby*, at next mini rndabt, *reset mileage (for station ⬆, after 200m ←)*

> To cycle directly to **York**, continue on page 74. To cycle to **Hull** and its ferry, go to page 78. From Hull you can also head for York, although this is an extra 78 km (48 miles)!

Tidal beach section of the route

Road closed due to coastal erosion

Route 8: Scarborough (Hunmanby) - York (Stamford Bridge)

63 km / 39 miles: 🚲 0%, 🚶 100%, 🚗 0%, 🚗🚗 0%
Stations: None

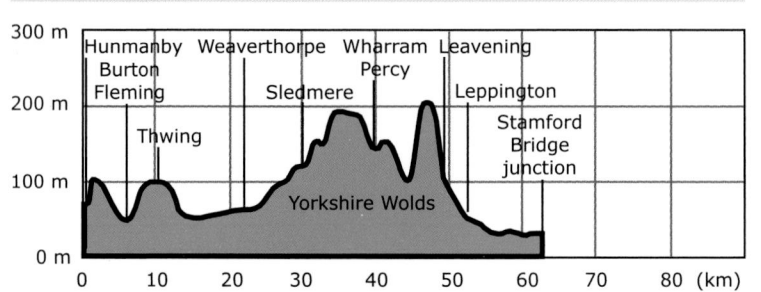

This route section takes you into the heart of the **Yorkshire Wolds**; a very rural area of pleasant rolling hills, which is sparsely populated. You will be on quiet country lanes and virtually empty roads, except for the 200m of cycle path at the very end; a unique route attribute even for this book!

Most villages on the way are in fact just hamlets. Get food and drink before leaving Hunmanby as you could find the only pubs in **Burton Fleming**, **Weaverthorpe** and **Sledmere** closed. You will encounter the stately home and gardens of **Sledmere House** on the midway point of this route (£10 pp). If you fancy a short walk to a special picnic spot, why not visit the deserted village of **Wharram Percy**? Landowners evicted their tenants in the 16th century, as sheep grazing was more profitable for them. Today, the lonely church ruins still stand. English Heritage provides a free audio tour.

0.0 *(14.6)* At mini rndabt *Hunmanby*: go west, → (New Rd, to Burton Fleming, **166**), 2x ↑

4.0 3rd rd ← (to Burton Fleming) (*ignore* signs route **166**!)

6.3 At end of rd ↗ (Front St)

6.5 At pub 🛏 🍴 **Burton Fleming**, at give-way jct, ↑ (Thwing Rd, to Kilham)

7.6 In bend to left, go ↗ (to Thwing)

10.6 At end of rd ↗ into **Thwing**, keep ↑

14.9 At T-jct → (see sign 'scenic byway')

16.4 At give-way jct ←

16.6 At T-jct cross main rd (🚗🚗!) ↑ (to Butterwick, **166**)

24.1 After **Butterwick**, 🛏 🛏 🍴 **Weaverthorpe** and **Helperthorpe**, 1st rd ← (to Sledmere, **166**)

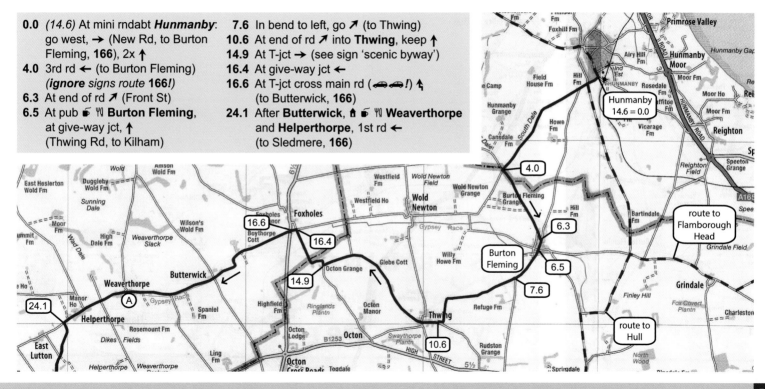

Route 8: Scarborough (Hunmanby) - York (Stamford Bridge)

26.2 At give-way jct ↑ (to Sledmere, **166**)

30.0 At T-jct → (to Malton, **166**), 🍺 *pub*

30.4 Just after hidden entrance on left of
⚞🍺 **Sledmere House** *reset mileage:*

0.0 *(30.4)* 1st rd →
(to Kirby Grindalythe, **166**)

4.0 At T-jct ← (to Duggleby, **166**)

6.0 1st rd ↖ (**166**)

6.9 At give-way jct ↑
(to Wharram le Street)
(*ignore signs route* **166***!*)

7.3 At T-jct ↖ (no signs)

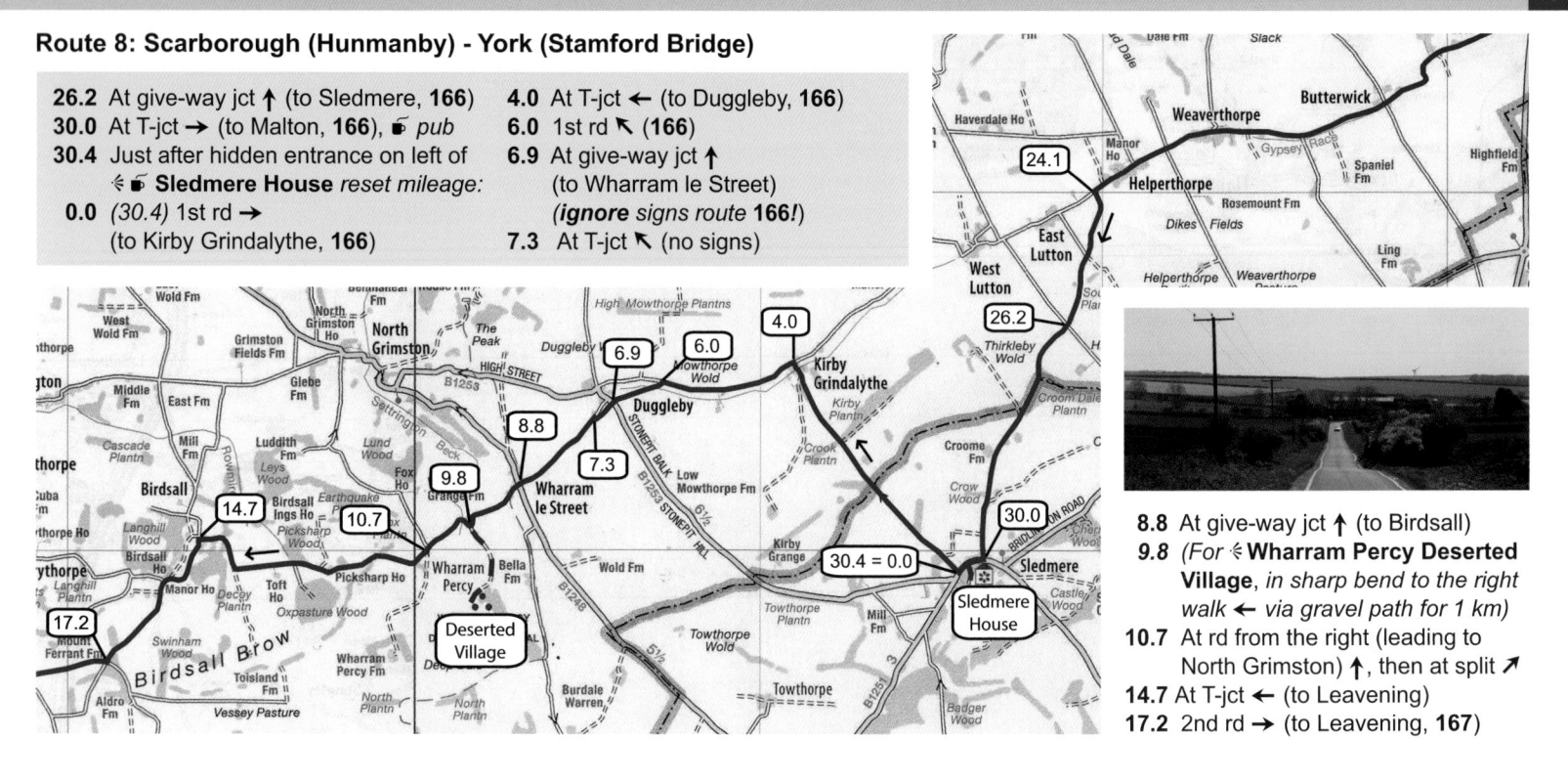

8.8 At give-way jct ↑ (to Birdsall)

9.8 *(For* ⚞ **Wharram Percy Deserted Village**, *in sharp bend to the right walk* ← *via gravel path for 1 km)*

10.7 At rd from the right (leading to North Grimston) ↑, then at split ↗

14.7 At T-jct ← (to Leavening)

17.2 2nd rd → (to Leavening, **167**)

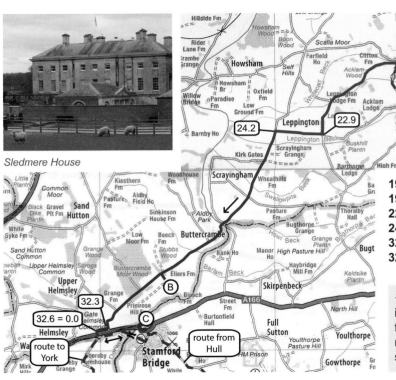

Sledmere House

19.4 On arrival in **Leavening** village, 2nd rd ↖ (Dam Ln)

19.6 At give-way jct ↑ (to Leppington)

22.9 At end of **Lepptington** village, 1st rd → (to Malton)

24.2 At T-jct ← (to Stamford Bridge), keep ↑

32.3 At T-jct → via 🚲 on right side of rd (to York, A166)

32.6 1st rd ← by crossing main rd (🚗🚗!), at start of dead end rd on other side of main rd *reset mileage, continue on page 91*

🚶 ⛺ 🛏 📷 🍴 **Stamford Bridge** (1.5 km from the end of this route section) is famous for a battle 1066 AD in which English rulers defeated Viking forces, before being defeated themselves by William the Conqueror. A monument can be found at the village square. To get there, follow the south-side 🚲 of the A166 to the east, leading onto a 🚲 into town.

Route 9: Scarborough (Hunmanby) - Hull

Direct route:
71 km / 44 miles: 🚲 36%, 🥾 59%, 🚗 5%, 🚗🚗 0%
Route via Flamborough Head and Bridlington:
100 km / 62 miles: 🚲 30%, 🥾 59%, 🚗 10%, 🚗🚗 1%
Stations: Bempton, Bridlington (both on the longer route)

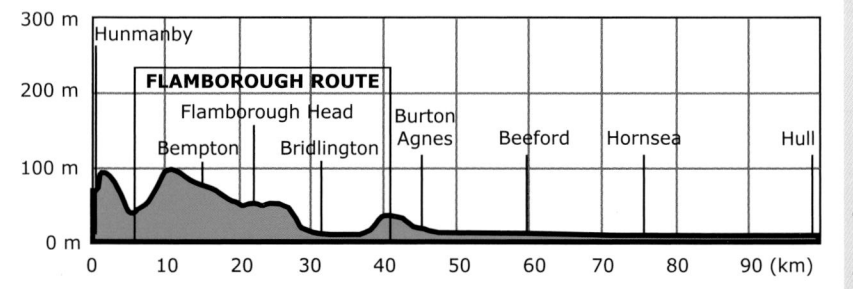

Heading south from Hunmanby you can choose between a direct inland route to **Burton Agnes** and its **Hall and Gardens** (£12 pp) or an optional coastal detour via **Flamborough Head** and **Bridlington**. Flamborough Head is a chalk promontory in the North Sea, famous for its impressive **Bempton Cliffs** and cape with scenic lighthouse. On the outskirts of Bridlington, **Sewerby Hall** features a scenic estate house, gardens and zoo (£9 pp). Bridlington itself features a pretty beach and all the usual coastal entertainment.

0.0 *(14.6)* At mini rndabt *Hunmanby*: go west, → (New Rd, to Burton Fleming, **166**)
0.4 1st rd ← (Bartindale Rd, to Grindale) **(ignore signs route 166!)**
5.4 At give way-jct choose your route: *For Flamborough Head, turn to next page* **For direct route to Hull:** ↑ (to Rudston)
7.9 At T-jct ← (to Rudston)
10.4 At T-jct ↖ (Middle St, to Village Hall)
10.6 At split of rds (see 'Waterside House' on right), at playground ↑ via narrow path
10.9 Ep → via bridge
11.1 At T-jct ←, imm ↖ (to Burton Agnes)
12.9 *Continue on page 80!*

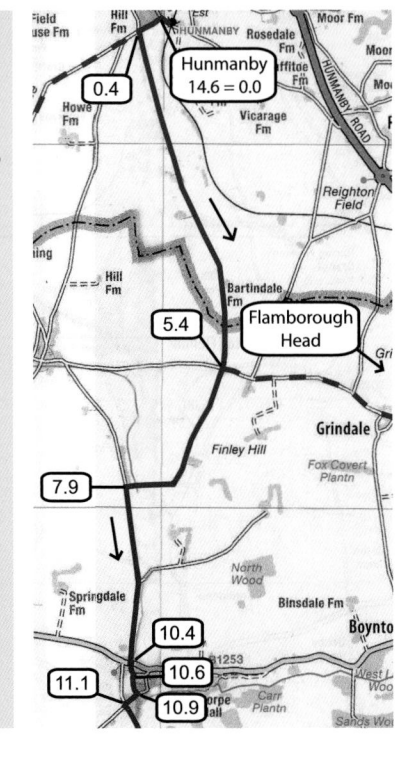

5.4 At give way-jct ← (to Grindale)

8.8 After Grindale 1st rd ↖ (**1**)

11.1 At give way jct ↑ (Grindale Rd, to Bempton, **1**) (🚗🚗 *!*)

13.5 At T-jct ← (to Bempton, **1**), 1st rd → (Pump Ln, **1**)

14.0 At T-jct → (to Bridlington, **1**) 🚗

14.9 At pub 🍴🍽 *Bempton* ↑ 🚗 (*ignore* signs route **1***!*) (For ⛵⛰ *Bempton Cliffs* ←)

19.1 In ⌂ 🏧 🍴🍽 *Flamborough* 2nd rd ← (Carter Ln, to Flamboro), then at rndabt ↑ (Post Office St), at next jct ↑ (Allison Ln), then at T-jct ↘

19.8 At give-way jct ← (Lighthouse Rd)

22.8 At ⛵⛰🏧 *Flamborough Head* car pk, after visit, turn around (go back)

25.9 At T-jct ↖ (to Bridlington) 🚗

26.4 Just before 40mph sign ↑ onto narrow path on right side of rd

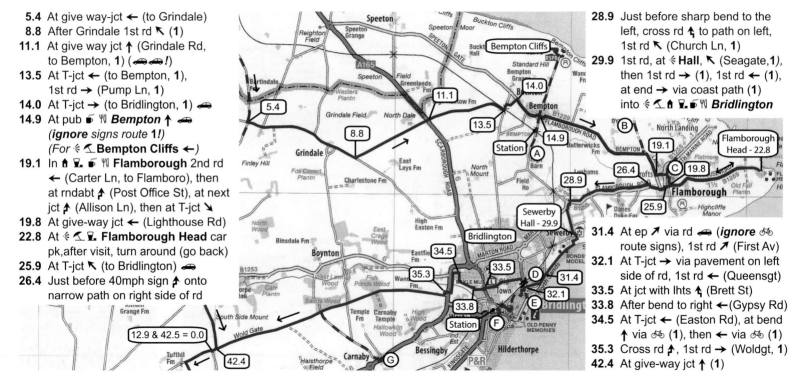

28.9 Just before sharp bend to the left, cross rd ↑ to path on left, 1st rd ↖ (Church Ln, **1**)

29.9 1st rd, at ⛵ *Hall*, ↖ (Seagate, **1***)*, then 1st rd → (**1**), 1st rd ← (**1**), at end → via coast path (**1**) into ⛵⛰⌂🏧🍴🍽 *Bridlington*

31.4 At ep ↗ via rd 🚗 (*ignore* 🚲 route signs), 1st rd ↗ (First Av)

32.1 At T-jct → via pavement on left side of rd, 1st rd ← (Queensgt)

33.5 At jct with lhts ↑ (Brett St)

33.8 After bend to right ←(Gypsy Rd)

34.5 At T-jct ← (Easton Rd), at bend ↑ via 🚲 (**1**), then ← via 🚲 (**1**)

35.3 Cross rd ↑, 1st rd → (Woldgt, **1**)

42.4 At give-way jct ↑ (**1**)

Route 9: Scarborough (Hunmanby) - Hull

The coast of Yorkshire's **East Riding** is dominated by low lying flats, stretching south all the way to Norfolk. This region has the fastest coastal erosion in Europe. Near **Skipsea**, a country lane part of the National Cycle Network fell prey of the waves only a few years ago. With main roads complicating the cause for traffic-calmed cycling further, we are forced to take you well inland, except for the coastal town of **Hornsea** where you will find a pleasant seaside vibe. It features the **Trans Pennine Trail monument**, which is the start for this official coast-to-coast cycle route to the west coast (Liverpool and Southport). It will regularly feature on our route to the Pennines. For now, we join this route for a pleasant traffic-free ride on a former railway all the way to Hull. Here, you can continue to the city centre for a continued route to York or head directly for the Hull international ferry terminal for ferries to Rotterdam.

12.9 and **42.5** at jct with sharp bend to the left *reset mileage:*

0.0 *(12.9 & 42.5)* At jct with sharp bend to the left ↑ (to Kilham, **1**)
0.8 1st rd ← (**1**)
2.8 At give-way jct ↑ (**1**)
3.6 After ⬥🚻 **Burton Agnes Hall** at T-jct ← via 🚲 on right side of rd (**1**), 1st rd → (to Lissett, **1**)
5.7 *Ignore* signs route **1**, keep ↑, 2nd rd → (to Lowthorpe, **1**)
8.1 At T-jct ← (to Kelk)
12.6 At T-jct ← (to Beeford)

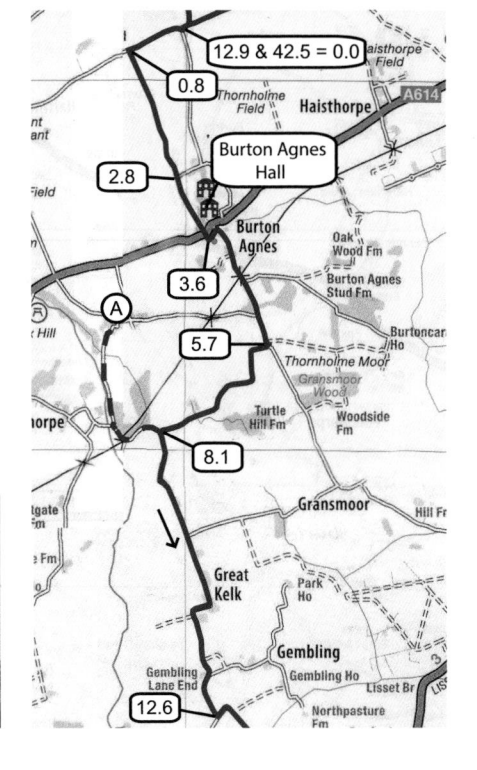

Flamborough Head

15.8 At give-way jct ↑ (Main St, to Skipsea) 🚗

17.4 Just before give-way jct → via lay-by rd in front of pub 🍺 ☛ 🍴 **Beeford**, join narrow path on right side of main rd, tarmac at first, then gravel, path keeps narrowing (🚗🚗!)

18.9 Where path ends, 1st rd ← (to Dunnington)

21.6 At jct, follow sharp bend → (to Dunnington)

24.2 At sharp bend to left, 1st rd ← (to Bewholme)

25.4 At T-jct ← (to Bewholme)

26.2 At T-jct → (to Skipsea Atwick), at next jct ↑ (to Seaton, see sign 🚲 route)

26.8 1st rd ← (to Hornsea, see sign 🚲 route)

30.3 At T-jct ← via narrow path on left side of rd (to Hornsea)

31.1 1st rd ↗ (cross rd 🚗🚗!) (Back Westgt)

31.5 At T-jct ←, at next T-jct ↑ (to Bridlington) 🚗, then 1st rd ↗ (Eastgt, to Seafront) 🚗

32.2 At give-way jct (🍺 **Cliff Rd**) ↑ 🚗

32.8 In 🌳 🏖 🏠 ☛ 🍴 **Hornsea**, 1st rd ← (Broadwy), then 1st rd ↗ (Parva Rd)

33.0 At give-way jct, cross ↑ to 🌳 **Monument** of start 🌳 **Trans Pennine Trail**; *reset mileage*

The Trans Pennine Trail to Hull is bumpy in places due to the tree roots pushing up the path surface.

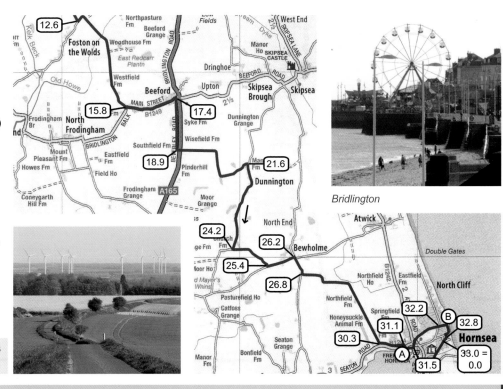

Bridlington

Route 9: Scarborough (Hunmanby) - Hull

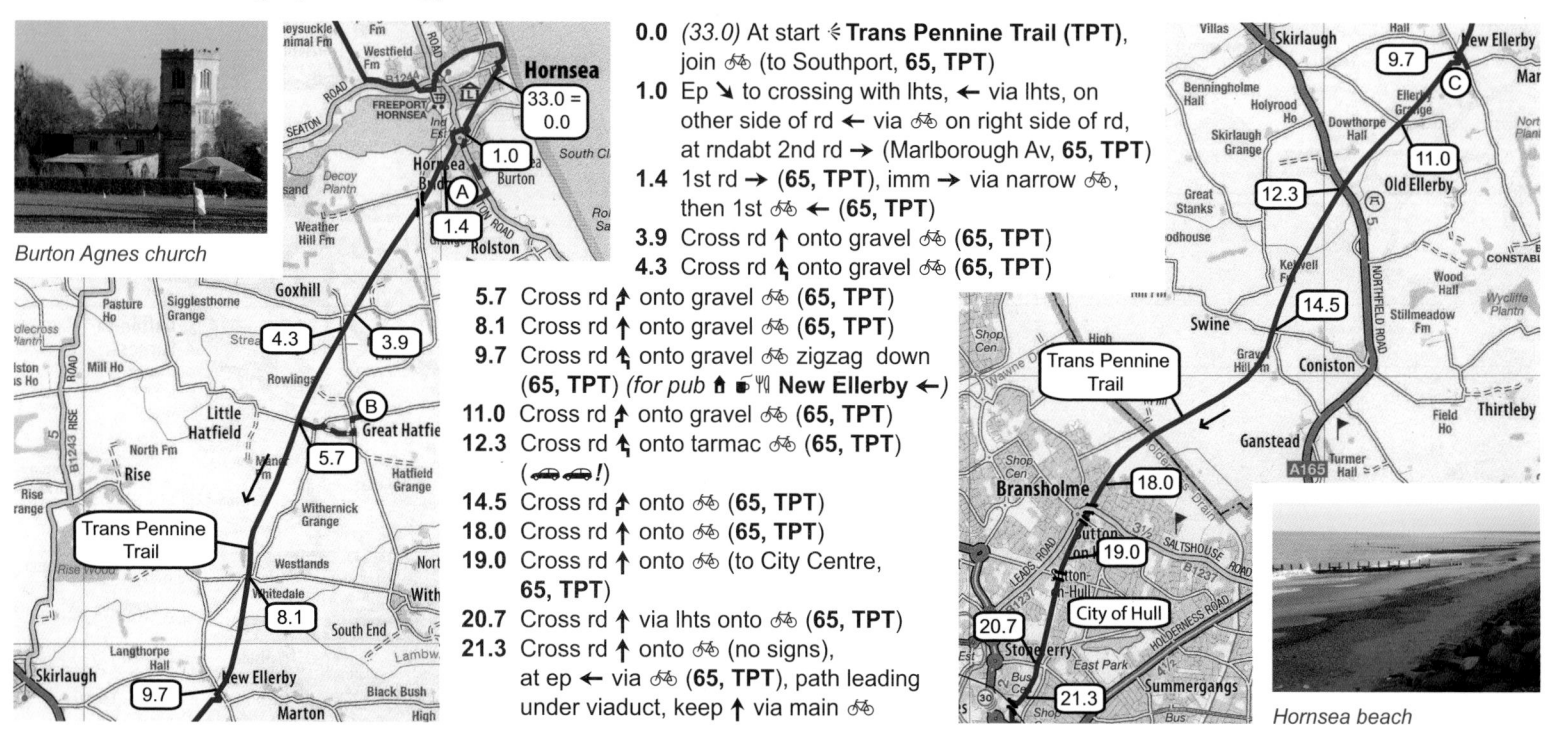

Burton Agnes church

0.0 *(33.0)* At start ⛟ **Trans Pennine Trail (TPT)**, join 🚲 (to Southport, **65, TPT**)

1.0 Ep ↘ to crossing with lhts, ← via lhts, on other side of rd ← via 🚲 on right side of rd, at rndabt 2nd rd → (Marlborough Av, **65, TPT**)

1.4 1st rd → (**65, TPT**), imm → via narrow 🚲, then 1st 🚲 ← (**65, TPT**)

3.9 Cross rd ↑ onto gravel 🚲 (**65, TPT**)

4.3 Cross rd ⬈ onto gravel 🚲 (**65, TPT**)

5.7 Cross rd ⬈ onto gravel 🚲 (**65, TPT**)

8.1 Cross rd ↑ onto gravel 🚲 (**65, TPT**)

9.7 Cross rd ⬈ onto gravel 🚲 zigzag down (**65, TPT**) *(for pub 🏠 🍺 🍴 **New Ellerby** ←)*

11.0 Cross rd ⬈ onto gravel 🚲 (**65, TPT**)

12.3 Cross rd ⬈ onto tarmac 🚲 (**65, TPT**) (🚗🚗!)

14.5 Cross rd ⬈ onto 🚲 (**65, TPT**)

18.0 Cross rd ↑ onto 🚲 (**65, TPT**)

19.0 Cross rd ↑ onto 🚲 (to City Centre, **65, TPT**)

20.7 Cross rd ↑ via lhts onto 🚲 (**65, TPT**)

21.3 Cross rd ↑ onto 🚲 (no signs), at ep ← via 🚲 (**65, TPT**), path leading under viaduct, keep ↑ via main 🚲

Hornsea beach

Start of the Trans Pennine Trail at the former station of Hornsea

Trans Pennine Trail between Hornsea and Hull

Art at the Hull Ferry Terminal

For Hull City Centre and York:

21.8 Ep ←, cross rd via zebra, then ↑ via 🚲, leading under viaduct, at rndabt ↑ via 🚲

22.4 Cross rd ↑ onto 🚲, ↑

22.6 Ep ↑ (Holborn St) *(ignore route TPT)*, at T-jct → 🚗, 1st rd ← (Blenkin St)

22.9 At T-jct ← (Hyperion St), at T-jct → (to City Centre) 🚌

23.2 At lhts ↑ (to City Centre) 🚗

24.0 At wide open square (Victoria Sq) *reset mileage:*
continue on page 85 at **0.0**

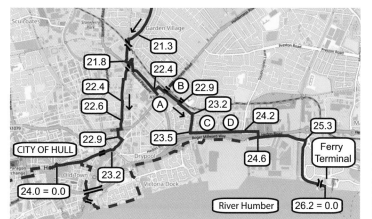

For Hull Ferry Terminal:

21.8 Ep ←, cross rd via zebra, then ← via 🚲 on right side of rd (**66**), 1st rd ↘ (Dansom Ln North), then 2nd rd ← (**66**)

22.4 1st rd ← (**66**), at T-jct → (Burleigh St), at end ↑ via 🚲

22.9 Ep ↑ (Newbridge Rd, **66**)

23.2 In bend → via 🚲 (to ferry), ↑

23.5 At T-jct ← via 🚲 on left of rd

24.2 At rndabt cross rd ↑ onto 🚲, then 1st 🚲 → cross via lhts

24.6 After ramp up ← via 🚲

25.3 At rndabt follow 🚲 →

Route 10: Hull - York (Stamford Bridge)

72 km / 45 miles: 🚲 18%, 🚶 73%, 🚗 8%, 🚗🚗 1%
Stations: *Hull Paragon Interchange, Cottingham, Beverley*

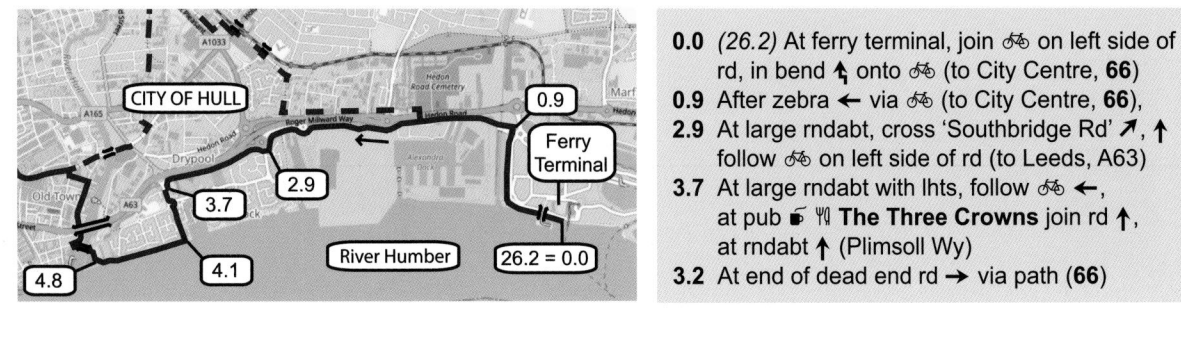

A warm welcome to those who are joining us from the **Rotterdam** ferry. This route section takes you via the urban sprawl of **Hull** into the lower **Yorkshire Wolds**. The pretty market towns **Cottingham**, **Beverley**, **Market Weighton**, **Pocklington** and **Stamford Bridge** make for a pleasant introduction to cycling in England. From Stamford Bridge, **York** is just a stone's throw away.

The National Cycle Network also provides a shortcut to **Selby**, further on our route and bypassing York. It starts on page 85. You rejoin us on page 95 when using this route. The route is branded as the Trans Pennine Trail (**TPT, 65**) and is 75 km/46 miles long. It is not part of our guidebook!

From the Hull ferry terminal, a cycle path takes you past the docks and a storage facility for blades of enormous wind turbines. Once our route has left the docks, you will enter a housing development. It features a riverside path with great views over the wide estuary of the **River Humber**.

0.0 *(26.2)* At ferry terminal, join 🚲 on left side of rd, in bend ↑ onto 🚲 (to City Centre, **66**)
0.9 After zebra ← via 🚲 (to City Centre, **66**),
2.9 At large rndabt, cross 'Southbridge Rd' ↗, ↑ follow 🚲 on left side of rd (to Leeds, A63)
3.7 At large rndabt with lhts, follow 🚲 ←, at pub 🍺 🍴 **The Three Crowns** join rd ↑, at rndabt ↑ (Plimsoll Wy)
3.2 At end of dead end rd → via path (**66**)

River Humber

4.8 Ep, in front of ⇇ 🔊 **The Deep** ↗, after 50m ↖ via 🚲 bridge (to City Centre)

5.0 Imm after bridge ↘ via rd (to City Centre)

5.5 On corner of entrance ⇇ **Museums Quarter**, 5th rd ← (Chapel Ln, to City Hall)

5.6 At T-jct →, at lhts ← (Alfred Gelder St) 🚗

6.0 At wide open square (Victoria Square) ⇇ 🏠 🍺 🔊 🍴 ⚡ 🅿 **Hull** reset mileage:

0.0 (6.0 or 24.0) Take bus lane route ← (**65**)

0.4 1st rd ← (Anne St, **65**) 🚗 (For station →)

0.5 At lhts 1st rd → 🚗, at next jct with lhts ↑ (Osborne St, **65**) 🚗, at mini rndabt ↑ (**65**)

0.8 1st rd → (Pease St, **65**, **TPT**), 1st rd ← (Cambridge St, to Hessle, **65**, **TPT**)

1.0 At T-jct ↗ (**65**), at next jct ↟ (Great Thornton St, to Liverpool, **65**, **TPT**)

1.6 In sharp bend to the left, → via 🚲 (**65**), ep cross rd ↑ via lhts, go ↑ via 🚲 (**65**)

1.7 Ep ← via rd, at end of rd ↑ via 🚲, imm bend →, **dismount** for narrow section!

1.9 Ep ← via rd, then 2nd rd → (Cholmley St, **65**, **TPT**), keep ↑ at rndabts and park

3.3 *Ignore signs route 65 TPT to the left*, at end of rd, at T-jct → (Hawthorne Av) 🚗

Hull (official name **Kingston upon Hull**) is a city with lots of maritime history. **The Deep** is a large aquarium (£15 pp), next to the **Hull Barrier**. The **Museum Quarter** in the **Old Town** features four museums. **Wilberforce House** is dedicated to the legacy of social reformer William Wilberforce. The **Arctic Corsair** is a fishing trawler with a remarkable history. The **Hull and East Riding Museum** displays local history and the **Streetlife Museum** focuses on transport. The **Maritime Museum** is located on Victoria Square (all free).

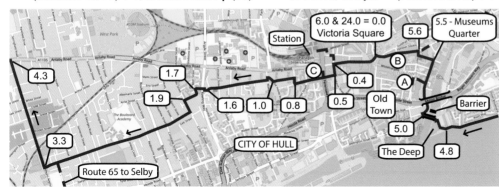

Hull Old Town

Route 10: Hull - York (Stamford Bridge)

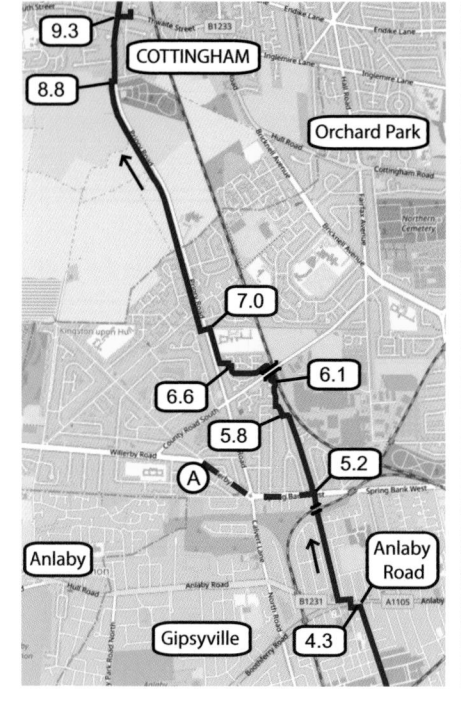

4.3 At T-jct *dismount*, ← via pavement on left side of 🚗🚗 🚅 🛒 🍴 **Anlaby Road**, after 50m cross rd ↑ at lhts, walk on footpath on right side of rd, just before 'Iceland' → via 🚲 on right side of car pk, keep ↑, becomes 🚲 in park

5.2 Cross rd ↑ via lhts, continue via park 🚲 ↑

5.8 Ep → (Rosedale Gr), 1st rd → (Lowdale Cl)

6.1 At end of rd ↖ via 🚲, follow main path under viaduct

6.6 Ep ← via rd (Shropshire Cl), after 50m at T-jct → via 🚲 on right side of rd (to Cottingham)

7.0 Cross rd via zebra ↟ onto 🚲 on left side of rd, keep ↑

8.8 Ep ↑ via main carriageway 🚗 (Hornbeam Dr on your right)

9.3 At mini rndabt ↟ (Kingtree Av) *(For station →, see map)*

9.7 At bend to the right ↑ via 🚲 (to Village Centre and Buses), ep ↟ via rd, at T-jct → King St 🚅 🛒 🍴 ***Cottingham*** 🚗🚗

9.9 After jct with lhts (↑), 1st rd ← (Long Stay P), go ↟ to far end of car pk, there via gap in fence onto quiet dead end rd ↑

10.3 At give-way jct (entrance 'Crescent St') → via through rd

10.5 At T-jct ← 🚗, 1st rd → (Park Ln, to Beverley, **66**)

12.3 At 'Burn Park Cottages' follow bend ↗ via tarmac rd (**66**)

13.2 At electric power sub station on right side of rd, 1st rd ← (**66**)

14.3 At farm shed of 'Poplar Farm' → via gate imm ↗ via tarmac rd, keep ↑, rough gravel sections with some tarmac

16.2 At jct with 2nd triangle grass island ↖ via through rd (**66**)

Hull's suburbs have absorbed towns as **Anlaby** and **Cottingham**. Only a few open fields near **Beverley** remain green, as you will discover on a path with rough gravel (see page 18). Discomfort will make way for amazement, with buildings such as the **Beverley Minster** and the **North Bar** town gate, both dating from the 15th century. Enjoy a break at Beverley's scenic squares before facing the low-lying hills of the **Yorkshire Wolds**. From **Cherry Burton**, leafy lanes will take you into unspoiled countryside.

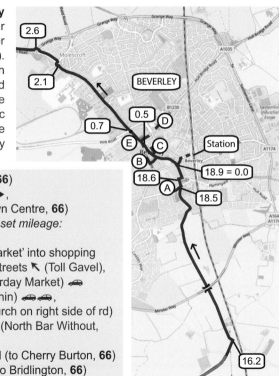

18.5 At T-jct →, imm 1st rd ← (St John St, **66**)

18.6 Imm after ⬳ **Beverley Minster**, 1st rd →, after bollards imm ← (Highgate, to Town Centre, **66**)

18.9 At square ⬳ ⌂ 🏛 📷 🍴 ⚹ 🛈 **Beverley** reset mileage: (For station →, see map)

0.0 (18.9) Go ↑ via square 'Wednesday Market' into shopping street, *dismount*, at split of shopping streets ↖ (Toll Gavel), resume cycling ↑ on next square (Saturday Market) 🚗

0.5 At lhts ↑ onto tarmac rd (North Bar Within) 🚗🚗, join left lane to go ↑ at next jct 🚗 (church on right side of rd)

0.7 After historic gate 'North Bar', ↑ at lhts (North Bar Without, to Yorkshire Wolds, **66**) 🚗

2.1 At rndabt ⬆, join path on right side of rd (to Cherry Burton, **66**)

2.6 At rndabt ↖ via 🚲 on right side of rd (to Bridlington, **66**)

Beverley Minster and North Bar town gate

Route 10: Hull - York (Stamford Bridge)

5.0 Cross ↑ to left side of rd (to Cherry Burton, 66) (🚗🚗!), 1st rd ← (Main St, 66)

6.2 In 🚉 **Cherry Burton**, 4th rd ↗ (Etton Rd, 66)

7.9 At T-jct ← *(ignore signs route 66!)*

8.8 1st rd → (to South Dalton)

9.4 1st rd ← (to Kiplingcotes)

12.5 At give-way jct ↖ (to Mkt Weighton, 66)

19.5 After school, 3rd rd → (The Green), follow road with bends, church on left side of the rd

19.8 At T-jct → (see house no 3 opposite T-jct) *(For High St 🏠 🚉 🛍 🍴 **Market Weighton** ←)*

21.8 At rndabt ↑ (🚗🚗!) (to Nunburnholme, 66)

23.8 At T-jct → (to Londesborough, 66)

24.0 1st rd ← (to Burnby, 66)

25.7 At T-jct ← (to Burnby, 66)

27.7 At T-jct ← (to Hayton, 66), keep ↑ to end

32.1 At T-jct ← (to Town Centre, 66), then after 50m 1st rd → (Dean's Ln, one-way st, 66)

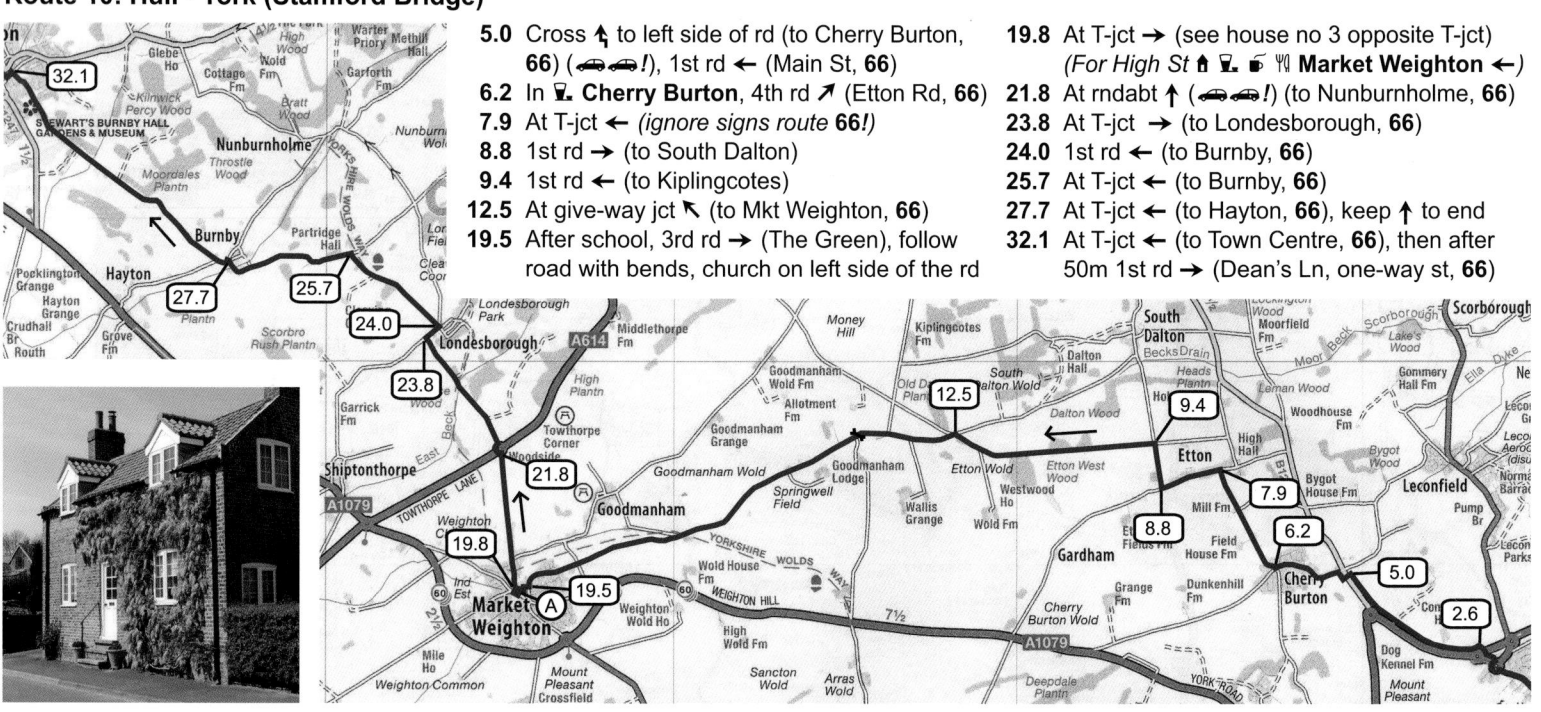

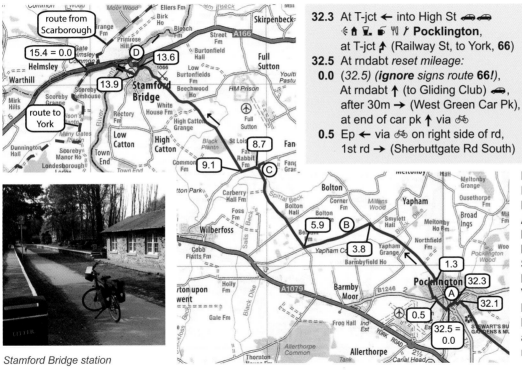

32.3 At T-jct ← into High St 🚗🚗 ⛽🏠🚏☕🍴🍝 *Pocklington*, at T-jct ↑ (Railway St, to York, **66**)

32.5 At rndabt *reset mileage:*

0.0 (*32.5*) *(ignore signs route **66**!)*, At rndabt ↑ (to Gliding Club) 🚗, after 30m → (West Green Car Pk), at end of car pk ↑ via 🚲

0.5 Ep ← via 🚲 on right side of rd, 1st rd → (Sherbuttgate Rd South)

1.3 After bend to the right, at T-jct ← 🚗

3.8 Out of town, 2nd rd ← (Feoffee Ln, **66**)

5.9 At give-way jct → (to Stamford Br, **66**)

8.7 At T-jct with triangle grass island ← (**66**)

9.1 1st rd → (to Stamford Br, **66**)

13.6 At T-jct ← (to High Catton, **66**) *(For ⛽🏪🚏☕🍴 Stamford Bridge →)*

13.9 At 'Old Railway Station' → via 🚲 (**66**), after river bridge ↖ via 🚲 in woods

15.4 At dead end rd on left side, *reset mileage*

Stamford Bridge station

Market Weighton is quiet market town, whilst **Pocklington** is busier, being a focus point for local tourism. The high street can be heaving. A road with some fast moving traffic cannot be avoided heading out of town, but then leafy empty lanes set the pace once again to **Stamford Bridge**. This village is famous for a battle 1066 AD in which English rulers defeated Viking forces, before being defeated themselves by William the Conqueror. The field where the battle happened is on your right, just before arriving in town. There is no museum, but a monument can be found at the village square.

Route 11: York (Stamford Bridge) - Doncaster

88 km / 54 miles: 🚲 48%, 🚶 37%, 🚗 14%, 🚗🚗 1%
Stations: York, Selby, Snaith

Elevation profile (0–80 km), labels: Stamford Bridge Junction, Dunnington, Bishopthorpe, York, Selby, Barlby, Riccall, Humberhead Levels, Carlton, Snaith, Bentley, Thorpe in Balne

This stage follows the signposted **Trans Pennine Trail** meticulously on its north-south journey across the **Humberhead Levels**. Just above normal sea level, this flat landscape originally consisted of inhabitable wetlands until Dutch engineers were invited to turn the area into productive farmland in the 1600s. The swamps were drained by rerouting rivers such as the Don and Went and by digging wide canals. Between York and Doncaster, you will be cycling the flattest section of our north-south journey, crossing the Ouse and Aire Rivers.

The Ouse River also flows through the city of **York**. York was founded by the Romans, taken by the Vikings and destroyed by William the Conqueror and is bursting with historic architecture. It is England's most popular city to visit after London. That you won't be the only one navigating its famous medieval city centre is an understatement. A two-night stay will allow time to do justice to some of the greatest sights!

Just before York, **Murton Park** is an open-air museum with traditional farming machinery on display (£8pp). A ride on the half-a-mile long **Derwent Valley Light Railway**, run by steam enthusiasts, is included in your ticket.

South from York, you cycle the old railway bed between **Bishopthorpe** and **Riccall**. To keep you entertained on this traffic-free tarmac highway, scale models of our solar system's planets are in the verges, placed proportionally from the Sun and from each other; can you spot them all? **Riccall** and **Barlby** are both 'by-passed' villages, providing a clear, direct road to **Selby**.

Jorvik Viking Museum and the 'Rocket' in the National Railway Museum, York

The town of **Selby** is a significant stop because of its **Abbey**. It enjoys the status of a parish church only, but is larger than some cathedrals. The abbey celebrated its 950th anniversary in 2019. Besides its regular services, the building can be visited during concerts (see www.selbyabbey.org.uk). Note: choice of accommodation in the Selby area is very limited; plan ahead!

Burn Airfield allows you to cycle next to a former runway. Then, we zigzag via the nondescript towns of **Carlton** and **Snaith** to be able to cross the River Aire by one of its very few bridges. Open horizons, great high skies and possible headwinds are your companions in the empty canal country of the **Aire and Calder Navigation Canal** and the **New Junction Canal**.

0.0 *(15.4 & 32.6)* 1st rd ← via dead end rd (see sign 'single track rd with passing places', to Dunnington, **66**)

2.4 1st rd → (**66**), at 'Limefield Farm' ↑ via gravel path (**66**)

3.6 Where wide gravel path turns sharp to the left, keep ↑ via narrow gravel path (**66**)

4.5 After passing through farm yard, keep ↗ via wide gravel path

5.5 At T-jct (end "Intake Ln") ←, at next T-jct imm → (**66**)

5.9 3rd ← (York St, to Murton, **66**) into ⌷ **Dunnington**, 🚗

7.6 Just before end of rd, join 🚲 on right side of rd, keep ↗ onto 🚲 on right side of rd of A1079, then 1st rd → (to Livestock Centre, **66**)

8.1 At T-jct → via 🚲 on right side of rd, after 30m, use crossing to take 1st rd ← (to Morton, **66**) 🚗

9.0 After entrances of York Lorry Park, ⛲ **Murton Park & Derwent Valley Railway**, 1st rd ← (Murton Wy, **66**)

10.5 1st rd ↗ (Osbaldwick, **66**) 🚗

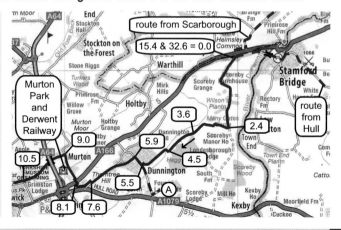

Route 11: York (Stamford Bridge) - Doncaster

The city of **York** has many great attractions. The architecture of **York Minster** can be greatly admired on a guided tour and Undercroft Museum combination ticket (£12 pp). To climb the cathedral's **Great Tower**, the cost is an additional £5 pp. World-class is the **National Railway Museum**, with over 100 historic locomotives on display (free). Its 'Great Hall' is located next to York's monumental railway station. **Jorvik** is York's popular Viking experience, where you can see, hear and smell (!) how things used to be in Yorkshire's Danish colony on British soil from 867 until 954 AD (advance timed tickets £13 pp).

York Castle Museum is housed in two former prisons, taking on the history of York beyond the Viking era (£11 pp). Right next to it, the historic **Clifford's Tower** can be climbed, with great views over the city (£7 pp). At the other end of town, the **Yorkshire Museum** has various themed displays and permanent collections on geology and archaeology (£8 pp). Ever popular is **The Shambles**, a narrow medieval shopping street which may remind you of Diagon Alley in Harry Potter. Also, not to miss are Britain's most intact medieval city walls. Its **Bootham Bar** and **Monk Bar** gates can be seen from our cycle route, but a city wall walk is recommended!

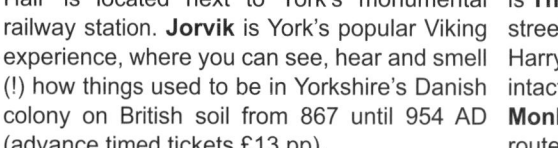

Bootham Bar gate, 'just a house' and York Minster

The crowded Shambles and Clifford's Tower

11.1 2nd rd → (to Meadlands & City Centre, **66**)
11.2 1st 🚲 ← (to Tang Hall & City Centre, **Foss Islands Path**, **658**), keep ↑
13.1 Keep 2x ↖ at two splits of paths, finally leading to bridge over stream
13.4 Ep, cross main rd ↑ via lhts, then ↗, follow bend around corner, continue on 🚲 on left side of bus lane route (zebra crossings)
13.7 Ep, cross main rd ↑ via lhts, then ← via 🚲 on pavement (to City Centre, **658**), *Note: confusing layout; stay on pavement, be careful at driveway crossings!*
13.8 1st rd → (Navigation Rd, to City Centre, **658**)

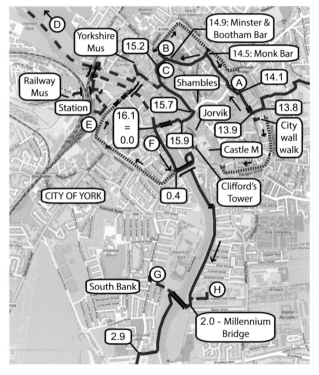

13.9 In sharp bend to the left → via 🚲 (Rowntree Wharf, to City Centre, **658**)
*(for ⮜ **York Historic City Walls walk** 2x ← into Rosemary Pl, see blue box below)*

To walk York's city walls in a full circle, turn left into Rosemary Place. Around the playground at the end you could lock up bikes away from the crowds. Walk the wall clockwise, walking via main roads at gaps in the wall. The wall is marked with a blue dotted line and short arrows on the map. The circle is about 4 km.

14.1 At T-jct ↟ via 🚲 (to City Centre, **658**),
at ep ↑ via rd and imm ↗ (dead end rd 'Aldwark', **658**)
14.5 At give-way jct (near ⮜ **Monk Bar**) ← (Goodramgate, to Minster, **658**), keep ↑
14.9 At front entrance ⮜ **Minster** ↖ (wide rd at Dean Crt Hotel, near ⮜ **Bootham Bar**)
15.2 On wide rd, 1st rd ↖ (Blake St) *(ignore signs route **658**)*
15.7 At end of wide 'Parliament St' ⮜ 🏠 🚻 📷 🍴 ⚕ 🅸 **York**
at lhts ↖ and imm ↗ (Coppergate) 🚗 *(for ⮜ **Shambles** ←, then 1st rd ←)*
15.9 At T-jct → (Ness Gt) 🚗🚗, follow bend to the left onto river bridge
16.1 Imm after river bridge, at traffic lhts, *reset mileage:*
*(For ⮜ **Railway Mus** and **Station** →, see map)*
0.0 *(16.1)* For continued route ← (Skeldergate)
0.4 At T-jct ← onto river bridge 🚗🚗, after bridge ↖ via 🚲 lane, imm after bus stop
← into park, then ↖ to riverside 🚲, keep following this route heading south
2.0 Via 🚲 ⮜ **Millennium Bridge** → (to South Bank), imm 1st 🚲 ↙ (to Bishopthorpe)

Route 11: York (Stamford Bridge) - Doncaster

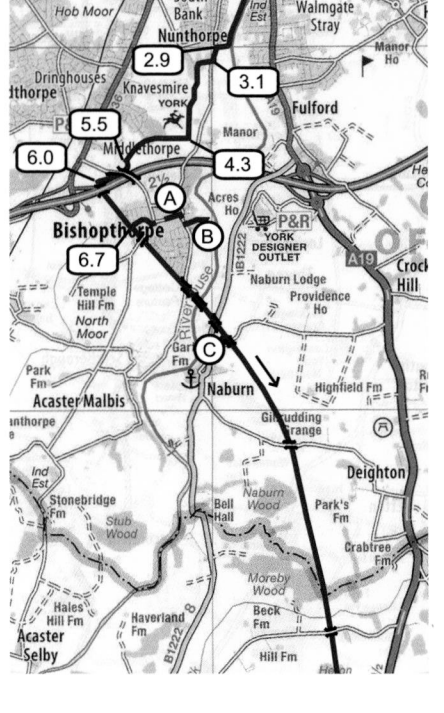

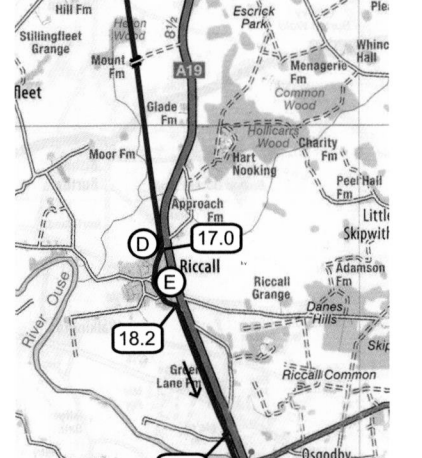

2.9 Ep ← via rd (to Selby, **65**, **Trans Pennine Trail** (**TPT**))

3.1 1st 🚲 → (to Selby, **65**, **TPT**)

4.3 Ep → via 🚲 (to Selby, **65**, **TPT**), cross racing course twice

5.5 1st 🚲 ← (to Selby, **65**, **TPT**), path leading under viaduct

6.0 Ep ← via 🚲 (to Selby, **65**, **TPT**), path leading under viaduct

6.7 Ep ↑ via rd (to Selby, **65**), end of rd ↖ via 🚲 (to Selby, **65**)

17.0 Ep ↑ onto rd (to Selby, **65**), at T-jct ↗ (to Selby, **65**, **TPT**)

18.2 At end of High St 🏠 🍺 🍴 **Riccall**, just before T-jct, ↑ to join 🚲 on right side of main rd (to Selby, **65**, **TPT**)

20.0 Ep ↑ onto dead end rd ('Newgrove Farm' on right side of rd)

20.9 At T-jct ↗ (**65**, **TPT**)

23.4 At end of High St 🍺 **Barlby**, just before rndabt ↗ via 🚲 (to Selby, **65**, **TPT**), ↑ via earth path onto river bank, keep ↑

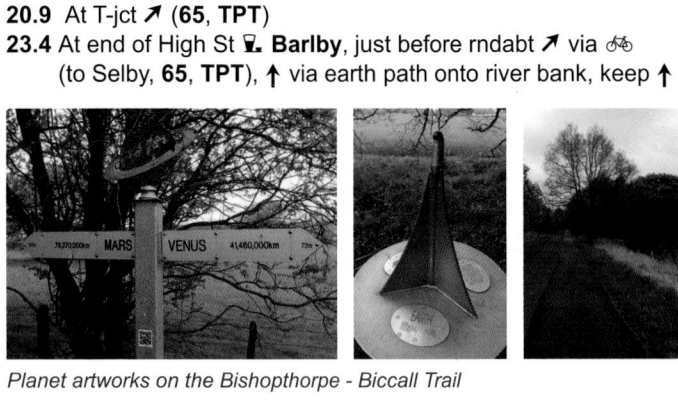

Planet artworks on the Bishopthorpe - Biccall Trail

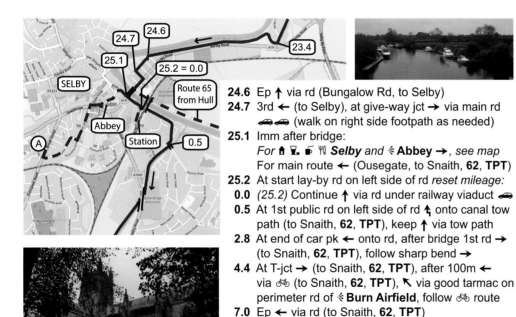

Selby Abbey

24.6 Ep ↑ via rd (Bungalow Rd, to Selby)

24.7 3rd ← (to Selby), at give-way jct → via main rd 🚗🚗 (walk on right side footpath as needed)

25.1 Imm after bridge:
For 🏨 🛏 📷 🍴 **Selby** *and* ⚑ **Abbey** →, *see map*
For main route ← (Ousegate, to Snaith, **62**, **TPT**)

25.2 At start lay-by rd on left side of rd *reset mileage:*

0.0 (25.2) Continue ↑ via rd under railway viaduct 🚗

0.5 At 1st public rd on left side of rd ↖ onto canal tow path (to Snaith, **62**, **TPT**), keep ↑ via tow path

2.8 At end of car pk ← onto rd, after bridge 1st rd → (to Snaith, **62**, **TPT**), follow sharp bend →

4.4 At T-jct → (to Snaith, **62**, **TPT**), after 100m ← via 🚲 (to Snaith, **62**, **TPT**), ↖ via good tarmac on perimeter rd of ⚑ **Burn Airfield**, follow 🚲 route

7.0 Ep ← via rd (to Snaith, **62**, **TPT**)

10.5 At T-jct ← (to Snaith, **62**, **TPT**) 🚗

15.3 On arrival in **Carlton** 1st rd → (to Snaith, **62**, **TPT**)

15.6 At T-jct → via pavement on left side of main rd (to Snaith, **62**, **TPT**) (🚗🚗!)

Route 11: York (Stamford Bridge) - Doncaster

River Aire bridge at Snaith

Crossing the New Junction Canal via a lock

17.0 After River Aire bridge, at jct just before railway crossing *reset mileage:*
(*For* 🏠 🍺 📷 🍴 *Snaith* ↑)

0.0 *(17.0)* For continued route → before railway crossing (to Gowdall, **TPT**) 🚗

2.2 2nd rd ← (Field Ln, to Sykehouse, **TPT**)

3.6 At T-jct ← (to Goole, **TPT**) 🚗

4.4 1st rd → (to Pollington, **TPT**) 🚗

5.8 At bend to the right, go ↖ (Willow Ln, **TPT**)

6.7 At sign 'Viking Fishery' ↗ via bridge (**TPT**)

7.4 At near end of rd → via gravel 🚲 (**TPT**)

7.9 At slight bend of path to the left ↙ via wider gravel 🚲 (to Doncaster, **TPT**)

9.0 Imm after bridge ↖ via narrow path, ep ← via rd, then 1st rd → (Bate Ln, to Doncaster, **TPT**)

9.9 1st rd ← (to Doncaster, **TPT**)

10.3 At T-jct ← (Broad Ln, to Doncaster, **62**, **TPT**)

11.5 1st rd → (Kirk Ln, to Doncaster, **62**, **TPT**)

12.4 Imm after bridge → onto canal tow path (**62**)

12.9 At canal locks cross via bridge or lock doors ↑ onto canal tow path on other side of ⋞ **New Junction Canal** (**62**)

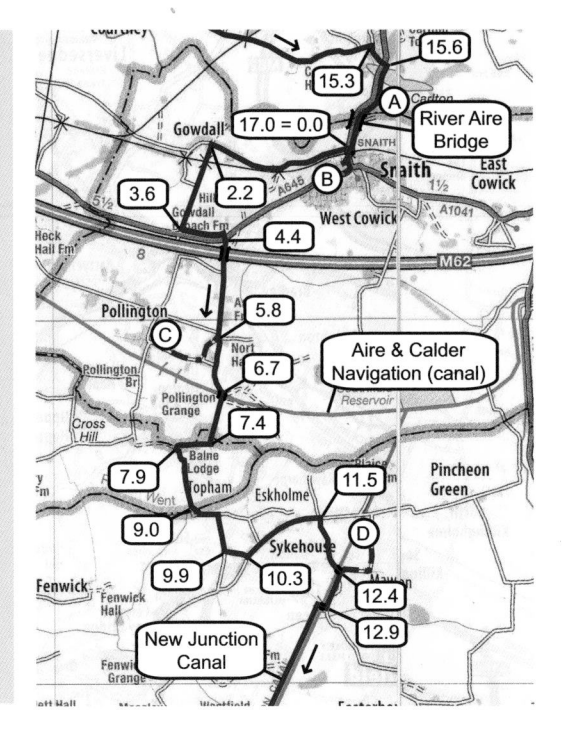

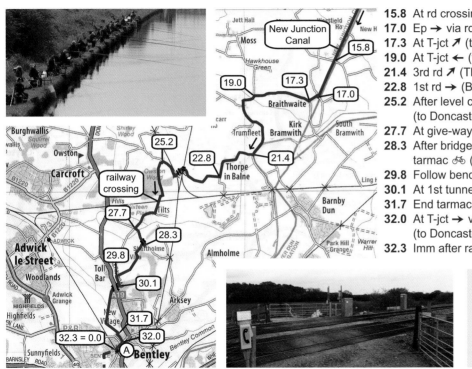

15.8 At rd crossing ↑ via canal tow path (**62**)

17.0 Ep → via rd (to Doncaster, **62**, **TPT**), 1st rd ← (to Braithwaite, **62**)

17.3 At T-jct ↗ (to Doncaster, **62**, **TPT**)

19.0 At T-jct ← (to Thorpe, **62**)

21.4 3rd rd ↗ (Thorpe Ln, to Doncaster, **62**, **TPT**)

22.8 1st rd → (Bell Croft Ln)

25.2 After level crossing and sharp bend to the right, 1st narrow 🚲 ↖ (to Doncaster, **62**, **TPT**), follow path; tarmac, gravel, then tarmac rd

27.7 At give-way jct ← (to Doncaster, **62**, **TPT**)

28.3 After bridge over dismantled railway, at end of down ramp ↘ onto tarmac 🚲 (to Doncaster, **62**, **TPT**)

29.8 Follow bend of tarmac 🚲 ← (to Doncaster, **62**, **TPT**)

30.1 At 1st tunnel, follow tarmac 🚲 → (to Doncaster, **62**, **TPT**)

31.7 End tarmac path → onto rd, 1st rd ← (Truman St, to Doncaster, **62**)

32.0 At T-jct → via main rd 🚗 (walk on right side footpath as needed), (to Doncaster, **62**, **TPT**) (For 🏠 🍴 🛒 🍽 **Bentley** ↑ via Chapel St)

32.3 Imm after railway crossing at **Bentley Station** *reset mileage*

Near **Bentley** you have to cross a railway without warning bells or lights. It is important to open both gates first before wheeling your bike across. Close both gates after you made the crossing with the bike. If you are on your own, you will end up crossing five times; **look and listen** for every crossing you make!

Route 12: Doncaster - Oughtibridge

58 km / 36 miles: 🚲 61%, 🚶 33%, 🚗 5%, 🚗🚗 1%
Stations: Bentley, Doncaster, Conisbrough, Wombwell, Penistone

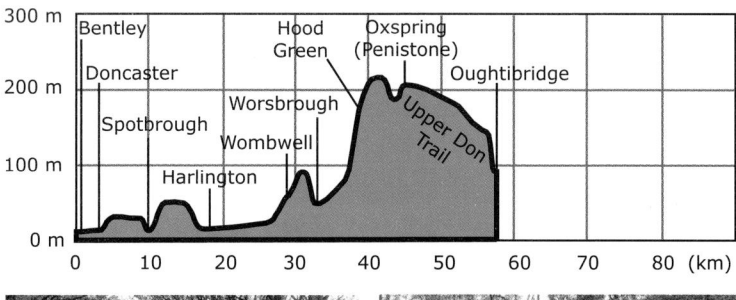

The **Trans Pennine Trail** keeps playing a major role on this section. We leave the trail regularly to avoid some rough sections or to enjoy some landmarks and local scenery. The large town of **Doncaster** is such a landmark. The Romans built a road here to its suitable crossing of the River Don in the 1st century. Today, Doncaster is still an important focus point on the York-London route for road and rail. Those who wish to avoid the upcoming long steep climbs across the Pennines and Peak District can best take their bikes on fast trains from Doncaster to Burton-on-Trent or Leicester. A change may be required at Sheffield. See page 7 to get an idea of these connections.

You will arrive in Doncaster from its suburb **Bentley**, once a mining village. Just east of Doncaster's busy town centre with many shops in and around the **Frenchgate** shopping mall, the **Doncaster Museum and Art Gallery** moved to a brand-new building in 2020, with a focus on natural and local history, combined with fine art (free). Fans of planes shouldn't miss the **South Yorkshire Aircraft Museum**, located on the old Royal Air Force site of Doncaster. It is just one kilometer further east via quiet estate roads to this wonderful collection of old planes, stacked in multiple hangars (£7 pp).

Whether you visit Doncaster town centre or wish to bypass it by staying on the Trans Pennine Trail, you will end up at the beauty spot of **Sprotbrough Falls**. To make shipping possible on the River Don, a short canal with locks and weir was built here in 1726. Located in a forested deep valley, the canal side is a good spot for a picnic, overlooking the fish pass next to the weir, popular with anglers. The scenic **Boat Inn** pub can be found at the far end.

Trans Pennine Trail

Upper Don Trail

0.0 *(32.3)* At **Bentley Station**, 1st rd ↗ (Pipering Ln East, **62**)
0.4 1st ⊕ ← (to Doncaster, **62**, **TPT**)
1.1 After bridge over ⊕, at split of paths, keep ↗ via ⊕ (no signs)
1.5 Imm after subway ← via ⊕ (to Town Centre)
    (For short-cut (city bypass) ↑ via ⊕, see map)
2.0 After petrol station ↑ via quiet rd
2.3 At end of rd ↑ via ⊕ crossings onto ⊕ on right side of rd
2.6 At Volkswagen dealer ↰ via ⊕ crossings to ⊕ on left side
3.3 After river and railway bridges, at lths via ⊕ crossings ↑
    into shopping area ⇙ ⌂ 🛒 🍴 ⚹ 🛈 **Doncaster** (French Gate)
3.5 1st rd rd → (to Station), keep ↑ *(For ⇙ **Museums** ↑, see map)*
3.8 At end 'St Sepulchre Gt' ← via ⊕ on left side pavement,
    take 1st ⊕ crossing →, at other side of rd ↖ via quiet rd
4.1 At traffic lhts, at end of one-way rd, *reset mileage:*
0.0 *(4.1)* At lhts, take rd ↗ (St Sepulchre Gt West) 🚗, keep ↑
2.2 After 2nd railway viaduct, 1st ⊕ → (to Warmsworth, **62**)
2.5 Ep ↟ onto next ⊕ (to Warmsworth, **62**, field on right)

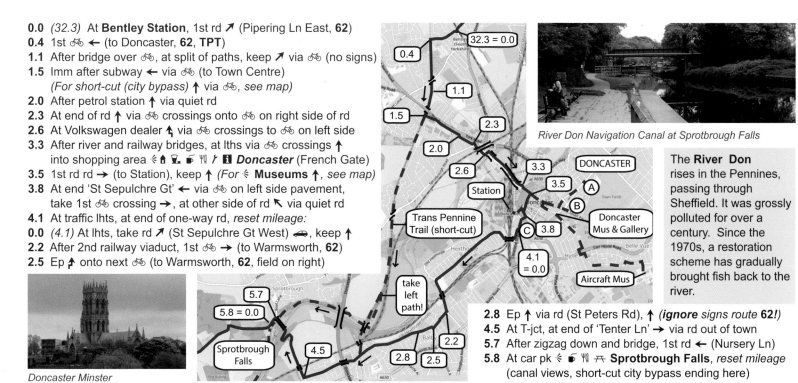

River Don Navigation Canal at Sprotbrough Falls

The **River Don** rises in the Pennines, passing through Sheffield. It was grossly polluted for over a century. Since the 1970s, a restoration scheme has gradually brought fish back to the river.

Doncaster Minster

2.8 Ep ↑ via rd (St Peters Rd), ↑ (*ignore signs route* **62***!*)
4.5 At T-jct, at end of 'Tenter Ln' → via rd out of town
5.7 After zigzag down and bridge, 1st rd ← (Nursery Ln)
5.8 At car pk ⇙ 🛒 🍴 ⛱ **Sprotbrough Falls**, *reset mileage*
    (canal views, short-cut city bypass ending here)

Route 12: Doncaster - Oughtibridge

At Sprotbrough Falls you have the choice to keep your ride on the move via our on-road route or to slow down on some rough paths in the deep valley of the River Don, only worthwhile if you wish to visit or view Conisbrough Castle.

Conisbrough Castle is a classic stronghold, dating from the 11th century. Built on a limestone spur, the castle rises 53m over the surrounding valley, with impressive baileys. The castle fell into disrepair in the 16th century, but gained fame after the publication of the novel **Ivanhoe** in 1819, which was set in the castle. The castle is worth a visit (£7 pp), but the rough **Trans Pennine Trail** features some quirky turns to cross the River Don and its industrial works; see the map on this page to get there.

0.0 (5.8) At car pk ⓧ 🖙 ⑪ 🛏 **Sprotbrough Falls** ↑ via rd uphill
(For ⓧ **Conisbrough Castle** *via ↟ onto tow path, use rough sections of route* **62**, **TPT**, *see map and inset)*

0.7 At T-jct ← (to Mexborough), keep ↑

4.6 At T-jct ← (Pastures Rd) 🚗

5.1 Before river bridge, 1st 🚲 → through gate, *reset mileage:*

0.0 (5.1) From gate next to cycle river bridge, join 🚲 on north side of river, gravel path heading down from bank, heading west

Willow Bridge near Oxspring

2.5 Ep feeds onto dead end rd, at T-jct ← (to Barnsley, **62**, **TPT**)

2.9 Beyond pub 🍺 🍴 **Harlington**, at T-jct → (to Barnburgh, **62**, **TPT**)

3.1 1st rd ← (**62**, **TPT**), then 1st 🚲 ←, through gate (**62**, **TPT**)

4.1 After cycle river bridge, 1st 🚲 → (to Barnsley, **62**, **TPT**)

5.8 Just before ep ↗ onto path under arch of viaduct, ep cross rd ⤊ (🚗🚗!), onto next 🚲 via gate (to Bentley, **62**, **TPT**)

7.1 Ep → via gate, cross rd via lhts, through gate, → via 🚲 (to Old Moor, **62**, **TPT**), keep ↑ via main path, ignoring side tracks

10.1 *(For 🚶 🍺 🍴 **Old Moor Reserve and Cafe**, after bridge over path, 1st gravel path →, before next bridge over path!)*

10.4 Cross rd ↑ (to Barnsby, **62**,**TPT**)

12.8 At rd crossing ← via rd (to Wombwell)

12.9 At rndabt ↗ via pavements onto ramp leading onto high 🚲 bridge, ep onto rd

13.5 At T-jct ↗, then at give way-jct ↑ (Cemetery Rd)
For High St 🏠 🚉 🍺 🍴 🏃 **Wombwell** ←

13.7 At T-jct → (cemetery on right side of rd)

14.0 At rndabt ↑ (see 'Summer Lane Center')

14.6 At give way-jct ↑ (no signs, see 🍺 *pub*)

15.2 After tunnel under railway, at T-jct ↗

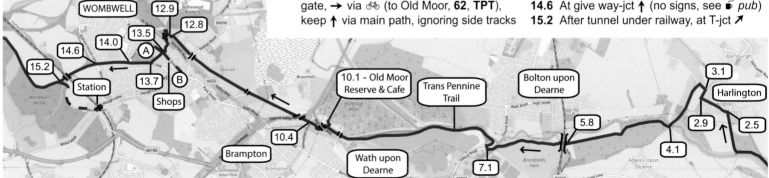

Route 12: Doncaster - Oughtibridge

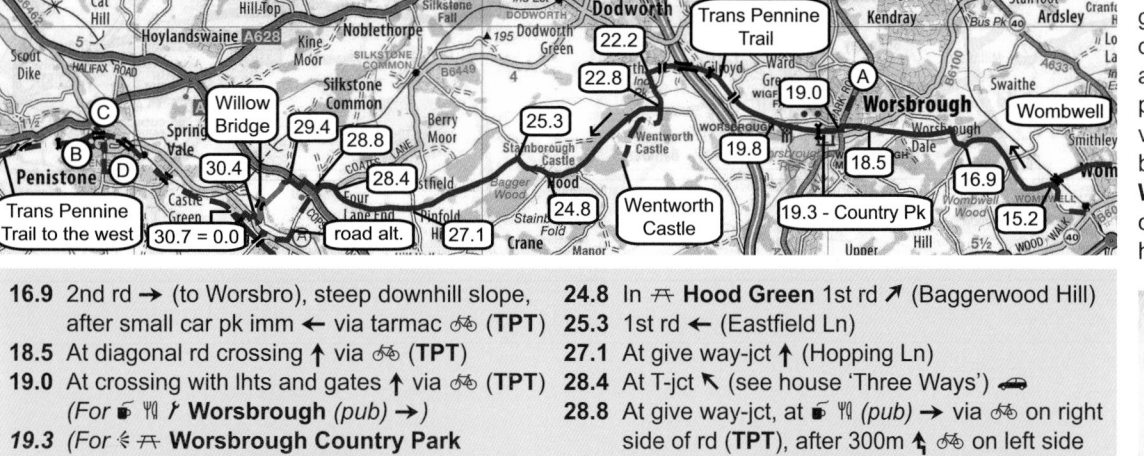

The **Trans Pennine Trail** is of reasonable quality from **Harlington**, guiding you through the urban sprawl of Barnsley. The path climbs gradually alongside the River Dearne. You will probably see a peaceful stream in its valley, but heavy rain can swell this backwater into a raging current. In **Wombwell**, you find a last collection of shops directly on our route before hitting the empty Peak District!

16.9 2nd rd ➔ (to Worsbro), steep downhill slope, after small car pk imm ← via tarmac 🚲 (**TPT**)

18.5 At diagonal rd crossing ↑ via 🚲 (**TPT**)

19.0 At crossing with lhts and gates ↑ via 🚲 (**TPT**)
*(For 🍴 🍽 ↾ **Worsbrough** (pub) ➔)*

19.3 *(For ⛶ 🌲 **Worsbrough Country Park** go ← at bridge over path)*

19.8 Just after 🍴 🍽 **Wigfield Farm Cafe** cross rd ↑ via 🚲 (**TPT**)

22.2 Ater M1 bridge, at four-way jct of paths ← (to Wentworth Castle), ep, join tarmac rd ↗ 🚗

22.8 At give-way jct ➔ (Lowe Ln, to Hood Green)
*(For ⛶ 🍴 🍽 **Wentworth Castle** ↑ (after 1km))*

24.8 In 🌲 **Hood Green** 1st rd ↗ (Baggerwood Hill)

25.3 1st rd ← (Eastfield Ln)

27.1 At give way-jct ↑ (Hopping Ln)

28.4 At T-jct ↖ (see house 'Three Ways') 🚗

28.8 At give-way-jct, at 🍴 🍽 (pub) ➔ via 🚲 on right side of rd (**TPT**), after 300m ⭧ 🚲 on left side

29.4 1st tarmac path ↖ (to Oxspring, **62**, **TPT**), before farm ↖ via gravel path, then open ground, leading to ⛶ 🌲 **Willow Bridge**

30.4 Ep ➔ via path on right side of rd (**62**, **TPT**), after 50m ⭧ via traffic island to path on left side, 1st rd ← (The Willows, **62**, **TPT**), 1st gravel 🚲 ↗ (**62**, **TPT**), 1st gravel 🚲 ➔, *reset mileage*

Thurgoland Tunnel

From **Worsbrough,** the **Trans Pennine Trail** is blessed with tarmac, but this surface will run out, with a rough gravel climb ahead. We leave the trail after **Worsbrough County Park** (a reservoir with pretty views) and the M1 motorway bridge. A serious on-road climb awaits you from the **Wentworth Castle Gardens**. These grounds belong to a country house dating from 1764, also featuring the sham ruins of **Stainborough Castle**, a folly completed in 1731 (£10 pp). Then, we go briefly on a short rough gravel descent (see page 18) to experience the **Willow Bridge** beauty spot; just walk it and be ready for a picnic! At **Oxspring**, you can turn to nearby **Penistone** for the last B&Bs before the empty Peak District. The scenic **Upper Don Trail** features the **Thurgoland Tunnel** and a scenic forest ride in the **Wharncliffe Woods**. At its end, we utilise a short rough forest track (see page 18) to get you to **Oughtibridge,** our gateway into the Peak District (avoiding Sheffield).

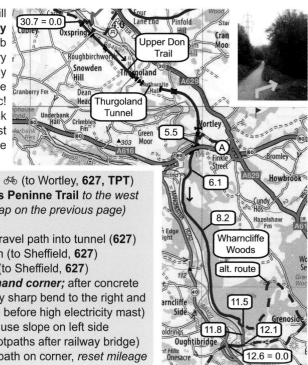

Wharncliffe Woods

0.0 *(30.7)* At start **Upper Don Trail** ← via 🚲 (to Wortley, **627, TPT**) (*For* 🏠 🍴 📷 🍺 ⚐ *Penistone and* **Trans Peninne Trail** *to the west coast and Manchester* →, *see also map on the previous page*)

2.5 ◁ **Thurgoland Tunnel**

5.5 At high bank of main rd ↟ onto wide gravel path into tunnel (**627**)

6.1 At split of paths ↗ via wide gravel path (to Sheffield, **627**)

8.2 At jct of paths ↗ via wide gravel path (to Sheffield, **627**)

11.5 *Pay attention*; *see picture on right hand corner;* after concrete bridge over narrow stream, followed by sharp bend to the right and curve to the left, take 1st path ↗ (50m before high electricity mast)

11.8 Keep ↑ via rough path, at steep drop, use slope on left side

12.1 Ep → via main rd down hill 🚗🚗 (footpaths after railway bridge)

12.6 After river bridge, *dismount* onto footpath on corner, *reset mileage*

Route 13: Oughtibridge - Ashbourne

100 km / 62 miles: 🚲 44%, 🥾 54%, 🚐 1%, 🚗🚗 1%
Stations: Hope Derbyshire (near Castleton)

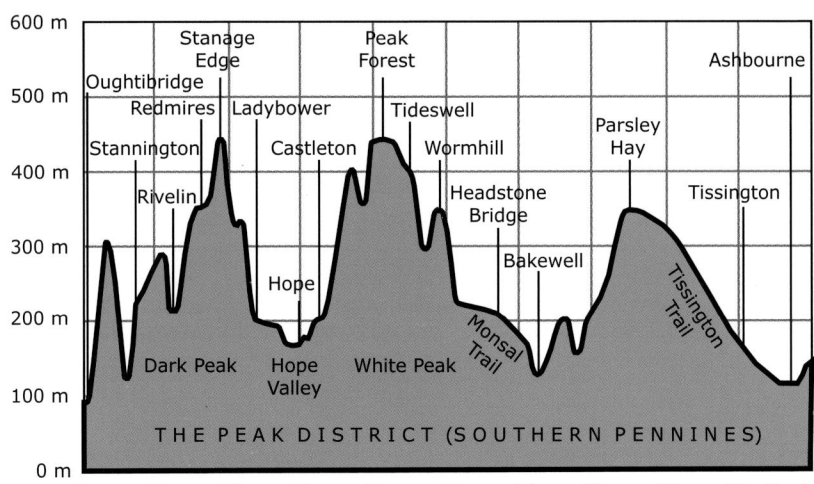

In the Peak District of the Pennines you twice reach an elevation of 445m above sea level. At the path across Stanage Edge (see picture), the point is clearly marked with a pole on the south side of the path. At Peak Forest, you will easily recognise the highest point of the pass in a sharp bend to the left.

This stage takes in the very best of **Peak District National Park**, the southern half of England's upland area of the **Pennines**. You will climb steeply towards the less-visited **Dark Peak** area. In the vicinity of Sheffield, **Rivelin** and **Redmires** are beautifully located drinking water reservoirs. Civilisation suddenly halts on the **Long Causeway** of **Stanage Edge**. This rough gravel track (see page 18) takes you onto a grit stone escarpment, popular with climbers. It is a stark visual evidence of the change from the grit stone of the northern 'Dark Peak' area to the softer limestone area of the 'White Peak' area.

Warning: treat Stanage Edge as an alpine crossing. Do not proceed in thunder and lightning, heavy rain, sleet, snow, low cloud or strong winds. Wait for better weather or use the alternative tarmac route!

Looking down to Oughtibridge

Stanage Edge

0.0 *(12.6)* At end of river bridge ⚑ 🍴 🍺 **Oughtibridge,** use zebra crossing, walk ↑ via path on left side of rd (Bridge Hill)

0.1 At give way-jct ↑ (Church St), resume cycling, steep climb 🚗

0.6 At near end of steep climb (you were allowed to walk ☺), keep ↑ (Burton Ln, to Bradfield)

2.1 Out of town, 1st rd ← (to Worrall), at T-jct ← (end 'Coal Pit Ln')

3.0 Just before 30 mph zone, 1st through rd →, follow through rd

4.2 At T-jct (opposite Hillsborough golf club) →

5.5 At T-jct → (Longley Rd, to Bradfield) 🚗, use path as needed

5.8 1st rd ← (Rowell Ln, to Stannington)

6.7 1st rd ← (Spout Ln, to Stannington), steep climb

7.7 At T-jct ↖ (for ⚑ **Stannington** ↑, *local shops after 500m*), imm 1st rd → (Bankfield Ln), 🍺 🍴 *(pub direct on route, on left)*

8.0 At T-jct ↗, imm 1st rd ↗ (Uppergate Rd, to Hollow Meadows), ↑

9.9 Out of town, 1st rd ↖ (Flash Ln)

10.5 After bend to the right, at sharp bend to left, ↑ via wide gravel rd (Moorwood Ln), rd downgrades to rough gravel (see page 18)

11.5 Ep, at Ronksley Hall Farm, ← via gravel rd, becomes tarmac rd

12.1 At T-jct ← via path on right side of rd (Manchester Rd) (🚗🚗!)

12.3 At 50 mph speed limit sign, ↖ to path on left side of rd (🚗🚗!)

12.9 1st rd → (🚗🚗!), narrow rd ≼ **Rivelin Dam**, lake on your right,

13.3 After dam → onto gravel path, becomes rough (see page 18)

14.2 At jct of gravel paths (with a wall at the jct) ↙, keep climbing

15.5 At end 'Wyming Brook' car park → via tarmac rd, keep ↑

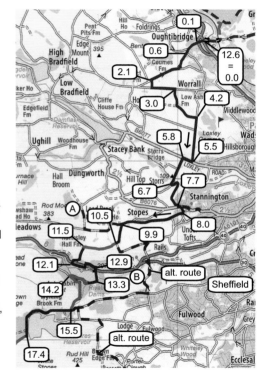

Route 13: Oughtibridge - Ashbourne

17.4 At end of rd → via gravel path (see sign 'unsuitable for motorised vehicles'), quality of ⛰ **Stanage Edge** path varies, take care!

21.3 Ep ('Dennis Knoll' car pk) ↑ via tarmac rd

21.6 1st rd ↗ (**6**)

24.6 At T-jct → via path on right side of rd (**6**)

24.9 After 🛏 🍴 **Yorkshire Bridge Inn** *(pub)*, at driveway 'Ladybower Lodge', ↖ to path on left side of rd (🚗 🚗 !)

25.2 After gate ← onto ⛰ **Ladybower Dam** (**6**)

25.6 At end of dam ← (**6**)

25.8 In descent, 1st gravel path ↗ (Thornhill Tr, **6**)

27.2 Ep ↗ via tarmac rd (**6**)

27.8 1st rd → (at red phone box, Carr Ln, **6**)

28.3 At sign 'Winhill House', ↖ via tarmac rd

30.8 At T-jct → via path on left side of rd (to Hope, A6187, **6**) *(Hope station ←)*

31.1 In 🏠 🚆 🛏 🍴 ⚑ **Hope** 1st rd ← (School Ln, **6**)

31.3 At T-jct ← (**6**)

33.6 At T-jct ↗ (no signs!)

34.0 At triangle square ↖, at end of square →

34.2 At T-jct ←, rnabt ⛰ 🏠 🏨 🚆 🛏 🍴 ℹ **Castleton**

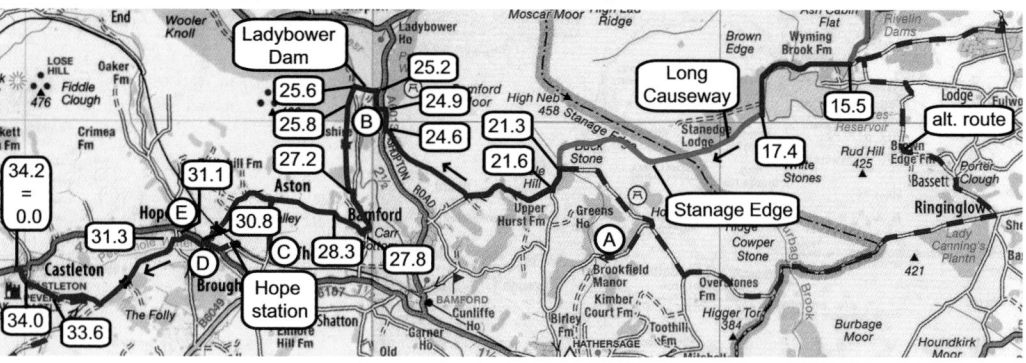

Hope Valley

Via scenic **Ladybower Reservoir** you arrive in **Hope Valley**, historically an important route across the Pennines between Sheffield and Manchester. Today, the A6187 is a dead end road to **Castleton** only, with its **caves** being a popular tourism destination. On the vault line between grit stone and limestone, just west of town, a continuous landslide occurs at **Mam Tor**, where the abandoned A6187 crumbles away since its forced closure in 1979.

Scenic **Castleton** is worth a two-night stay. **Speedwell Cliff Cavern** and **Peak Cavern Caves** are both within a 1km walk from town (£20 pp for joined ticket), as is **Treak Cliff Cavern Cave**, where the **Blue John** mineral can be seen (£12 pp). Do not miss wild and rocky **Winnats Pass**, **Mam Tor** and the 11th century ruins of **Peveril Castle**. With stunning views over the valley, the keep and the castle museum are worth a visit (£7 pp).

Speedwell Cavern

Winnats Pass

0.0 *(34.3)* From rndabt next to visitor centre of Castleton go east to town centre, 1 1st rd → (CastleSt)

0.2 At 'Market Place' triangle square ↖ **(6)**, follow rd uphill (Pindale Rd, with white house 'Bray Cottage' on left side of rd)

0.7 At next jct, keep ↑ (see sign 'unsuitable for HGVs') *(**ignore** signs route **6**)*

5.1 1st rd → opposite black sign 'lorries A625')

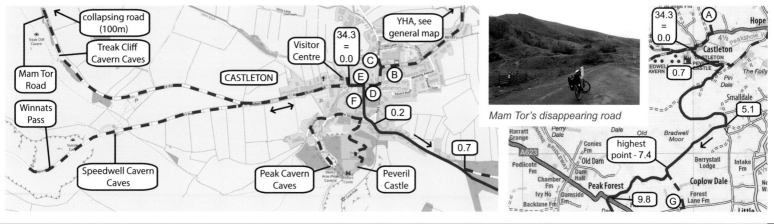
Mam Tor's disappearing road

Route 13: Oughtibridge - Ashbourne

Heading south into **White Peak**, highland country lanes take you to the **Monsal Trail**, deep in the valley of the **River Wye**. **YHA Ravenstor** is possibly England's most beautifully located hostel. The **Monsal Trail** is also possibly the most scenic cycle path of the country. It opened in 1981, but only became truly possible to cycle in 2011, when its old railway tunnels finally opened to the public. You will cycle in three of them on your way to **Bakewell**, with **Headstone Bridge** as the most striking point. Allow extra time to take in this very special place!

River Wye views from Headstone Bridge, Monsal Trail

9.8 At give-way jct, cross main rd A623 ↑ (🚗🚙!)

12.6 At T-jct ← (to Tideswell)

12.9 1st tarmac rd → (no signs!)

14.0 At four way-jct, where rd straight on continues as a gravel path, → via tarmac rd (Pennine Bridleway)

16.0 At four way give way-jct ← (to Wormhill)

19.1 In descent, 1st car pk ↗ (Millers Dale), at end car pk ← onto 🚲 **Monsal Trail** (to Bakewell, **680**)

21.7 🚲 **Litton Tunnel**

22.4 🚲 **Cressbrook Tunnel**

24.3 🚲 **Headstone Bridge/Tunnel**

The Monsal Trail 'rollercoaster' cycling experience

28.1 At 🚲 🍽 **Hassop Station Cafe & Bike Hire** ↑
29.8 At Bakewell station, just before station building,
→ onto car pk, at end car pk ← (Station Rd)
30.4 At end of rd ← onto river bridge 🚗🚗
(use footpath as needed)
30.5 Imm after bridge *dismount*, pull onto footpath
on left side of rd, walk ↙ onto riverside path
30.6 At riverside piazza ⇇ 🏠 🎡 🚲 🍽 ℹ **Bakewell** →,
↖ resume cyling on rd (to Toilets/Stall Market)
30.8 At T-jct → 🚗🚗 (use footpath as needed),
1st rd ← (King St) 🚗
31.0 1st rd ← (Butts Rd, 'dead end, no turning space'),
rd becomes tarmac path, steep climb, keep ↑
31.5 *Reset mileage* at end of tarmac path:
0.0 ↖ onto tarmac through rd, climb continues

Bakewell is bustling on market days, with the riverside walk always popular with tourists. From Bakewell, you will have to climb once more onto the heights of the Peak District. On these heights, **Arbor Low** is the 'Stonehenge of the peaks', with fifty large flat-lying limestone blocks making up an egg-shaped circle, dating from 2000BC (£1 pp).

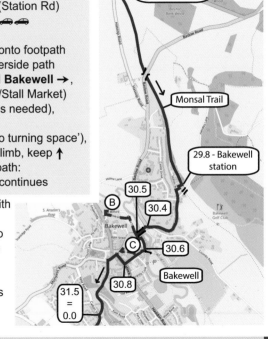

Route 13: Oughtibridge - Ashbourne

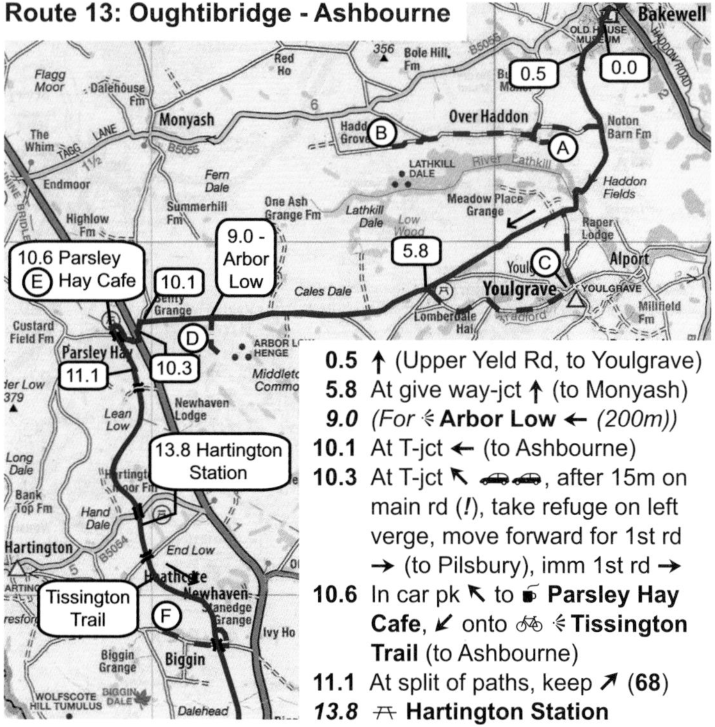

Bakewell

0.5 ↑ (Upper Yeld Rd, to Youlgrave)
5.8 At give way-jct ↑ (to Monyash)
9.0 *(For ⚲ Arbor Low ← (200m))*
10.1 At T-jct ← (to Ashbourne)
10.3 At T-jct ↖ 🚗🚗, after 15m on main rd (*!*), take refuge on left verge, move forward for 1st rd → (to Pilsbury), imm 1st rd →
10.6 In car pk ↖ to ☕ **Parsley Hay Cafe**, ↙ onto 🚲 ⚲ **Tissington Trail** (to Ashbourne)
11.1 At split of paths, keep ↗ (**68**)
13.8 🚉 **Hartington Station**

The **Tissington Trail** is one of England's oldest railway cycle paths. It has been open since 1971. Although less spectacular than the Monsal Trail, it forms a worthy finale to your ride across the Peak District National Park. The trail cuts deep into the limestone on a regular basis, allowing a continuous comfortable gradual descent to **Ashbourne**. The trail is dotted with picnic areas in the old station yards and an abundance of campsites to choose from too. It ends in style with a journey through **Ashbourne Tunnel**. From the tunnel's end, you can visit the centre of this market town. Note that **Alton Towers**, England's largest and most famous theme park, is just ten miles to the west (online tickets from £34 pp). Do not cycle there, as a section of main road cannot be avoided. Stay for two nights in Ashbourne and take a taxi or bus from the bus station if you are up for some serious theme park fun!

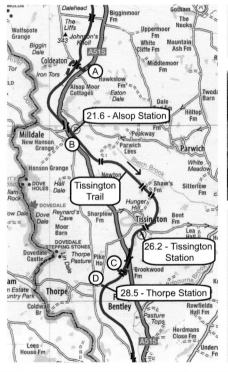

21.6 At 🚏 **Alsop Station** ↑
26.2 At 🚲 🚏 **Tissington Station** ↑
28.5 At 🏠 🚏 **Thorpe Station** ↑

32.5 At 🚲 **Ashbourne Cycle Hire** ↑ into 🚇 **Ashbourne Tunnel**

33.0 Ep after tunnel:
For 🏠 🍴 🚲 🍽 🍴 **Ashbourne** *imm* ← and ← up the hill
For continued route ↑ across car pk, keep ↗ on car park rd
33.3 At rndabt ←, at T-jct → 🚗🚗 **(68)**, use footpath on left side of rd as needed
33.8 2nd rd ← (just before large rndabt ahead, no signs!)
34.0 At T-jct ← **(68)**, 1st rd ↗, imm → onto 🚲 **(68)**, then 1st 🚲 ← **(68)**
34.6 Ep, join rd, at T-jct → **(68)**
34.8 At T-jct (end 'Duncombe Dr') ← **(68)**, *reset mileage at* **34.9**

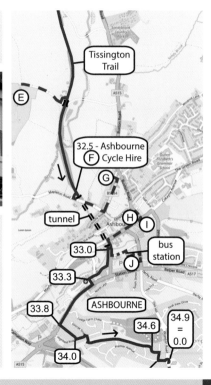

Route 14: Ashbourne - Leicester

94 km / 58 miles: 🚲 23%, 🚶 60%, 🚗 16%, 🚗🚗 1%
Stations: *Burton-on-Trent, Leicester*

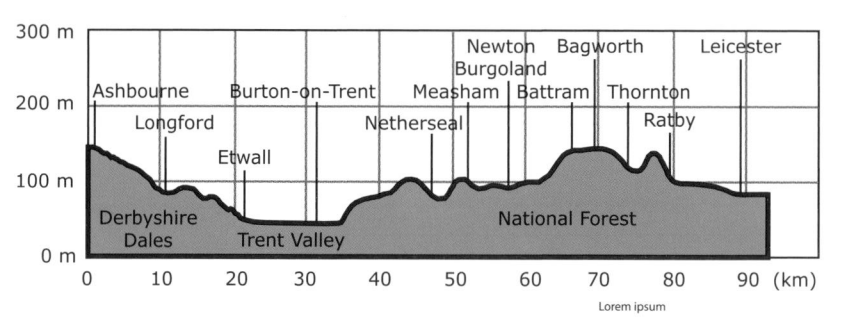

Lorem ipsum

s0.0 *(34.9)* At rndabt → **(68,** see 'Ashbourne Hilltop School')
2.6 At T-jct → (to Edlaston, **68**)
3.9 3rd rd ← (to Rodsley, **68**), keep ↑ via tarmac rd
9.2 At T-jct ← (to Longford, **68**)

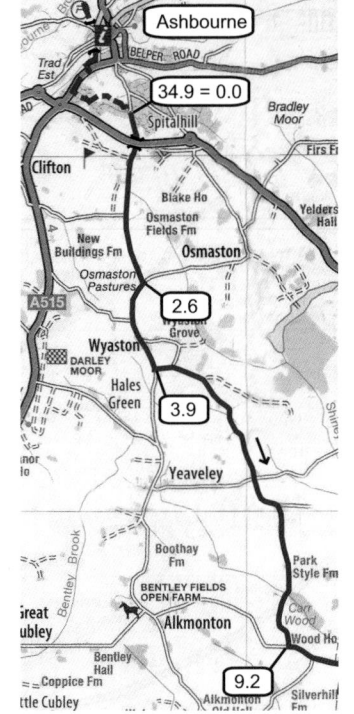

The elevation of the **Derbyshire Dales** is considerably lower than the Peak District, but up to **Etwall** it breathes a similarly empty feel. Then, the busier **Trent Valley** awaits you. The River Trent was canalised in 1712, making mass cargo transport possible. Local beer brewers experimented with adding sulphate to water used for beer production. Helped by the chemical composition of the local water, this process allowed the beer's hops to develop its own distinctive taste, making beer from **Burton-on-Trent** a favourite across Britain and its empire in the 18th and 19th century. Today, the industry still survives. The **National Brewery Centre** tells the full story, including the local invention of **Marmite**, which was created from the by-products of beer production (£12 pp).

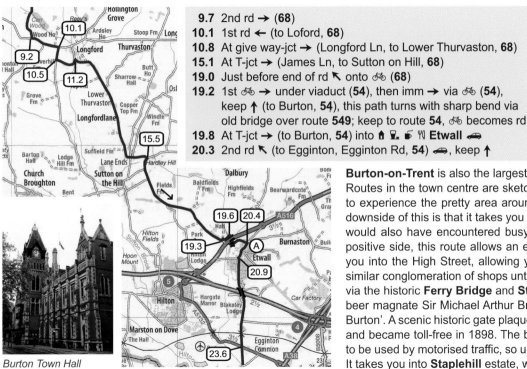

Burton Town Hall

9.7 2nd rd → (**68**)

10.1 1st rd ← (to Loford, **68**)

10.8 At give way-jct → (Longford Ln, to Lower Thurvaston, **68**)

15.1 At T-jct → (James Ln, to Sutton on Hill, **68**)

19.0 Just before end of rd ↖ onto 🚲 (**68**)

19.2 1st 🚲 → under viaduct (**54**), then imm → via 🚲 (**54**), keep ↑ (to Burton, **54**), this path turns with sharp bend via old bridge over route 549; keep to route 54, 🚲 becomes rd

19.8 At T-jct → (to Burton, **54**) into 🏠 🚂 🛒 🍴 **Etwall** 🚗

20.3 2nd rd ↖ (to Egginton, Egginton Rd, **54**) 🚗, keep ↑

National Brewery Centre, Burton-on-Trent

Burton-on-Trent is also the largest town on this route to Leicester. National Cycle Routes in the town centre are sketchy, so we created our own route, allowing you to experience the pretty area around **St Paul's Church** and the **Town Hall**. The downside of this is that it takes you by the busy road at the railway station, but you would also have encountered busy roads without cycle paths otherwise. On the positive side, this route allows an easy train exchange as needed and it will take you into the High Street, allowing you to catch the local vibe. You won't see any similar conglomeration of shops until your arrival in Leicester. You will leave Burton via the historic **Ferry Bridge** and **Staplehill Viaduct**. The link was funded by local beer magnate Sir Michael Arthur Brass, who later simply became known as 'Lord Burton'. A scenic historic gate plaque will inform you that the bridge opened in 1889 and became toll-free in 1898. The bridge's structure and width made it impossible to be used by motorised traffic, so up until today, it is a pedestrian and cycle haven. It takes you into **Staplehill** estate, with some nice views over the River Trent.

Route 14: Ashbourne - Leicester

Trent & Mersey Canal

23.6 At give-way jct, cross main rd ↑ (to Egginton, **54**) (🚗🚗!)
25.7 At end of rd → via 🚲 on right side of main rd (to Burton, **54**)
27.2 At side rd 'Claymills Rd', cross this side rd, keep ↑ via 🚲 on right side of main rds (**54**), leading onto bridge
27.4 After bridge, cross side rds, following tarmac 🚲 ↗, into bushes, via ramp down (to Burton, **54**), *dismount* for steps!
28.2 Ep ← via rd (**54**)
28.3 At rndabt ↑ (Hillfield Ln, **54**), then 1st rd → (Alderholme Dr)
28.5 At end of rd ↖ onto tarmac path, then → via canalside path
29.1 Ep → via rd closed for cars, then imm ← via cut through to dead end rd (**54**), keep ↑ (house no 40 on left side of rd)
29.5 At end of rd 'Kingsmead' ← via 🚲 on left side of rd (**54**)
29.6 After bridge, 1st 🚲 ← (**54**), at end of ramp leading down ← via canal tow path route (to Lichfield, **54**)
29.8 Use 🚲 ↖ onto quiet rd (to Lichfield, **54**), later rejoining tow path route ↗, keep following canal route

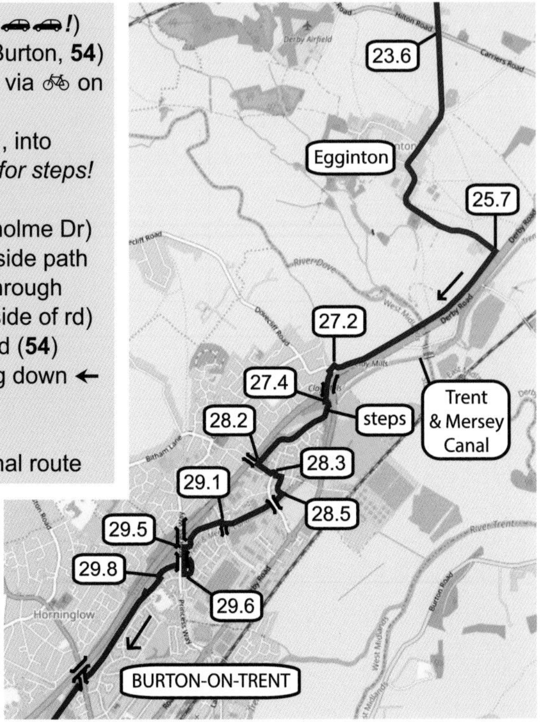

The National Forest is a forestry project in the rural area between Burton and Leicester. Over 8 million trees have been planted since 1995 and woodlands should cover 20% of the area once the project is completed. The transformation is slow, but some short trails will actually take you into the woods. **Beehive Woodlands Lakes** is ideal for camping, while

Thornton Reservoir is a perfect picnic spot. The **Ivanhoe Trail** is a cycle route under development on dismantled railways. Large sections remain not surfaced and are hard-going, so up to the town of **Measham** we keep you away from it. Only from **Ratby** the trail is tarmac. Our route as a whole has some busier roads, which we cannot avoid.

31.5 Imm after canal locks ↖ via wider tarmac onto 🚲 on higher bank (with tow path on your right, **54**)

31.9 At split of 🚲 paths ↖ (**63**)

32.1 Ep, cross rd ↑ (Casey Ln, **63**), then 1st rd → (Grange St, **54**)

32.4 At give way jct ← (St Paul's St West) (*ignore signs route **54** and **63**!*)

32.5 At T-jct ↟ into one-way rd (St Paul's Sq, to Station)

32.6 At T-jct ↟ into one-way rd (King Edward Pl, to Station)

32.8 At end King Edward Pl, *dismount*, use crossings to walk ↑ on path on right side of rd (Borough Rd)

32.9 At next jct cross via lhts ↟, join rd ↑ 🚗🚗 or walk on path on left side

33.6 At next jct with lhts ↑, at next lhts ↑ (*For ⚲ **Brewery Centre** ← at 1st jct with lhts, 300m ↑ to museum*)

34.0 At end of shopping st → (High St) 🏠 🚉 🚲 🍴 ***Burton-on-Trent***

34.2 At rndabt ↑ (Lichfield St), at start of bend to the right ↑ (Abbey St, **63**)

34.4 At end of Abbey St, *reset mileage*

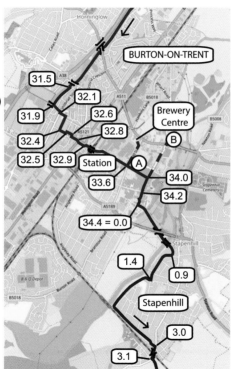

Ferry Bridge, Burton-on-Trent

0.0 *(34.4)* At end 'Abbey St' ← (Fleet St, to Stapenhill, **63**), at end of rd ↑ via 🚲 (**63**), keep ↑

0.9 At T-jct → (Ferry St, one-way) (*ignore signs route **63**!*)

1.4 At house no 161 on left side of the rd, → (Heath Rd)

3.0 Follow tarmac rd to end, at T-jct → 🚗

3.1 After railway bridge 1st rd ↖ (Rosliston Rd South) 🚗

Route 14: Ashbourne - Leicester

4.7 1st rd ← (Caldwell Rd) 🚗
5.4 1st rd ↗ (to Caldwell) *(difficult right turn!)*, keep to tarmac rd
7.6 At T-jct → (no signs) 🚗
8.5 In sharp bend to the right, 1st rd ← (to Botany Bay and ▲)
10.8 At give way jct ← (to Netherseal)
12.6 3rd rd ↗ (to Netherseal)
13.9 At T-jct → (to 🛏 🍴 **Netherseal**), follow through rd
16.1 At T-jct → via narrow path on left side of rd (🚗🚗!),
(to Nueneton, A444), 1st rd ↖, rejoin rd (to Measham) 🚗
18.3 2nd rd ← (Coronation Ln)
19.6 In 🛏 🛏 🍴 **Oakthorpe**, just before end of rd at T-jct,
join pavement on right side of rd and turn → (to Measham),
keep to narrow path on right side of rd
20.3 1st rd → (Blackthorn Wy), 1st rd ← (Poplar Dr), at end of
rd ↗ via narrow tarmac path through park (no signs!)
20.6 Ep join rd ↑, 1st rd ← (Oak Cl), imm → via tarmac path,
then 1st tarmac path ↖, ep join rd and keep ↑ to end
20.9 At T-jct → into High St 🛏 🛏 🍴 ⚡ **Measham** 🚗
21.0 At 'Bosworth Rd' (1st rd on left side of rd) *reset mileage*

Measham is a small town with just some local shops and pubs.

0.0 *(21.0)* 1st rd ← (Bosworth Rd, to N. Burgoland, **63**)
1.1 At T-jct, cross main rd ↑ (to Newton Burgoland, **63**)

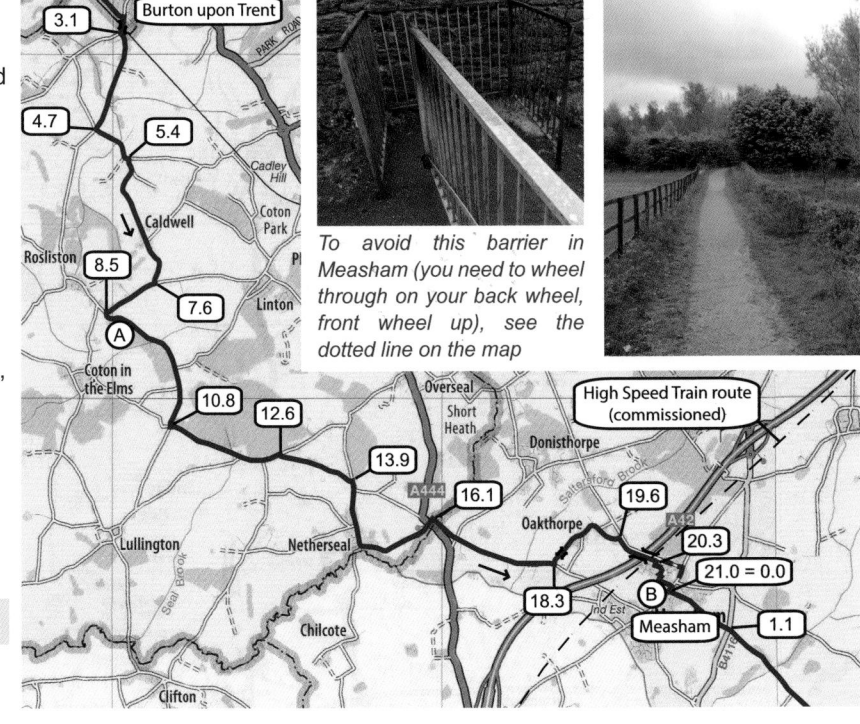

To avoid this barrier in Measham (you need to wheel through on your back wheel, front wheel up), see the dotted line on the map

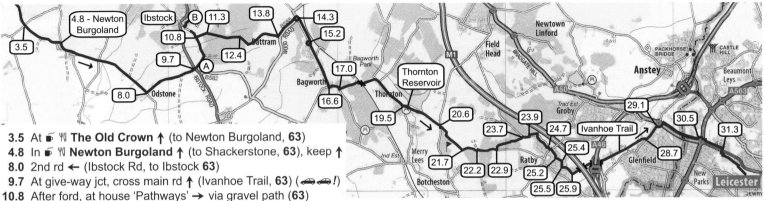

3.5 At 🍴 🍽 **The Old Crown** ↑ (to Newton Burgoland, **63**)

4.8 In 🍴 🍽 **Newton Burgoland** ↑ (to Shackerstone, **63**), keep ↑

8.0 2nd rd ← (Ibstock Rd, to Ibstock **63**)

9.7 At give-way jct, cross main rd ↑ (Ivanhoe Trail, **63**) (🚗🚗!)

10.8 After ford, at house 'Pathways' → via gravel path (**63**)

11.3 1st wide gravel path ↗ (through gate, **63**)

12.4 At split of gravel paths ↗, then at ep ← (car pk with rocks), ep ↑ via rd through village **Battram**

13.8 At T-jct ← via path on left side of rd (to Coalville, **63**)

14.3 At rndabt → via path on left side of rd (to Bagworth, **63**)

15.2 At rndabt ↑ (**63**), rejoin rd ↑ through village **Bagworth**

16.6 At T-jct ← (to Thornton, Ivanhoe Trail, **63**)

17.0 2nd tarmac rd ← (Thornton Ln, to Thornton, **63**)

19.5 In 🍺 🍴 🍽 **Thornton**, 4th rd ↖ (Reservoir Rd, to Markfield, **63**), at ⛵ 🌲 **Thornton Reservoir** ↑

20.7 At T-jct → (to Botcheston), imm ← via tarmac 🚲 (**63**)

21.7 1st tarmac 🚲 ← (**63**)

22.2 Ep ↗ via rd (Ivanhoe Trail, **63**)

22.9 After car pk, 1st gravel 🚲 ↖ (**63**)

23.7 1st rd → *(ignore signs route 63!)*

23.9 At sign 'Ratby' ↑ via lay-by rd, at end cross ↑ (lay-by on other side)

24.7 At end lay-by rd ↑ rejoin rd, at rndabt ← (→ *for* 🍺 🍴 🍽 **Ratby**), 1st rd → (Dane Hill, **63**)

25.2 4th rd ← (Ferndale Dr, **63**)

25.4 2nd rd → (Nicholas Dr, **63**)

25.5 2nd rd ← (Tylor Rd, **63**)

25.9 At T-jct → (Taverner Dr), imm ← via gravel 🚲 (⛵ **Ivanhoe Trail**, to Glenfield , **63**), keep ↑ to end

28.7 Ep ← via rd 🚗 (**63**), at rndabt ↑

29.1 At lhts → follow 🚲 on right side of rndabt, cross Station Rd and main rd, then → via 🚲 on left side of main rd (to Leicester, **63**)

30.5 At next rndabt ↑ by using two 🚲 crossings on left side of rndabt (**63**)

Route 14: Ashbourne - Leicester

Leicester is one of England's oldest cities, with an Iron Age settlement developing from 2nd or 1st centuries BC. During the Roman era, a forum and bathhouse was constructed. The ruins of the Roman baths can be visited at the **Jewry Wall Museum** (free). More ruins can be viewed in **Abbey Park** (free). This is where Leicester Abbey stood proud until 1538, when Thomas Cromwell convinced King Henry VIII of immoral behaviour in England's monasteries and all were dissolved.

Leicester is truly famous for the remains of King Richard III. The **King Richard III Museum** tells the tale of a king who only reigned for two years, died in battle and whose remains were found in 2012 under the tarmac of a local car park (£10 pp). Whilst you are at it, also visit **Leicester Cathedral** opposite, where the unfortunate king was reburied. Nearby is the beautiful timber-framed **Guildhall Museum**, with exhibitions on the history of the city (free).

North of the city centre, you can visit the **National Space Centre** with rockets, satellites, meteorites, space suits and so on. The iconic Rocket Tower and the largest planetarium of the UK are a must (£16 pp).

All attractions can be visited via our circular city centre route, also featuring the main shopping area around the scenic **Clock Tower**.
It is possible to bypass all the city centre stuff and cycle on. The cycle routes in and out of the city are straightforward and pretty green.

Leicester has something to offer for all!

31.3 At 🚲 🍴 **Heathley Park** cross ↑ via lhts onto 🚲 on right side of main rd (to City Centre, **63**)

31.4 → via 🚲 (**63**), ep ← via rd (Copeland Av, to City Centre, **63**), at next jct ↑ (Stokes Dr, to City Centre, **63**)

32.1 At house no 1a → via 🚲 (Stokewood Park, to City Centre, **63**), after entrance gate imm ← via 🚲, keep ↑, at playground ↖

33.5 On arrival at riverside with cobbled rd, *reset mileage:* *(For short-cut (city bypass)* ↑ *via riverside 🚲, at bridge* ↗*)*

0.0 *(33.5)* For **City Centre Route** ← via bridge (**6**), ep keep ↑ via rd

0.3 At lhts ↑ onto pavement to cross main rd ↑ (Sanvey Gate) 🚗

0.6 At lhts ← via 🚲 on left side of rd (Riverside Wy), keep ↑ (**6**)

1.1 Ep → via 🚲 under viaduct main rd

1.2 ← via bridge, after bridge → via gate into 🚶 **Abbey Park** (**6**)

1.6 At 🚲 🍴 **Abbey Park cafe**, *reset mileage:* *(For* 🚶 **Abbey ruins** ↑ *and for* 🚶 **National Space Centre** ↑*)*

0.0 For **City Centre Route continued** → via 'weak bridge', keep ↖, 3rd tarmac path ↗, at 'mini rndabt' of paths ← via wide tarmac path, which keeps bending to the right

0.8 After car pk, 1st tarmac path ↖ (to City Centre), path leading over canal bridge, ↑

1.2 At 'Archdeacon Ln' ↑ onto piazza, via 🚲 lhts ← onto 🚲 in middle of rd, at next 🚲 lhts ↑ onto pavement, then 1st rd →(Chapter St)

1.7 At give way jct, 2nd rd → (Russell Sq), at end of rd ↑ to 🚲 lhts ↑, cross main rd ↑ onto rd

2.2 At lhts →(Humberstone Gt), use right side 🚲 lane of left side carriageway (**!**) 🚗🚗

2.4 At lhts ↑ into pedestrianised zone 🏠 🚻 🚲 🍴 ⚕ 🛈 *Leicester* (Humberstone Gt)

2.6 At 🚶 **Clock Tower** ↑ (East Gates), 1st rd ← (Cheapside), 1st rd →(Cank St), keep ↑

3.1 After 🚶 **King Richard III Mus & Cathedral**, 1st rd → (Apple Gt), after 50m ↖ via piazza, at end ↖, via lhts onto 🚲 on right side of rd, keep ↑, after river bridge *reset mileage*

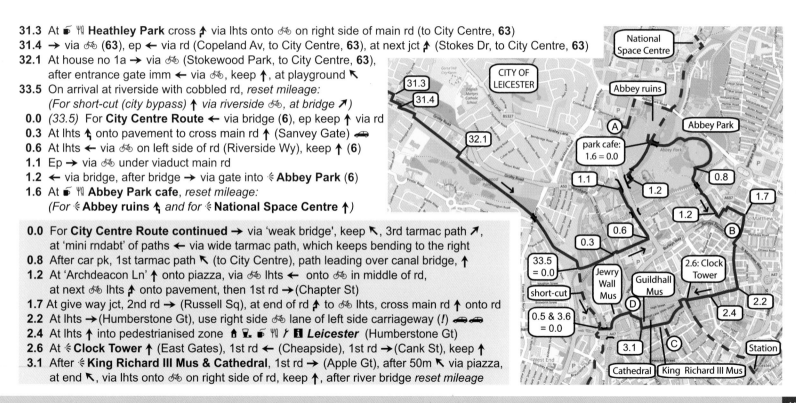

Route 15: Leicester - Stratford-upon-Avon

99 km / 61 miles: 🚲 36%, 🚶 48%, 🚗 15%, 🚃 1%
Stations: *Rugby, Royal Leamington Spa, Warwick*

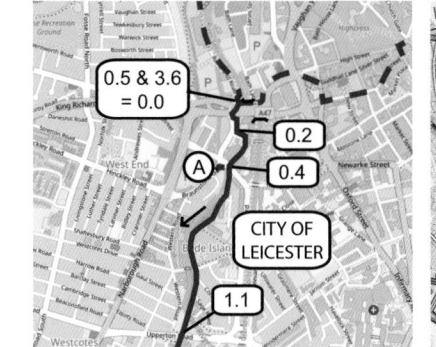

0.0 *(0.5 & 3.6)* Just west of river bridge, at jct with lhts, cross main rd via 🚲 lhts to the south, onto 🚲 on left side of rd (**6**)
0.2 1st rd ← (Westbridge Cl), follow 🚲 ↗ (**Great Central Way, 6**)
0.4 At lhts ↑ via 🚲 (to Bede Park, **Great Central Way, 6**), keep ↑
1.1 At rd crossing with lhts ↑ via 🚲 (to Narborough, **6**), keep ↑
6.1 Ep ↑ via rd (**Guthlaxton Trail, 6**)
6.4 At T-jct → (Cork Ln, to Blaby, **6**), keep ↑

7.2 Ep ← on rd, at end of rd ↑ via lay-by(**6**)
7.5 Cross main rd ↟ via lhts onto 🚲 on other side of rd, at rndabt, cross ↑, then → via 🚲 next to bus stop (**6**), 1st rd ← (Northfield Rd), ↖ (Chapel St)
8.1 At T-jct ← (**6**, Mill Ln, dead end rd)
8.6 1st 🚲 → (**Guthlaxton Trail, 6**), ↑
9.2 Ep →, cross rd ↗ onto rd (**6**)
10.2 At end of lay-by ← via 🚲 on left side of rd (to Countesthorpe, **6**)
10.3 Cross rd ↟, 🚲 on right side (**6**)

11.5 At end of 🚲, join rd ↑ (Winchester Rd, **6**)

15.2 After **Willoughby Waterleys**, at jct ↑ (to Ashby Magna, **50**)

17.4 In **Ashby Magna**, 2nd rd ← (Peveril Rd, to Gilmorton, **50**), after bend to →, imm 1st rd ← (Gilmorton Rd, to Gilmorton, **50**)

18.5 At T-jct ↖ (to Gilmorton, **50**) 🚗

20.8 In 🍴 **Gilmorton**, at 🛏 🍴 **Crown Inn**, → (Lutterworth Rd, **50**)

22.1 At T-jct ← (to Kimcote, **50**) 🚗

22.4 1st rd → (to Walcote, **50**)

25.2 At T-jct → via narrow path on right side of rd (to Walcote, **50**)

25.5 In 🛏 🛏 🍴 **Walcote**, opposite house no 30, cross main rd ↟ to narrow path on left side (🚗 🚗!), then 1st rd ← (Swinford Rd, **50**)

26.8 At split of rds ↗ (to Swinford, **50**)

28.0 At T-jct ↗ *(ignore signs route 50!)*, imm 1st rd ↖ (to Shawell)

29.8 At give way-jct ↖ (to Shawell)

30.7 At give way-jct ↑ (Catthorpe Rd)

31.9 At T-jct ←

32.4 1st rd → under motorway viaduct

33.4 In 🛏 🍴 **Catthorpe**, a T-jct → 🚗, 1st rd ← (to Catthorpe Manor)

35.6 At *pub* 🛏 🍴 **Lilbourne** → via rd (Chapel Ln), then at T-jct ←, at give way-jct ↑ (Hillmorton Ln)

The **Great Central Way** leads you into an area with modest rolling hills. Between **Shawell** and **Catthorpe** you pass under the 'motorway of the north', the **M6**, which merges here into the M1. Welcome to the south! A rough 'Unclassified Country Road' (see picture and page 18) leads to Rugby. This is not a 'public right of way' by law, but its west end has been turned into a cycle path. Use the alternative route when told to!

Private or public? Fact is that this is a handy link. You proceed at own risk!

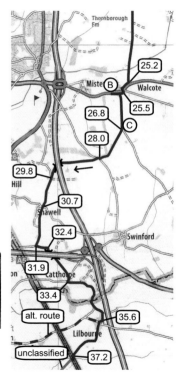

Route 15: Leicester - Stratford-upon-Avon

37.2 At T-jct ← (to M. Keynes, A5) 🚗🚗, use 🚲 lane,
imm → (Waitling Meadows), if shut, shut gate behind you,
keep ↑ via rough gravel 'unclassified rd', becomes 🚲

39.2 Cross rd ↑ onto 🚲, becomes rd, bridge ⛵ **Grand Union Canal**

40.0 At T-jct →, 1st rd ← (Coton Rd), 1st rd → (Jenkins Rd)

40.4 At T-jct (end of Jenkins Rd) ←

40.6 2nd rd → (Bromwich Rd)

41.0 At T-jct ←, at next T-jct (end of Vere Rd) →

41.3 At T-jct ←, at T-jct → 🚗🚗, see 🍴 **Hillmorton**

41.7 2nd rd ← (Fisher Av), 1st rd ↗ (St Johns Av),
then 1st rd ← (Vernon Av)

42.2 At T-jct → via 🚲 on left side of rd (Ashlawn Rd)

43.0 At side rd to Crematorium, *reset mileage:*
(For ⛵ 🏠 🍴 📷 🍴 ⚡ Rugby ← via small gravel car pk,
*down via zigzag (follow signs route **41**), see map)*

0.0 *(43.0)* **For continued route** ↑ via 🚲 (to Dunchurch, **41**)

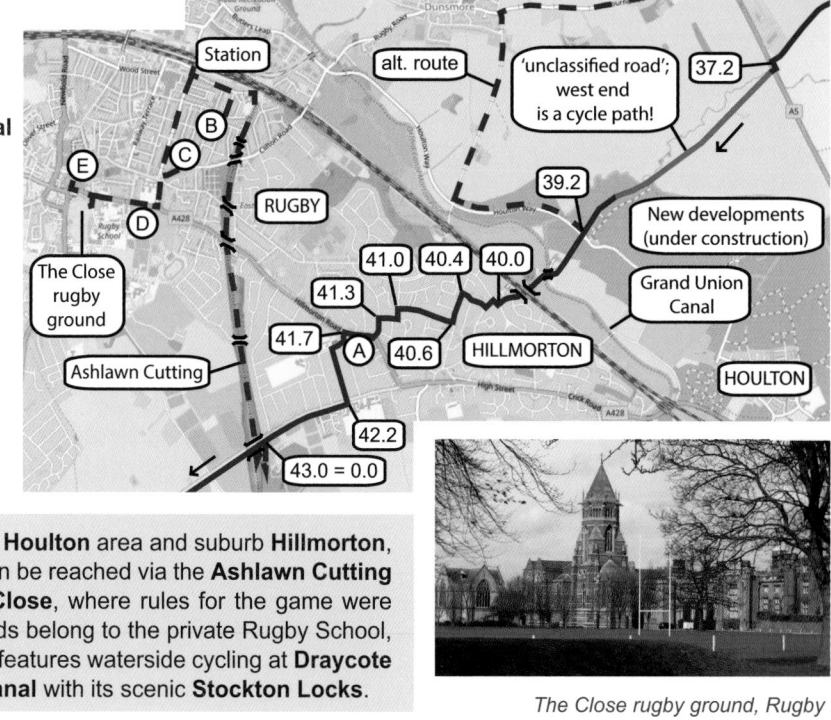

Station

alt. route

'unclassified road';
west end
is a cycle path!

37.2

A5

39.2

RUGBY

New developments
(under construction)

The Close
rugby
ground

41.0 40.4 40.0

41.3

Grand Union
Canal

41.7

40.6

HILLMORTON

A

HOULTON

Ashlawn Cutting

42.2

43.0 = 0.0

A428

The Close rugby ground, Rugby

Rugby is a spread-out historic market town. We travel via the new **Houlton** area and suburb **Hillmorton**, but we bypass the town centre. The central area and the station can be reached via the **Ashlawn Cutting** cycle path. Via this route you can also visit rugby ground, **The Close**, where rules for the game were defined and recorded in 1845, hence the sport's name. The grounds belong to the private Rugby School, but you can peek over the wall (on **Barby Road**). The next stretch features waterside cycling at **Draycote Water** (water reservoir and country park) and the **Grand Union Canal** with its scenic **Stockton Locks**.

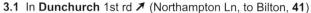

3.1 In **Dunchurch** 1st rd ↗ (Northampton Ln, to Bilton, **41**)

3.4 2nd rd ↖ (Northampton Ln, **41**)

3.8 At T-jct ↑ via gravel path (**41**), becomes rd

5.0 At T-jct → via 🚲, after 30 m, make U-turn onto 🚲 on other side, (🚗🚗!), then 2nd rd → (Halfway Ln, to Draycote Water, **41**), ↑

5.9 After viaduct M45, at ep ↗ via tarmac rd (**41**)

8.8 At start dam ⛵ **Draycote Water** → (to Draycote, **41**), onto gravel path

9.5 Ep ← via rd (*ignore* signs route **41**!)

9.8 At 'Draycote Farm', 1st rd ↗, (keep *ignoring* signs route **41**!)

10.9 At T-jct ← (to Birdingbury), keep following tarmac through rd

13.2 At give-way jct in ☛ 🍴 **Birdingbury** ← (to Leamington, **41**) 🚗, 1st rd → (to Stockton, **41**)

Pub near the Stockton Locks, Grand Union Canal

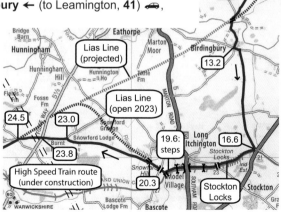

16.6 Just before T-jct ↘ onto tow path (**41**)

19.6 After ⛵ **Stockton Locks** and ☛ 🍴 **Two Boats Inn**, just before bridge '26a', ↗ via steps up (**41**), → onto tarmac 🚲 on former railway

From this point, the **Lias Line** will open in 2023. How it will cross the new **High Speed Train route** we do not know. The route as seen in May 2022 is shown!

20.3 Follow path from railway bank, ep ↖ via rd (to Leamington, **41**)

23.0 At T-jct ← (to Leamington, **41**) 🚗

23.8 At large rndabt via 🚲 crossings ↑ (**41**) 🚗

Route 15: Leicester - Stratford-upon-Avon

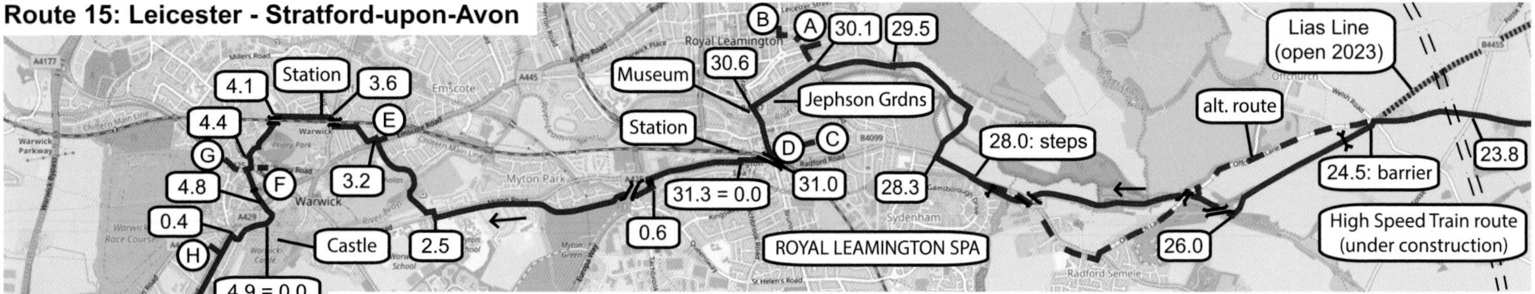

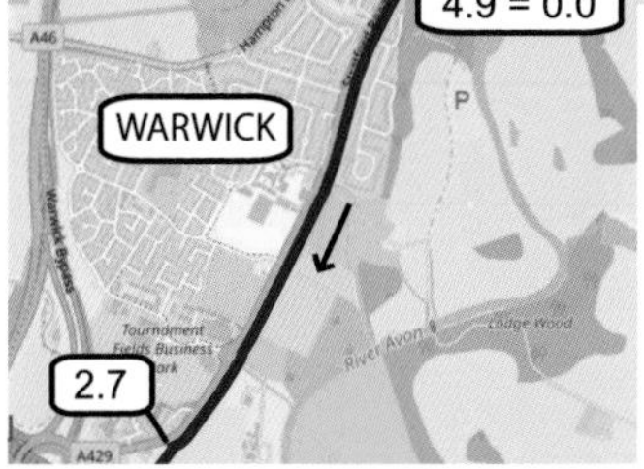

Map labels:
- A4177
- Skillers Road
- Station 4.1
- 3.6
- 4.4
- Emscote
- A445
- Royal Leamington
- Warwick
- Priory Park
- E
- G
- 4.8
- F 3.2
- 0.4
- H
- Warwick
- Castle
- 2.5
- Myton Park
- River Avon
- WARWICK
- A429
- A46
- 4.9 = 0.0
- 2.7
- B
- A 30.1 29.5
- 30.6
- Museum
- Jephson Grdns
- Station
- D C
- 31.3 = 0.0
- 31.0
- 28.3
- 0.6
- ROYAL LEAMINGTON SPA
- B4099
- Radford Road
- Sydenham
- Radford Semele
- 28.0: steps
- 26.0
- alt. route
- Lias Line (open 2023)
- 24.5: barrier
- 23.8
- High Speed Train route (under construction)

24.5 1st rd ← and imm → via 🚲 (to Leamington, **41**) *(tricky barrier and steps; see map for alt. route!)*
26.0 Ep → onto tow path (**41**)
28.0 Use steps ↑ to join 🚲 on left side of main rd (**41**)
28.3 At house no 162, → into car pk (**41**), ↑ onto 🚲, at ep, join rd through park
29.5 After leisure centre, ↟ join 🚲 on left side of rd
30.1 Ep at jct with lhts ↑ via rd (to Town Centre, **41**)
30.6 ♿ 🏨 🚻 ☕ 🍴 ⚲ 🛈 *Royal Leamington Spa*, at T-jct *dismount*, ← via footpath on left side of rd (entrances ♿ **Museum & Jephson Gardens**)
31.0 At lhts under bridge → (High St), walk on the left
31.3 At lhts opposite station, *reset mileage:*
0.0 *(31.3)* Resume cycling ↑ via 🚲 on left side of rd

0.6 1st 🚲 ↖ (opposite lhts), after bridge → (**41**), ↑
2.5 Ep → via lths onto 🚲 into park (Myton Fields, **41**)
3.2 Ep cross rd via lths, then ← via 🚲 leading to 1st rd → (Broad St, to Warwick, **41**)
3.6 At end 'Cuy's Cliffe Terrace' → via 🚲 on left side of rd, 1st rd ← (Lakin Rd), imm ↖ via tarmac path
4.1 After station, 1st path ← under railway, keep ↑
4.4 At end of drive ← via rd, at T-jct → 🚗, 1st rd ← (Northgate St), ↑ via gate ♿ **St Marys Church**
4.8 At give-way jct cross rd ↑ (🚗🚗!) (Castle St)
4.9 After bend to ↗, enter car pk, *reset mileage:* (For ♿ **Warwick Castle** use 'Town Gate' in wall)
0.0 *(4.9)* **For continued route**, from car pk ↑ via rd
0.4 At T-jct ← via pavement on left side, later 🚲

Royal Leamington Spa grew rapidly into a busy town in the early 19th century due to its water springs with assumed healing powers. The **Royal Pump Rooms and Baths** opened in 1814 and the neighbouring **Jephson Gardens** opened in 1834. The royal prefix to the town's name was granted by Queen Victoria in 1838. The park and museum (art gallery included) have free access.

Famous **Warwick Castle** is one of England's finest castles. William the Conqueror commissioned the first stronghold on this site in 1068 and the current stone keep was constructed in the late 12th century (£20 pp). Back on the lanes, **Charlecote Park** is a 16th century country house with a deer park (£10 pp). Try to avoid the road between Loxley and Stratford during rush hours.

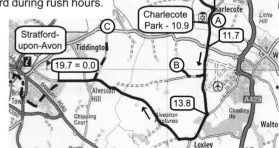

2.7 At end of 🚲 on left side of main rd
   ↖ via quiet rd (to Stratford, 41), at end
   of rd ↑ via 🚲 bridge (41), keep to 🚲
3.7 On 🚲 on left side side of main rd, use
   1st crossing ↑ to 🚲 on right side of rd
   (to Stratford, 41), ep ↑ via rd
   (Fulbrook Ln, to Sherbourne, 41), ↑
8.5 At T-jct ↖ (to Hampton Lucy, 41) 🚗

9.4 In 🛏 🍴 **Hampton Lucy** ↑ (to Charlecote)
   (For 🛏 🍴 pub → via Church St, 200m)
10.5 At T-jct → (to Wellesbourne, 41) 🚗
10.9 At ⬱ 🛏 🍴 **Charlecote Park** ↑ 🚗
11.7 At give way jct ↑ (to Airfield, 41)
13.8 At T-jct → (to Loxley) 🚗 , keep ↑
19.7 After arrival in Stratford-upon-Avon,
   at house no 180, *reset mileage*

Route 16: Stratford-upon-Avon - Oxford

100 km / 62 miles: 🚴 20%, 🔌 75%, 🚗 4%, 🚗🚗 1%
Stations: Stratford-upon-Avon, Moreton-in-Marsh, Hanborough, Oxford

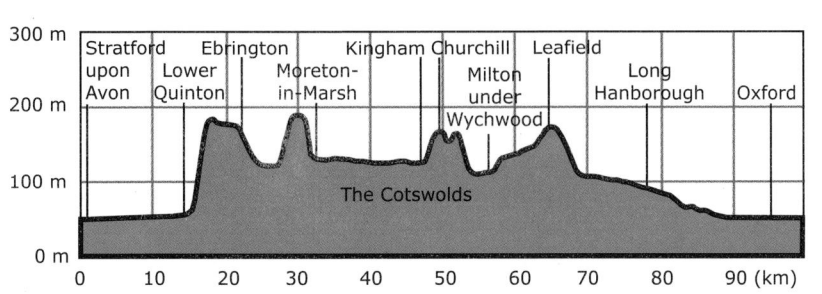

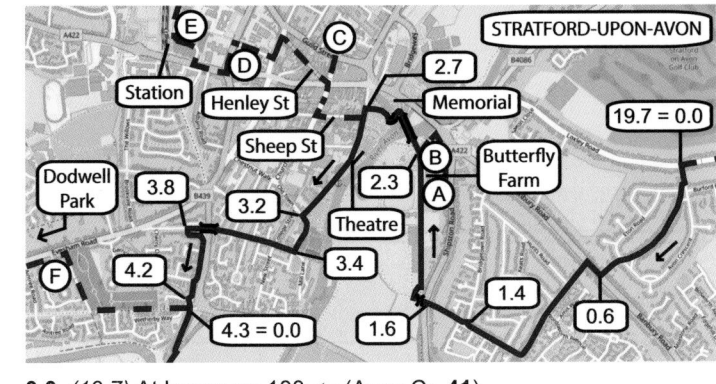

Stratford-upon-Avon is the birthplace of **William Shakespeare**. After passing **Butterfly Farm** (£8 pp), you will arrive in town via the historic river bridge and the historic canal lock basin, where the **Gower Memorial** pays tribute to the great writer. Head via **Sheep Street** (see map) for **Tudor World** (£6 pp) where the 16th century is brought to life for all ages. The **Mechanical Art Museum** (£8 pp) can be found on our station route via crowded Henley St, as is **Shakespeare's Birthplace Home** (£18 pp). The **Royal Shakespeare Theatre** is on the riverside, with regular performances of Shakespeare plays. It's tower (£3 pp) offers beautiful views over the town centre, famous for its Tudor buildings, see Sheep Street and Henley Street.

0.0 *(19.7)* At house no 180 ← (Avon Cr, **41**), 1st rd ↗ (at house no 53, **41**)
0.6 At T-jct → 🚗🚗 (Bevan Rd), 1st rd ← (Rushbrook Rd, **41**)
1.4 At 2nd sharp bend to the right, go ↑ via tarmac 🚴 (**41**)
1.6 Cross rd via 🚴 lhts ↑ under viaduct, → up ramp, ↖ via 🚴
2.3 Ep, cross rd diagonally ↑ (to Boat Club), *dismount* for bridge ⬅🏠 🚉 📷 🍴 🚲 ℹ *Stratford-upon-Avon*, imm ← via bridge, ↑
2.7 At end of locks ← (Waterside, **41**), keep ↑ *(⬅ Sheep St →)*
2.9 At T-jct ← (to Milcote Picnic Area) *(ignore signs route 41!)*
3.4 Follow bend → (College Ln), at give-way jct ↑
3.8 After bridge, 1st rd ← (Sandfield Rd), then 2x 1st rd ←
4.2 At steps ← via ramp, cross rd ↑ onto 🚴, *reset mileage*

Stratford-upon-Avon Greenway

The **Stratford-upon-Avon Greenway** takes you comfortably out of town on the course of an old railway. Ahead are **The Cotswolds**, a rural area with rolling hills, protected as an area of Outstanding Natural Beauty. Back on the country lanes, **Kiftsgate Court Gardens** and **Hidcot Manor Gardens** are directly on our route, facing each other. Kiftsgate features rare and unusual plants (£9 pp), whereas Hidcot is about the idea of a garden as a series of outdoor themed 'rooms' (£14 pp). **Moreton-in-Marsh** is a historic market town, with a scenic and busy High Street. 'Fuel up' here, as it is a long way to the next shop in Long Hanborough.

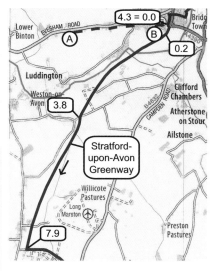

Stratford-upon-Avon: Shakespeare's Birth Place Home and Tudor architecture

0.0 (*4.3*) From crossing ↑ via ᗧᗣ
0.2 Keep ↗ (see ᗧᗣ hire in train)
3.8 Ep → to avoid gate, imm ←
via next entrance, rejoin main
ᗧᗣ after 100m) **(5)**
7.9 Ep ← via through rd **(5)** 🚗

Route 16: Stratford-upon-Avon - Oxford

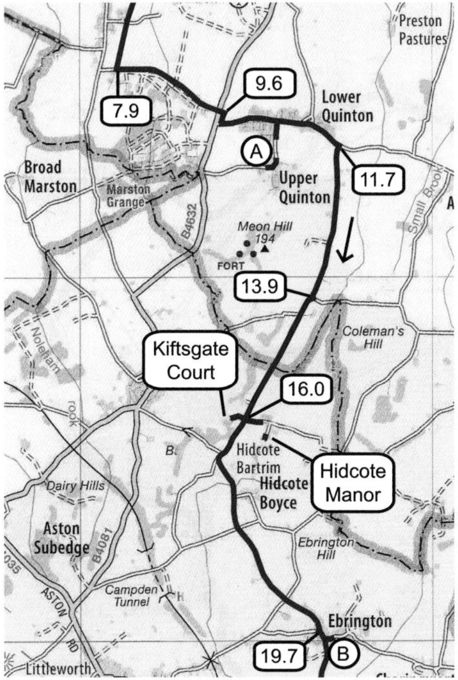

9.6 After 🛢 **The Barn**, at T-jct, cross ↑ (🚗🚗!) onto 🚲 →, ep ← (5) 🚗, use path on right side of rd as needed

11.7 After ⌂ 🚉 🍴 **Lower Quinton**, 1st rd ↗ (to Hidcote, 5)

13.9 At T-jct → (to Hidcote) *(ignore signs* route **5***!)*, in bend to the right, 1st rd ↖ (to Hidcote)

16.0 At ⬳ **Kiftsgate Court & Hidcot Manor Gardens** ↑, *(ignore signs route **442***!)*

On the horizon on the right you can see **Wales** on a clear day!

19.7 In ⌂ 🛢 🍴 **Ebrington** at T-jct ↖, 1st rd ↗ (to Paxford)

20.9 At T-jct ← and imm → (to Paxford)

22.0 At T-jct → (to Paxford) 🚗 into ⌂ 🛢 🍴 **Paxford**

22.2 1st rd ↖ (to Aston Magna), 1st rd ↖ (at tiny triangle)

25.3 At T-jct → (to Draycott)

25.8 After bridge over railway, 1st rd ← (to Batsford, **442**)

29.8 At T-jct *dismount*, → via footpath on right side of rd (🚗🚗!), after 100m resume cycling ↱ on lay-by rd

30.3 In ⬳ ⌂ 🚉 🛢 🍴 ♪ 🚻 **Moreton-in-Marsh**, at house no 16a (corner 'Corders Ln'), ←, cross High St ↑ onto Oxford St, at end Oxford St, *dismount*, ↖ via footpath on left side of rd *(for **station** ← at Station Rd)*, keep walking ↑

31.1 After railway bridge, at 1st through rd → *reset mileage*

0.0 *(31.1)* 1st through rd → (to Evenlode, **48**), ↑

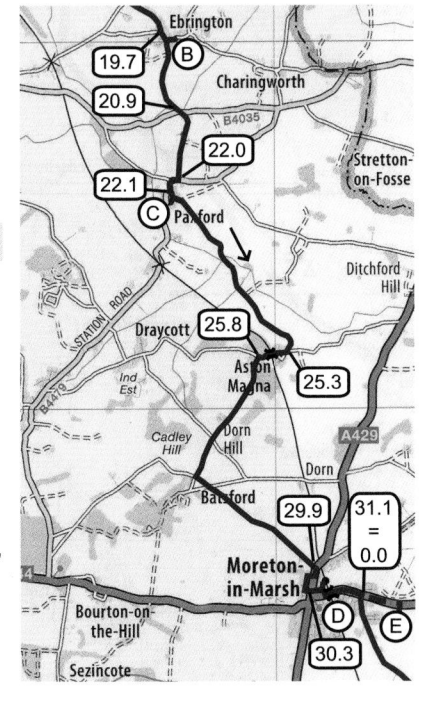

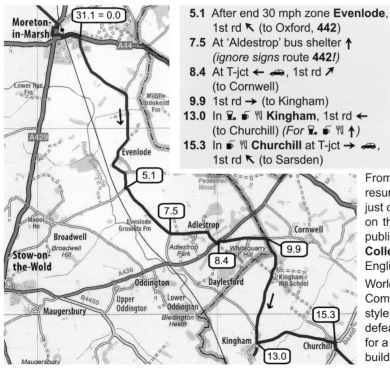

5.1 After end 30 mph zone **Evenlode**, 1st rd ↖ (to Oxford, **442**)

7.5 At 'Aldestrop' bus shelter ↑ (*ignore signs* route **442**!)

8.4 At T-jct ← 🚗, 1st rd ↗ (to Cornwell)

9.9 1st rd → (to Kingham)

13.0 In 🚆 ☕ 🍴 **Kingham**, 1st rd ← (to Churchill) (*For* 🚆 ☕ 🍴 ↑)

15.3 In ☕ 🍴 **Churchill** at T-jct → 🚗, 1st rd ↖ (to Sarsden)

Blenheim Palace

From Moreton-in-Marsh, you cycle temporarily on a flat plain, but then the hills resume. Beyond the hills, you can walk to the ruins of **North Leigh Roman Villa**, just off our country lane route (free). **Combe Mill Museum** is a historic saw mill on the River Evenlode (£5 pp). The **Oxford Bus Museum** has 130 years of public transport in Oxfordshire on display, also featuring the **Faulkner Cycle Collection**. This bicycle collection features a Penny Farthing and a Singleton English velocipide, also known as the 'boneshaker' (£5 pp).

World Heritage **Blenheim Palace** is one of England's largest country houses. Commissioned by Queen Anne, it was built between 1705 and 1722 in Baroque style to celebrate the achievements of the 1st Duke of Marlborough, who defeated the French in battle in 1704. You will have to travel away from our route for a visit. Admission is a hefty £27 pp, but there is a way to get a glimpse of the building for free; see page 130 to get to know the 'public right of way'.

Route 16: Stratford-upon-Avon - Oxford

Blenheim Palace World Heritage

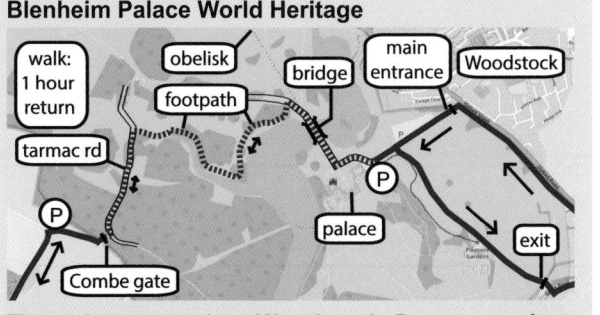

- walk: 1 hour return
- obelisk
- footpath
- bridge
- main entrance
- Woodstock
- tarmac rd
- P
- P
- palace
- exit
- Combe gate

The main entrance is at **Woodstock**. Best access from our route is at **Yarnton**. From there, you can cycle on cycle paths next to the A44 (12 km round trip). Only do so if you are happy to pay the entrance fee, intending to see the building from inside. Avoid Bladon Road, due to a lack of roadside paths! To get a glimpse of the building and grounds for free, use **Combe gate**. Note **no bicycles** are allowed; lock up on the lane 'triangle' north of Combe Mill, taking vital belongings with you. From the gate, walk the tarmac road north and turn right via the footpath. You will see the palace from the bridge.

16.3 1st rd ↗ (to Sarsden)
16.6 1st rd → (to Merriscourt)
19.3 At T-jct ← (to Lyneham)
(*ignore signs* route **442!**)
19.8 1st rd → (to Bruern)
21.9 1st rd ↖ (to Milton-u-W)
23.8 In 🍴 **Milton under Wychwood** at T-jct ↗ (to Fyfield) (*For* 🍴 ↖)
24.7 3rd rd ← (to Taynton)
25.6 1st rd ← (to Shipton-u-W)
27.5 Cross ↑ (🚗🚗!) (Upper End)
28.1 At T-jct ← (end 'Fiddlers Hill')
28.4 At give-way jct ↘ (to Leafield)
29.4 At give-way jct ↑ (to Leafield)
32.7 In 🍴 **Leafield** at T-jct ↖ (to Finstock)

North Leigh Roman Villa

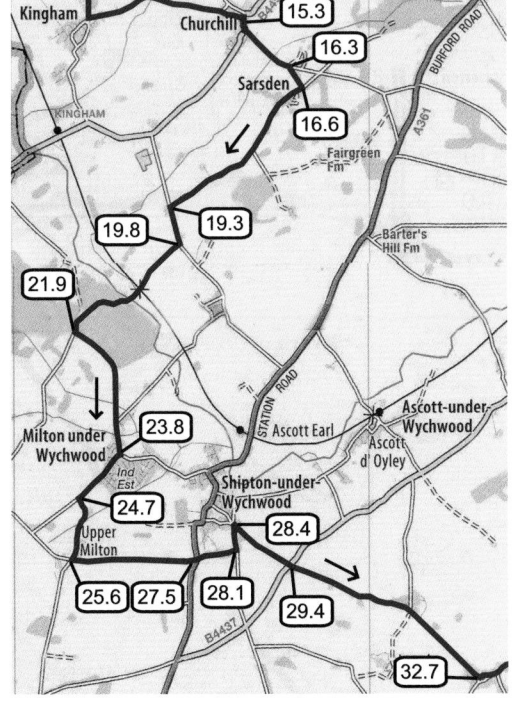

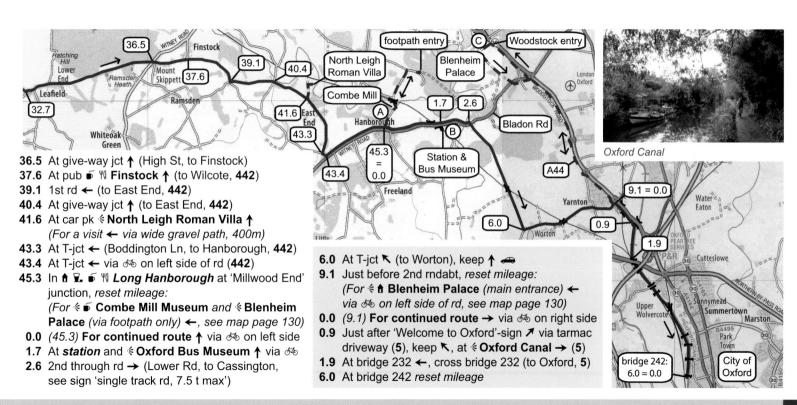

Oxford Canal

36.5 At give-way jct ↑ (High St, to Finstock)
37.6 At pub 🍺 🍽 **Finstock** ↑ (to Wilcote, **442**)
39.1 1st rd ← (to East End, **442**)
40.4 At give-way jct ↑ (to East End, **442**)
41.6 At car pk ⚲ **North Leigh Roman Villa** ↑
    (For a visit ← via wide gravel path, 400m)
43.3 At T-jct ← (Boddington Ln, to Hanborough, **442**)
43.4 At T-jct ← via 🚲 on left side of rd (**442**)
45.3 In 🏠 🚉 🍺 🍽 ***Long Hanborough*** at 'Millwood End' junction, *reset mileage:*
    (For ⚲ 🍺 **Combe Mill Museum** *and* ⚲ **Blenheim Palace** *(via footpath only)* ←*, see map page 130)*
0.0 (45.3) **For continued route** ↑ via 🚲 on left side
1.7 At *station* and ⚲ **Oxford Bus Museum** ↑ via 🚲
2.6 2nd through rd → (Lower Rd, to Cassington, see sign 'single track rd, 7.5 t max')

6.0 At T-jct ↖ (to Worton), keep ↑ 🚗
9.1 Just before 2nd rndabt, *reset mileage:*
    (For ⚲ 🏠 **Blenheim Palace** *(main entrance)* ← via 🚲 on left side of rd, see map page 130)*
0.0 (9.1) **For continued route** → via 🚲 on right side
0.9 Just after 'Welcome to Oxford'-sign ↗ via tarmac driveway (**5**), keep ↖, at ⚲ **Oxford Canal** → (**5**)
1.9 At bridge 232 ←, cross bridge 232 (to Oxford, **5**)
6.0 At bridge 242 *reset mileage*

Route 16: Stratford-upon-Avon - Oxford

The city of **Oxford** is world-famous for the **University of Oxford**, the oldest university in the English speaking world, with teaching known to be established from 1096. The academic community has shaped the city for centuries, with stunning architecture as a result. Over 9 million tourists visit the relatively small city centre annually, making for very crowded streets. The city also features more people on bicycles than anywhere else on our route, with the sting that risk of bike theft is higher; always lock up securely! Other than signposted route 5, our own route takes you via Oxford's most famous landmark buildings, such as the **Radcliffe Camera**, **Bridge of Sighs** and **Christ Church Cathedral** (£10 pp). On Broad Street, **Blackwell's** is a famous bookshop with the largest number of books in one room. Both our route and route 5 are shown on the map.

Many museums in Oxford are departments of the university. The **University Museum of Natural History**, the adjoining cultural **Pitt Rivers Museum** and the **History of Science Museum** can all be found on our main cycle route. The **Ashmoleum Museum** is the oldest of all, focusing on art and archaeology. The **Museum of Oxford** is run by the city council, with displays on the city's past. The **Modern Art Museum** and the **Story Museum** are other museums. All museums listed above are free of charge. **The Bodleian Library** is a working university library where copies of every book published in the United Kingdom are held. Tours can be booked from two weeks in advance (£6-15 pp). The longest tour features the **Radcliffe Camera**, Oxford's most iconic landmark.

Broad Street

Radcliffe Camera, Bodleian Library

Blackwell's

Bridge of Sighs

0.0 *(6.0)* After passing under bridge 242, at bench with bin, go ↘ up the ramp (to Jericho), ep → over bridge 242
*(For **Oxford station** and 🏛 continue ↑ via towpath south, see map)*

0.2 At rndabt ↑ via one-way rd (St Bernards Rd)
*(For route 5 south via ⌐ and ⸖**Ashmoleum Museum** go →, see map)*

0.6 At give-way jct, cross ↑ (🚗🚗!), via 🚲 onto quiet rd (Bevington Rd)

0.8 At T-jct → 🚗🚗, use 🚲 lane (Banbury Rd)

0.9 1st rd ↖ (Parks Rd), at bend, join imm 🚲 on left side of rd (Parks Rd)

1.4 At ⸖**Natural History & Pitt Rivers Museum** at end 🚲 ↑ rejoin rd 🚗

1.8 At mini rndabt ↑ (Catte St)
*(For ⸖**Blackwell's**, ⸖**History of Science Museum** and ℹ →, see map)*
*(For ⸖**Bridge of Sighs** look into 1st street on your left after mini rndabt)*

2.1 After ⸖**Bodleian Library** and ⸖**Radcliff Camera** on right side of rd ↑, rd becomes alley way, at end of alley way via lights onto rd → 🚗

2.4 Follow sharp bend ← (St Aldates) 🚗 *(For ⸖🚉 📷 🍴 **Oxford City** ↑)*

2.6 After ⸖**Oxford Museum** on left side of rd 1st rd → (Pembroke St)
*(For ⸖ **Christ Church Cathedral** ↑, entrance via park after 50m on left)*

2.8 After ⸖**Story and Modern Art Museums** 1st rd ← (St Ebbe's St, 5)

2.9 In sharp bend to the left, go ↗ (Littlegate St, 5), imm ↖ via 🚲 (5)

3.0 Ep → via 🚲 on right side of rd, at lhts cross rd via lhts ← (5), after lhts ↗ onto quiet rd (Blackfriars Rd, 5), follow quiet rd with bends

3.4 After playground on right side of rd 🚶 via Thames path *(ignore route 5!)*

3.9 Ep, **walk** → via path on right side of rd, at end of bridge *reset mileage*

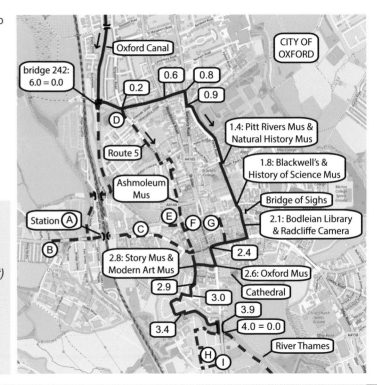

Oxford Canal

CITY OF OXFORD

bridge 242: 6.0 = 0.0

0.6 0.8 0.2 0.9

D

1.4: Pitt Rivers Mus & Natural History Mus

Route 5

1.8: Blackwell's & History of Science Mus

Ashmoleum Mus

Bridge of Sighs

Station (A)

E F G

2.1: Bodleian Library & Radcliffe Camera

B

C

2.4

2.8: Story Mus & Modern Art Mus

2.6: Oxford Mus

2.9

3.0

Cathedral

3.9

3.4

4.0 = 0.0

H I

River Thames

Route 17: Oxford - Alton Barnes

97 km / 60 miles: 🚲 56%, 🥾 41%, 🚗 3%, 🚗🚗 0%
Stations: Didcot Parkway

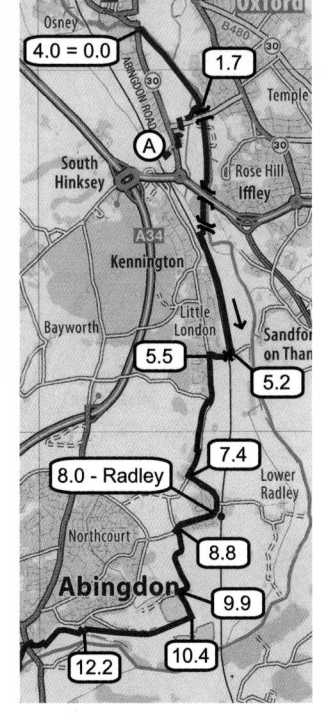

0.0 *(4.0)* At end of bridge ← via lhts onto 🚲 (← **Thames Path**, 5), ↑
1.7 *(For ▲ → via ramp, see map)*
5.2 Ep → via rd (to Abingdon, 5)
5.5 At end 'Sandford Ln' ↙ 🚗 (to Abingdon, 5), keep ↑
7.4 1st rd ← (Church Rd, 5)
8.0 At station 🚉 🍴 **Radley** ↑ (5)
8.8 In bend to the left, go ← (Thrupp Ln, 5)
9.9 After 2nd sharp bend to the right, 1st 🚲 ← (5)
10.4 Ep → via 🚲 (5), keep ↑

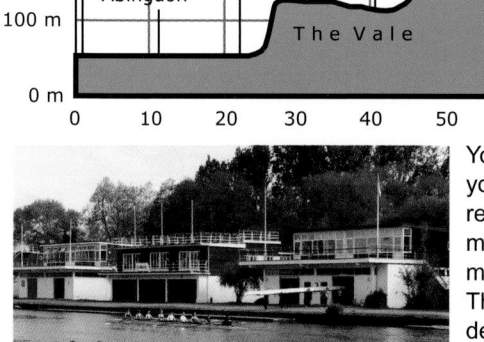

You will leave **Oxford** via the short, but very scenic **Thames route**, making your way to pretty **Abingdon**. Its 17th century **County Hall** is home to a regional museum, with pretty rooftop views (free by donation). Some bleak miles of cycling around a former power station site take you to **Didcot**, a modern service town, worth a visit because of its historic **Railway Centre**. The large collection of locomotives in the original setting of the former depot of the Great Western Railway makes this a must for steam train buffs (£7 pp). Empty lanes at the base of the **North Wessex Downs** take you to historic market town **Wantage**. Just beyond the pretty main square, the **Vale and Downland Museum** (free by donation) provides great context to your upcoming ride in the **Vale of White Horse**.

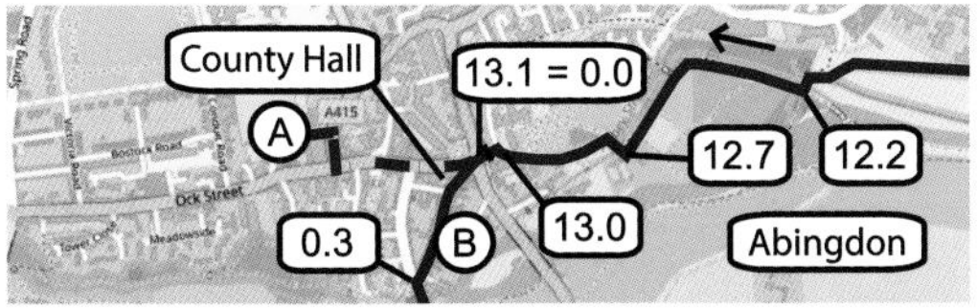

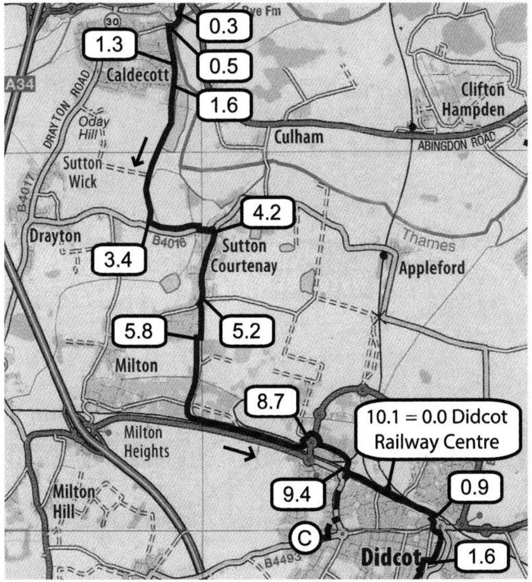

12.2 After narrow bridge → (The Vale Way, **5**)
12.7 Ep ↑ via bridge to car pk (to Town Centre, **5**)
13.0 On square ↖ via historic gate (**5**)
13.1 At square **Abingdon** ('Bridge St'), *reset mileage*
0.0 *(13.1)* ↑ into rd on left side of **County Hall**
0.3 At end of rd ← ('pedal cycles only', **5**)
0.5 1st rd ← (Wilsham Rd, **5**)
1.3 End of rd ↑ via 🚲 (**5**), ep join rd ↑
1.6 In sharp bend to the right, 2nd rd ↖ (to Didcot, **5**), keep ↑ (becomes 🚲)
3.4 Ep ← via 🚲 on left side of rd, **5**), ep onto rd
4.2 2nd rd ↗ (High St, **5**) 🚗
5.2 *Ignore signs route* ***5!***, ↑, at mini rndabt ↖ 🚗
5.8 At end village ↑, join 🚲 on right side of rd
8.7 At 3rd rndabt, take 3rd exit via 🚲 on left side of rd, see sign '7.5t weight limit') 🚗
9.4 After narrow bridge, join pavement on left side of rd, after next bridge ← via 🚲 on left side of rd, keep to most left side path (**5**)
10.1 At station ***Didcot*** *reset mileage*
0.0 *(10.1)* ↑ via 🚲 on left side of rd (**5**, later **544**)
0.9 Just before rndabt cross ↑ via lths, take 3rd exit on rndabt (Jubilee Wy), imm ↗ via 🚲 up the ramp (to Upton, **544**), at sharp bend ↗

The **Ridgeway** is an ancient trading route running for 139 km on the high edge of the North Wessex Downs. Not exactly the perfect cycle way; expect all variations as shown on page 18. The worst stretches are shown on our map as a continuous red line. Where things are not too bad, the maps show a red-blue dotted line. It is the total distance of discomfort what makes the route truly hard. Alternative routes are all far from perfect, but these are shown on the maps, further information in the table on page 18.

We included the Ridgeway because of both its extremely scenic and historic value and its premium access to **Uffington White Horse**. The famous chalk figure dates back to the bronze age (free). **Barbury Castle** is an ancient settlement of which only the earth works remain (free). **Chiseldon** is the only town on this exposed stretch.

The route ends near the ancient stone circle of World Heritage site **Avebury**; a tarmac road will never feel so comfortable again!

Route 17: Oxford - Alton Barnes

1.6 Ep cross rd ↑ via narrow path onto other rd, there ← (to Upton, **544**), after 50m ↖ via narrow tarmac ⬝⬝ (**544**), then keep following narrow ⬝⬝ ↗ (**544**)

2.6 At four-way jct of paths → (**544**)

2.7 At next four-way jct of paths ← (**544**)

4.7 At end of tarmac ↖ via wide gravel ⬝⬝ (**544**)

4.9 Ep → via tarmac rd into ⌂ **Upton** (**544**)

5.3 At T-jct ↗ (Chilton Rd, to Wantage, **544**)

6.4 At give way jct ↑ (**544**), later gravel surface

8.4 Ep, cross main rd ↑ via lhts onto narrow ⬝⬝, imm ↖ (to Wantage, **544**), onto lay-by rd

8.6 At next jct → (industrial estate rd)

9.0 1st rd → (to 'building 587'), at end ←

9.1 Where rd bends to the left, go ↗ via gravel path, follow bend ← through fields

11.2 At tarmac rd crossing ← (to Wantage, **544**)

12.6 1st private rd → (ignore access signs, **544**)

13.8 At jct of gravel paths → (**544**), imm 1st tarmac rd ← (to Wantage, **544**)

16.9 In **East Lockinge** 1st rd ← (to West Lockinge, **544**)

17.7 In sharp bend to right, ↑ via ⬝⬝ (**544**)

18.7 At T-jct ←, then 1st rd → (Springfield Rd)

19.3 1st rd →, then ← into 1st car pk, ↑ into ⬝⬝ on right side of scouts hut

19.4 Keep ↑, at end of 'Icknield Ln' ↖ ⊞

20.0 Imm after fire station → via driveway, keep to left onto path, keep ↖ to join dead end rd

20.2 At T-jct → ⊞, at T-jct ↖ onto town square

20.4 ↑, at end ⑄ ⌂ 🏧 ☕ 🍴 ⚕ ⓘ **Wantage** square *reset mileage* at 'no entry'-sign:

0.0 *(20.4)* **Walk** into one-way rd, ← (Church St)

0.1 At ⑄ **Vale and Downland Museum** →

0.3 At T-jct → (Locks Ln), becomes path, after footbridge ↖, at end of 'Locks Ln' ← via rd

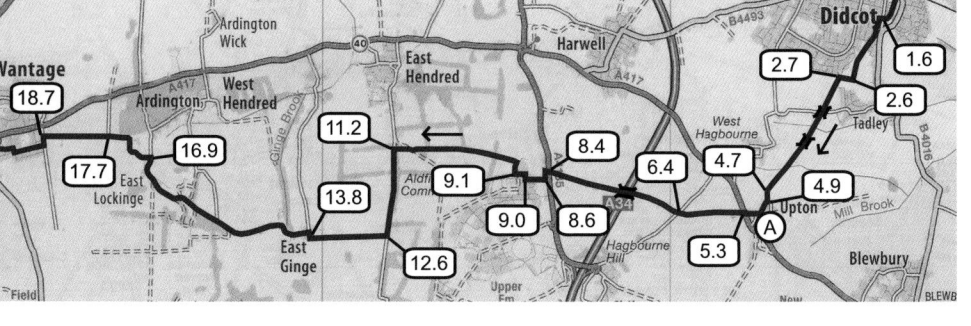

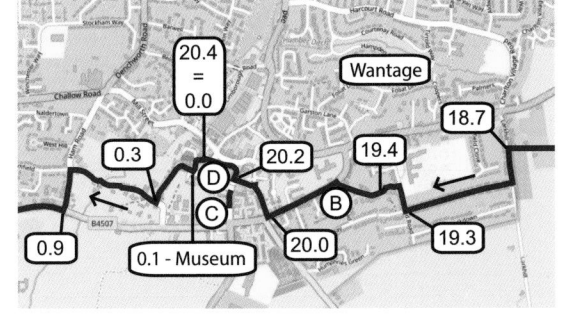

0.9 At T-jct → (Ickleton Rd) 🚗

1.3 1st rd ← (to Letcombe Regis)

2.8 In 🏠 🍴 🍺 **Letcombe Regis** follow bend → (to Letcombe Bassett)

5.0 After rd 'Knoll Cl' on right side of rd, 1st rd ↖ (to Downs Church), ↑

5.6 After leaving village, at split of rds ↗ (see sign 'Ridgeway closed to motor vehicles')

6.3 1st gravel path → (see sign 'Restricted Byway'), keep ↑, path narrows, becomes grass, then gravel again

9.4 Cross rd ↑ via tarmac rd (to Sparsholt), 1st gravel path ↖ (Ridgeway), ↑ becomes rough

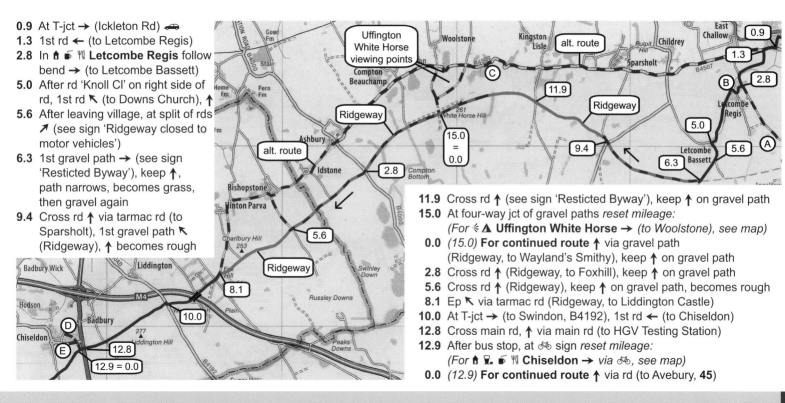

11.9 Cross rd ↑ (see sign 'Restricted Byway'), keep ↑ on gravel path

15.0 At four-way jct of gravel paths *reset mileage*: (For ☕ ⛺ **Uffington White Horse** → (to Woolstone), see map)

0.0 *(15.0)* **For continued route** ↑ via gravel path (Ridgeway, to Wayland's Smithy), keep ↑ on gravel path

2.8 Cross rd ↑ (Ridgeway, to Foxhill), keep ↑ on gravel path

5.6 Cross rd ↑ (Ridgeway), keep ↑ on gravel path, becomes rough

8.1 Ep ↖ via tarmac rd (Ridgeway, to Liddington Castle)

10.0 At T-jct → (to Swindon, B4192), 1st rd ← (to Chiseldon)

12.8 Cross main rd, ↑ via main rd (to HGV Testing Station)

12.9 After bus stop, at 🚲 sign *reset mileage*: (For 🏠 🍴 🍺 🍴 **Chiseldon** → via 🚲, see map)

0.0 *(12.9)* **For continued route** ↑ via rd (to Avebury, **45**)

Route 17: Oxford - Alton Barnes

Ridgeway scenery

0.9 At next jct ↑ (to Draycot Oliat), rd widens

1.3 In bend to the left ↗ via tarmac rd
(*no signs*), becomes very rough gravel

4.4 Ep ← via rd, imm → via gravel path (**45**)

6.0 Cross rd ↑ (Ridgeway, to Hackpen Hill),
keep ↑ via gravel ⚲
(*For* ⚑ **Barbury Castle Country Park** ←)

8.5 Cross rd ↑ (Ridgeway), keep ↑ on gravel
path, becomes very rough gravel and grass

12.7 At four way-jct of paths → via ⚲
(to Avebury, **403**), rough gravel, becomes rd

15.3 At end of rd, *reset mileage:*
For ⚑ ⌂ 🛏 🍴 🍽 ℹ **Avebury** ↑ (*see next page*)

0.0 (15.3) **For continued route** ↖ via rd 🚗

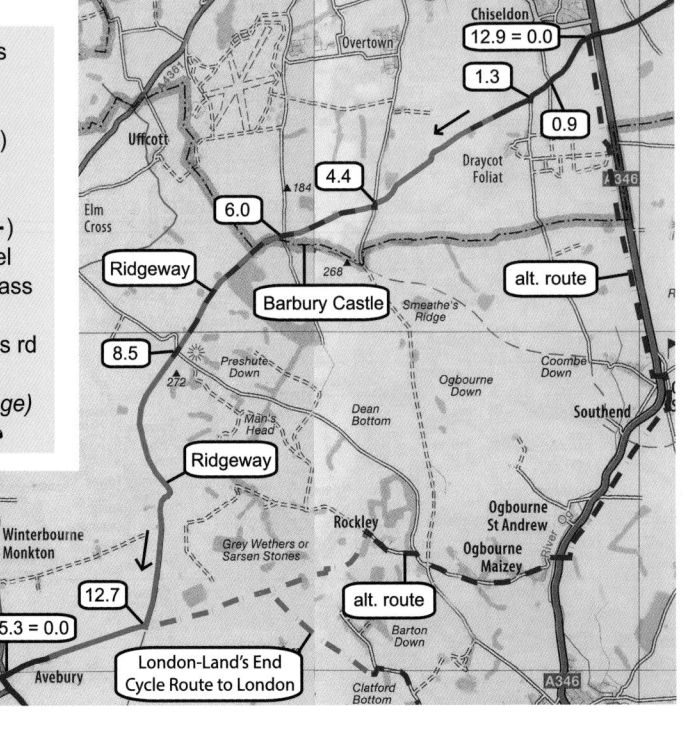

Uffington White Horse

Avebury World Heritage

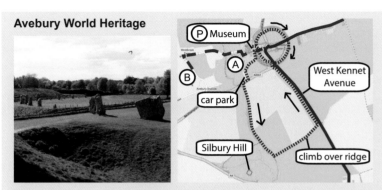

For a worthy visit to Avebury, cycle straight on from your arrival in the village ('Red Lion' pub on right hand side of the road). Beyond the pub, turn right via a wide path to the **Keiller Museum** (£5 pp). The museum courtyard is a good place to park bikes. For a circular walk, leave the courtyard via the main gate and turn left for a clockwise walk around the stone circle (about 30 minutes). Just before completing the circle, near the Keiller Museum, you can also walk to the ancient burial mound of **Silbury Hill**. In this case, follow signs to the left (to car park). At the car park exit, cross the road straight on onto footpath south. After visiting Silbury Hill, cross the ridge to the west and return via **West Kennet Avenue** with more impressive sarsen stones. This anti-clockwise walk takes about one hour. Do not bring bikes on walks!

0.2 Heading south, imm after leaving Avebury's historic stone circle, in sharp bend to the right, ↑ via quiet rd 'West Kennet Avenue' (*no signs*)

1.9 At T-jct ← (to Marlborough, **45**) (*use lay-by rd ahead in climb, then prepare for difficult right turn!*)

2.4 1st rd → (to East Kennet, **45**)

5.0 At T-jct → (to Alton Barnes, **45**)

10.1 After steep descent, at first road to the right *reset mileage*

London-Land's End Cycle Route: Our other long-distance cycle route, between **London** and **Land's End**, crosses your path at **Alton Barnes**. All change here for Bath, Bristol and the West Country.

If you wish to head east for London (or even Harwich or Dover) check the maps on pages 138 and 141.

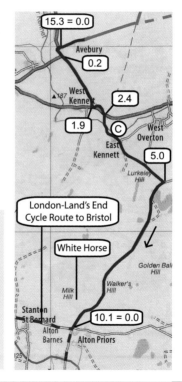

Route 18: Alton Barnes - Salisbury

47 km / 29 miles: 🚲 18%, 🚶 74%, 🚗 8%, 🚗🚗 0%
Stations: *Salisbury*

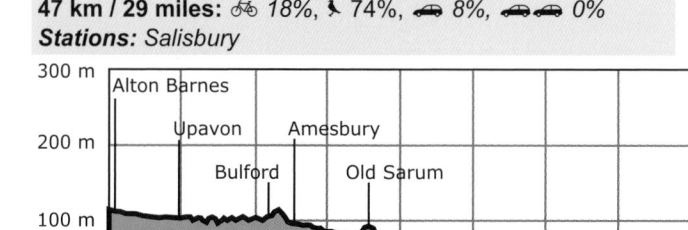

Alton Barnes White Horse is a 1812 tribute to Uffington White Horse. You will need to walk west at the Alton Barnes junction for about 30m to be able to see it. The horse is located on **Milk Hill**, Wiltshire's highest hill. From here, the route heads south via the **Avon Valley**, cutting through the **Salisbury Plains** to **Amesbury**, a town mostly serving the military on the plains and tourists visiting **Stonehenge**. This world famous World Heritage site is poorly accessible by bike. You need to cross a hazardous main road and you will have to leave your bikes locked up against a fence, covering the last mile on foot. Buy your timed ticket in advance, so you can access the epic stone circle without having to walk to the main entrance, another mile or so to the west (£21 pp).

0.0 *(10.1)* After looking back at ◁ **Alton Barnes White Horse** go south via rd ↑
0.8 At 🍴 🍽 **Barge Inn** *(pub)* ↑, keep following through rd ↑ (Honey St)
7.2 At rndabt △ 🍴 🍽 **Woodbridge Inn** ↑ 🚗 (to Salisbury, A345)
9.4 In 🏠 🚉 🍴 🍽 **Upavon** 1st rd ← 🚗 (Andover Rd, to Andover, A342)
10.6 Just after end of built-up area, in sharp bend to the left, ↑ (to Enford)

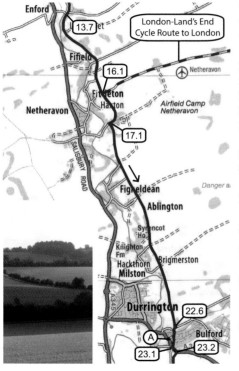

13.7 In Enford ↑ (to Netheravon)

16.1 At give-way jct with "stop" signs ↑ (to Airfield Camp)

17.1 After main entrance of army camp, 1st rd ←
(to Figheldean), keep ↑

22.6 At T-jct ↗, 2nd rd ↖ (Salisbury Rd)

23.1 At give-way jct 🏠 🍴 **Bulford** ← (to Bulford Camp) 🚗

23.2 1st path ↗ via steps with bike channel onto 🚲

24.3 At rndabt cross ↑ onto 🚲 on right side of rd

24.6 Cross rd ↑, then → via 🚲 on left side of rd
(to Town Centre)

25.0 After rndabt 🍴 *super store*, at ep, join rd ↑

26.2 At lhts, cross ↑, then *dismount* immediately,
walk ↑ via pavement on left side of rd against flow

26.4 At next jct 🏠 🍴 🛏 🍴 ⚡ 🛈 **Amesbury** ↑
(Church St, to The Woodfords, **45**)

27.3 At West Amesbury jct (town end), *reset mileage*

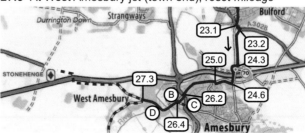

Beyond Amesbury and Stonehenge, **Old Sarum** is an iron age hill fort, home to the Romans, Saxons and Normans. The site was abandoned in 1217, in favour of a new town to be built in the valley: Salisbury. You can explore the Old Sarum ruins (£5 pp) or walk the banks for free. Use the alternative route if you wish to avoid Old Sarum's rough paths (see page 18). **Salisbury**, the 'new town', is famous for its cathedral having the highest spire in England. The beautiful **Salisbury Cathedral** is also home to a historic copy of the **Magna Carta**. This document dating from 1215 defines the rights and duties of the English King (free access by donation). On the square leading to the cathedral park you will also find the **Salisbury Museum** (local artifacts, £8 pp) and the **Wardrobe Museum**, displaying military weapons and uniforms (£5 pp).

Route 18: Alton Barnes - Salisbury

Stonehenge World Heritage

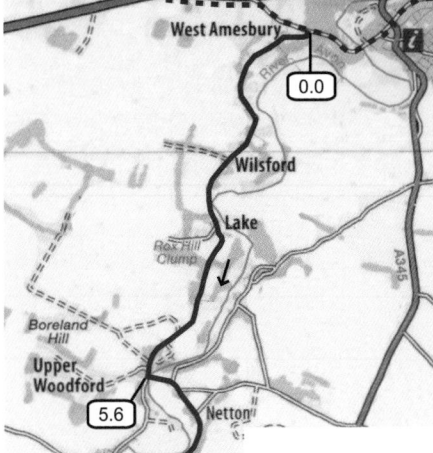

To access Stonehenge by bike, follow Old Stonehenge Rd to the end. On arrival at the A303, use the path on the south side of this busy road. For a free **walk** with great Stonehenge views (12 km) cross the A303 at the point where four lanes merge into two lanes. Opposite there is a gate on the left side of some woodland. Lock up bikes here and do the anti-clockwise walk as suggested on the map. For a **visit** follow the south-side path of the A303 to the end. Cross the A303 here and lock up bikes at the gate opposite. Walk via the grass path to Stonehenge and report with your pre-purchased tickets at the gate.

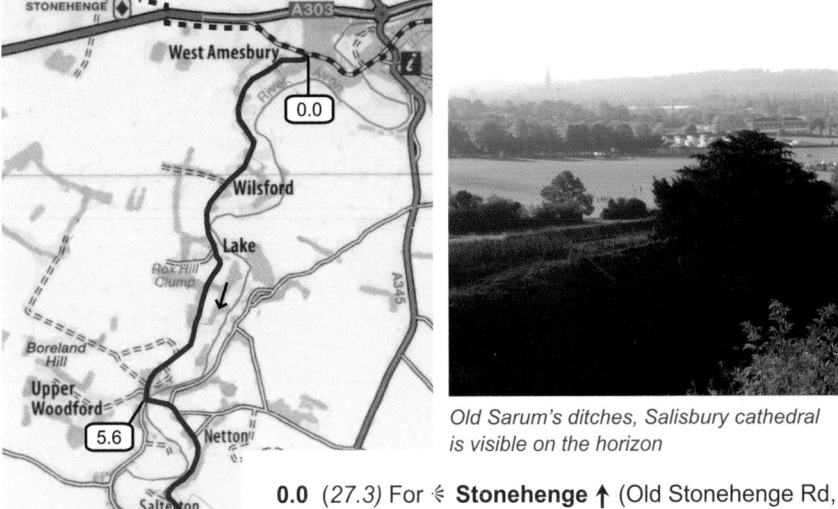

Old Sarum's ditches, Salisbury cathedral is visible on the horizon

0.0 (*27.3*) For ⮜ **Stonehenge** ↑ (Old Stonehenge Rd, see inset), for continued route, 1st rd ← (West Amesbury, to Woodford, **45**)

5.6 In 🛏 🍴 **Upper Woodford** (*pub*) 1st rd ← (**45**)

9.4 In descent ← via private rd (Little Dunford Est, to Old Sarum, **45**)

10.1 At end of climb → via gravel path (**45**)

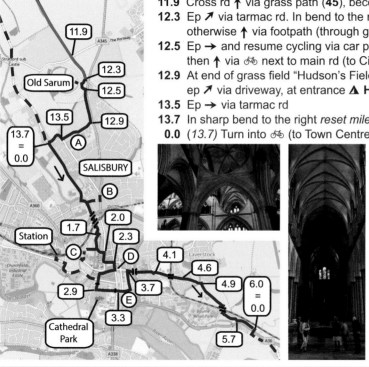

11.9 Cross rd ↑ via grass path (**45**), becomes rough

12.3 Ep ↗ via tarmac rd. In bend to the right, ↗ for ⛪ **Old Sarum**, otherwise ↑ via footpath (through gate, *dismount,* **45**)

12.5 Ep → and resume cycling via car pk on right hand side of main rd, then ↑ via 🚲 next to main rd (to City Centre, *ignore signs* route **45!**)

12.9 At end of grass field "Hudson's Field" → via 🚲 (The Golden Way), ep ↗ via driveway, at entrance ▲ **Hudson's Field** ↗ via tarmac path

13.5 Ep → via tarmac rd

13.7 In sharp bend to the right *reset mileage*

0.0 (*13.7*) Turn into 🚲 (to Town Centre, **45**), keep following 🚲

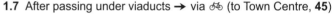

1.7 After passing under viaducts → via 🚲 (to Town Centre, **45**)

1.8 Ep ↑ via rd, ep ← via rd (**45**)

2.0 At T-jct → (**45**) 🚌, at jct with lhts keep ↑, following main rd 🚗

2.3 At end of square, 1st rd → (Queen St, **45**), next jct → (Mlford St, **45**)

2.7 In sharp bend to the right, ← via pedestrian shopping st (**45**)

2.8 At lhts ↑ and pass under old gate (*for **station**: at lhts →, see map*)

2.9 In front of cathedral park entrance ⛪ 🏠 ▲ 🚻 ☕ 🍴 ⚡ ℹ️ *Salisbury,* go ← via quiet tarmac rd (*ignore signs route 45!*)

3.3 At end of rd *dismount,* after gate ↑, walk via pavement on right side, on corner "Brown St" resume cycling ↑, at "Conservative Club" ←

3.7 At end of "Giant St" → (Milford St) 🚌, under viaduct, then uphill

4.1 At rndabt → (Shady Bower), imm ← via tarmac path (Milford Hollow)

4.6 After narrow bridge over railway, at ep ↑ (Milford Hill Rd)

4.9 After narrow bridge with lhts → (Milford Hill Rd), 1st rd ← (**24**)

5.7 At T-jct ↖ via 🚲 on left side of rd (**24**); at 🚲 lhts *reset mileage*

Route 19: Salisbury - Lymington Pier (New Forest)

64 km / 39 miles: 🚴 *15%,* 🥾 *76%,* 🚗 *8%,* 🚙 *1%*
Stations: Brockenhurst, Lymington Pier

Heading south from Salisbury, the Avon Valley ride continues briefly to **Downton**. You are then climbing up onto the plateau of the **New Forest National Park**. Its landscape is made up by open heath lands and the largest forest of southern England. The area is well known for its villages and hamlets where wild ponies and cattle roam free on its commons (see picture).

The area received National Park status in 2005, protecting the area from overdevelopment. Packed in between the cities of Southampton and Bournemouth, also within a (very stretched) commuting distance from London, the New Forest villages are very much a playground for the rich. Although looking picturesque, many villages appear to be socially dead. Homes are often only lived in during weekends or at night. Away from the occasional pub, you won't find any shops until you arrive in Brockenhurst. With limited choice availabe, accommodation in the park is expensive, often exclusively catering for the well-off. Also, campsites can be for members or caravans only. We have only listed cycle-friendly B&Bs and campsites. When cycling, watch out for cattle grids and wildlife!

0.0 *(6.0)* At 🚴 lhts cross rd ⬆, go east via 🚴 on south side of A36 main rd **(24)**
0.2 Ep ↗ via lay-by rd **(24)**, at T-jct ↗ **(24)** 🚗
1.2 1st rd ↗ (to Downton) *(ignore signs route 24!)*
4.8 🍴 **Witherington Farm** *(cafe on fishing lakes)*
9.8 At T-jct 🛏 🍴 🍽 **Downton** ⬅ (Lode Hill) 🚗
10.1 On narrow rd with lhts, 1st rd ➡ (Slab Ln)
11.1 1st rd ↖ *(note: no signs!)*

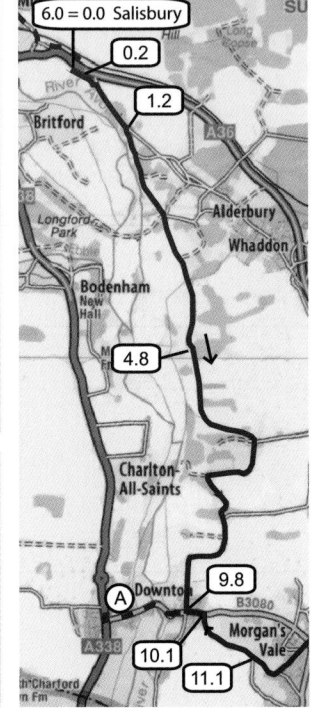

Route 19: Salisbury - Lymington Pier (64 km / 39 miles)

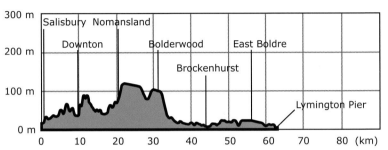

Bolderwood and Rhinefield Ornamental Drive.

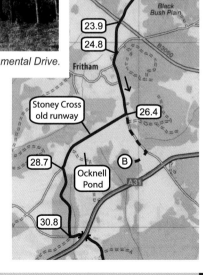

12.2 At T-jct, at end of "Morgans Vale", cross rd ↟ (Bowers Hill, to Hamptworth)

12.5 In descent, 1st rd → (Princes Hill, later Vicarage Rd) (☛ ♨ **Kings Head** *on corner*)

14.7 At T-jct → (to Lyndhurst)

18.0 1st rd → (Lyburn Rd)

21.7 At T-jct (end of North Ln) → 🚌 *(for ▲ ←)* ☛ ♨ **Nomansland** *(pub and restaurant)*

23.9 At give-way jct ↑ (to Fritham)

24.8 At T-jct ↗ (to Fritham) 🚌

26.4 3rd → (to Linwood, ⬲ **old runway**) *(for ▲ ↑)*

28.7 After car pk "Ocknell Pond" on left side of rd, 1st wide gravel 🚲 ←

Route 19: Salisbury - Lymington Pier (New Forest)

Beyond **Nomansland** you cycle on a road on the old runway of WWII airfield **Stoney Cross**. The **Canadian Memorial** is a reminder of the days that allied bombers took off from here to occupied Europe. **Bolderwood** is the best loved picnic site of the New Forest. A walking trail takes you to the nearby **deer sanctuary**. The **Ornamental Drive** is a scenic forest road, busy on sunny weekends, but empty most other times. Although small in size, **Brockenhurst** is a busy gateway for the New Forest. Its railway station with popular bike rental is served by the cross-country service up north and fast services to London. Beyond Brockenhurst, you will be cycling on the scenic gravel **forest tracks** of the New Forest. You will definitely see wild ponies and probably some deer too! At **Lymington Pier**, a ferry departs for the Isle of Wight.

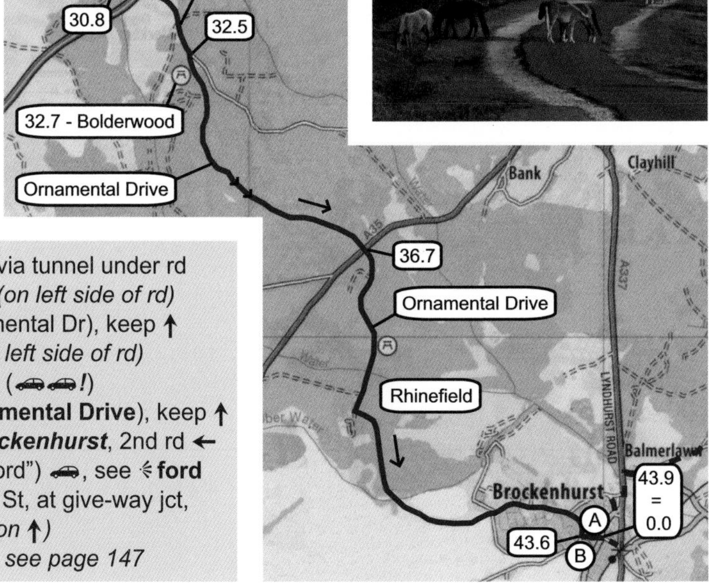

30.8 Ep ← via tarmac rd, ↑ via tunnel under rd
32.1 ⋨ **Canadian Memorial** *(on left side of rd)*
32.5 1st tarmac rd ↗ (Ornamental Dr), keep ↑
32.7 ⋨ 🌲 **Bolderwood** *(on left side of rd)*
36.7 At give-way jct, cross ↑ (🚗🚗!)
　　　(⋨ 🌲 **Rhinefield Ornamental Drive**), keep ↑
43.6 In ⋨▲🏠🚻🛒🍴🚲 *Brockenhurst*, 2nd rd ←
　　　(to "Village Centre via ford") 🚗, see ⋨**ford**
43.9 At end of shops in High St, at give-way jct,
　　　reset mileage (For station ↑)
　　　For continued route ←, see page 147

32.1 = Canadian Memorial
30.8
32.5
32.7 - Bolderwood
Ornamental Drive
36.7
Ornamental Drive
Rhinefield
Bank
Clayhill
Brockenhurst
Balmerlawn
43.9 = 0.0
A
43.6
B

0.0 *(43.9)* At end of shops in High St, at give-way jct, ← go north (Grigg Ln, to Beaulieu, B3055) 🚗

0.4 At jct at start of open green, 2nd rd ↖ (Wates Green) *(do NOT turn into rd with ford!)*

0.6 At T-jct ↘ around open green

0.8 At T-jct *dismount*, ← via footpath on right side of rd (🚗🚗!)

1.1 1st rd → (Balmer Lawn Rd, to Beaulieu, B3055) *(for ▲ ↑)*

1.5 In bend to the right (see house "Windrush") ↖ via gravel rd

2.5 At "Standing Hat Car Pk", in front of gate, imm → via gravel 🚲 (Foresty Commission sign 291), ↑ via gate

4.7 At 2nd gravel four-way jct → (Foresty Commission sign 324, **2**)

5.2 After bridge over railway, 1st gravel 🚲 ← (Foresty Commission sign 326) *(ignore signs route 2!)* *(for ▲ ↑)*

6.4 1st gravel 🚲 → (Foresty Commission sign 330)

7.4 At gravel four-way jct ← (Foresty Commission sign 332)

8.0 At jct (Foresty Commission sign 337) ↖ (steep climb)

8.8 At jct (Foresty Commission sign 340) ↗

9.6 Ep ↑ via car pk, ↗ via tarmac rd (Foresty Commission sign 342)

10.3 At jct ↑ (to Lymington, B3054) 🚗, *(watch fast 🚗 from the left!)*

10.6 1st rd ↖ (to East Boldre), keep ↑ at next jct

11.9 At church ⛪ 🏛 ⛽ 🍴 **East Boldre,** keep ↗ (to East End)

15.3 In "East End" 1st rd → (Norleywood Rd, to Boldre)

16.4 1st rd ↖ (see sign "single track road"), after 200m at ford ↖

17.7 At T-jct → (next to South Baddesley school)

19.8 ↙ to ⛴ 🚲 *Lymington Pier Ferry* for Yarmouth (Isle of Wight)

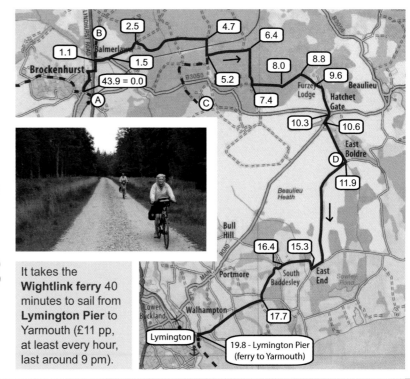

It takes the **Wightlink ferry** 40 minutes to sail from **Lymington Pier** to Yarmouth (£11 pp, at least every hour, last around 9 pm).

Route 20: Isle of Wight & Portsmouth

71 km / 44 miles: 🚴 31%, 🚶 57%, 🚗 12%, 🚗🚗 0%
Stations: Sandown, Ryde Esplanade, Portsmouth Harbour

0.0 *(19.8)* After ferry, at rndabt 🏨 🚲 🛒 🍴 / ℹ️ **Yarmouth**
    ↖ (to Ryde, A3054) 🚐
0.2 After bend, 1st rd → (Mill Rd), at end ↑ via gravel 🚴
0.6 Ep ↗ via gravel 🚴 (to Freshwater) *(for* 🚶 🚴 *hire* ↙ *)*
3.0 At rd crossing → via rd (Freshwater Causeway)
3.4 At T-jct visually ↑ (Hooke Hill, to Freshwater) *(for* ▲ → *)*
3.8 Rndabt 🏨 ▲ 🚲 🛒 🍴 / **Freshwater** ↖, imm → (Stroud Rd)
4.0 1st rd ↗ (Camp Rd)
4.6 At T-jct ↖ (Queens Rd, to Alum Bay)
4.8 At T-jct → (to Alum Bay) *(for short-cut **without** visit to
    ♟ The Needles* ←, *see after 14.8 km on next page!)*
6.2 At 🏨 🛒 🍴 **Highdown Inn** ↑ (to Alum Bay) *(for* 🏨 → *)*
7.2 At T-jct ↖ (to Needles) 🚐
8.1 At toll gate (free for 🚴) ↖, steep up via path
    (to The Needles Headland & Old Battery, Nat. Trust)
9.2 At split jct ↖ steep up (to Needles View point),
    (for ♟ 🛒 **Old Battery Museum** ↑ *)*
9.6 Via zig zag up, at split jct ↗ on flat path (to View point),
    beyond ♟ **New Battery** ↗ via zig zag down
9.8 At end of path you are at ♟ **The Needles**

Yarmouth is a small, friendly town, welcoming you to the **Isle of Wight**. The island is known for being cycle-friendly, but the signposted Wight cycle route (see sign) is sketchy, including long sections on main roads and missing out on the best landmark of all: **The Needles**. Stick to our route and do not miss out on this magical place, the final great landmark of your ride. Views over **Alum Bay** are striking and the cliff edge is magnificent. The **Old Battery Museum** (£7 pp) is also worth a visit.

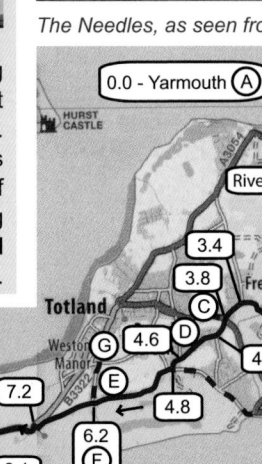
The Needles, as seen from the sea.

The red-coloured Alum Bay cliffs.

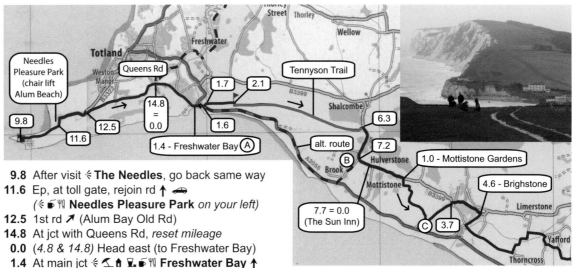

At the **Needles Pleasure Park** you can take a **chairlift** down to **Alum Beach**, providing more striking views (£6 pp). From quiet **Freshwater Bay** our route takes on the exposed **Tennyson Trail**. It is a steep climb up, but stunning views are your reward (see picture on right). Some sections of poor gravel/grass and the steep drop at the end can be challenging, as can wet and windy conditions (see page 18).

9.8 After visit ⇇ **The Needles**, go back same way

11.6 Ep, at toll gate, rejoin rd ↑ 🚗 (⇇ ☕🍴 **Needles Pleasure Park** on your left)

12.5 1st rd ↗ (Alum Bay Old Rd)

14.8 At jct with Queens Rd, *reset mileage*

0.0 *(4.8 & 14.8)* Head east (to Freshwater Bay)

1.4 At main jct ⇇ 🗻🏠 🛏️☕🍴 **Freshwater Bay** ↑ (to Ventnor, A3055) 🚗 *(use footpath as needed)*

1.6 In climb, 1st rd ↖ (Southdown Rd, to Freshwater Golf Club, becomes rough gravel)

1.7 ↗ via Bridleway F32 (Tennyson Trail), keep ↑

2.1 At split jct ↗ via Bridleway F54 (Compton down), keep following main track

6.3 Ep → via rd 🚗

7.2 Follow bend ↖ (to Brighstone, B3399) 🚗

7.7 At ☕🍴 **The Sun Inn** *(pub)*, *reset mileage*

0.0 *(7.7)* Head east through Hulverstone 🚗

1.0 After ⇇ ☕ **Mottistone Gardens** (£6 pp), 1st rd → (Hoxall Ln, later Chilton Ln), follow tarmac rd

Route 20: Isle of Wight & Portsmouth

Have a break or stay in lively **Brighstone**. The next stretch via the island's interior is very rural.

3.7 At T-jct → (to Shorwell) 🚗

4.6 At end village centre 🏠🏨⛺🅿️🛒🍴 **Brighstone**, on corner, at church, → (New Rd, Shorwell 🚲)

5.1 1st rd ← (Mill Ln, Shorwell 🚲) *(for* ⛺🏨↑*)*

7.7 2nd rd ← (Thorncross, to Shorwell, Wight 🚲)

8.6 1st rd → (Mill Ln, to Shorwell, Wight 🚲)

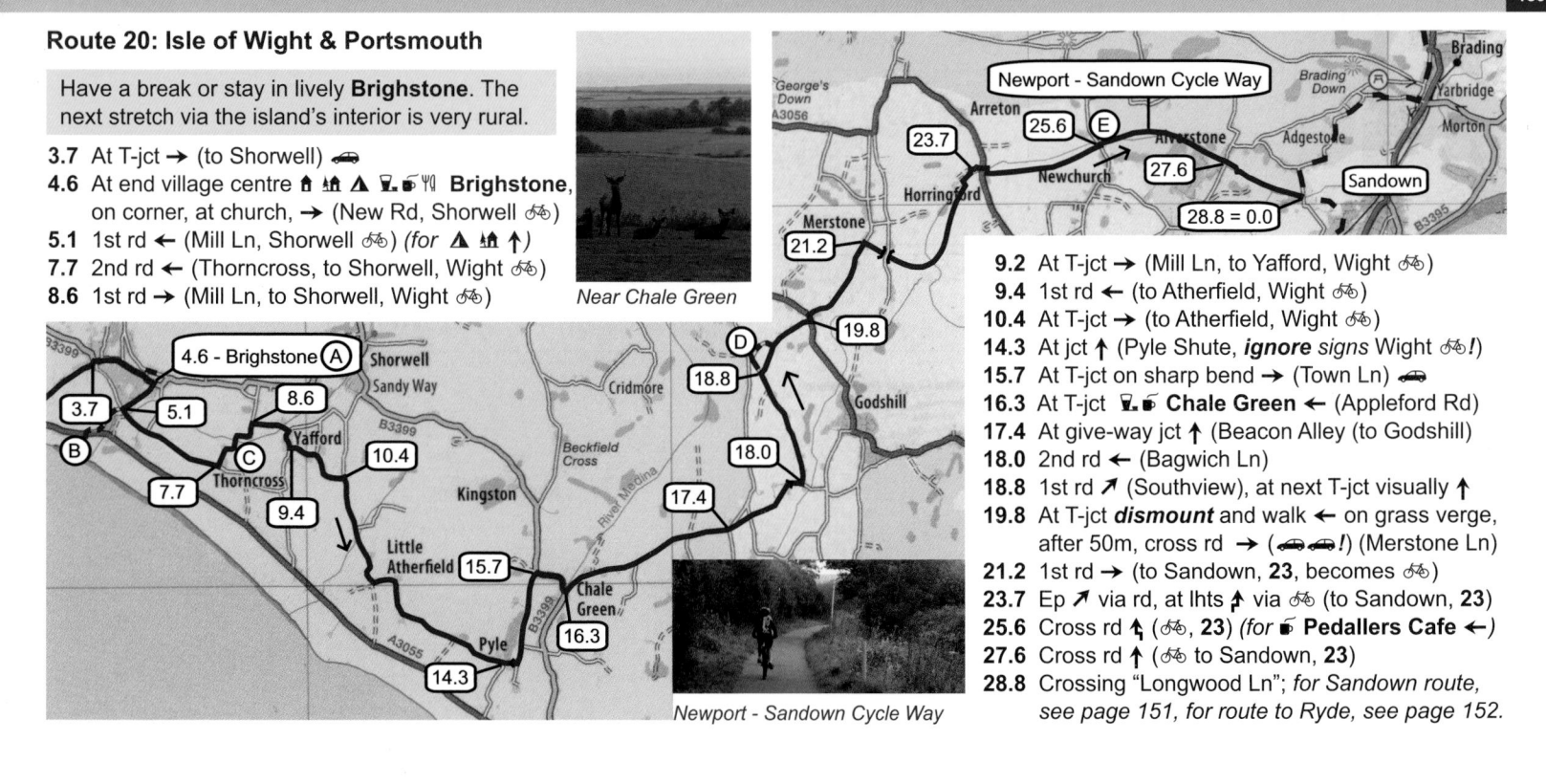

Near Chale Green

Newport - Sandown Cycle Way

9.2 At T-jct → (Mill Ln, to Yafford, Wight 🚲)

9.4 1st rd ← (to Atherfield, Wight 🚲)

10.4 At T-jct → (to Atherfield, Wight 🚲)

14.3 At jct ↑ (Pyle Shute, *ignore signs* Wight 🚲!)

15.7 At T-jct on sharp bend → (Town Ln) 🚗

16.3 At T-jct 🅿️🛒 **Chale Green** ← (Appleford Rd)

17.4 At give-way jct ↑ (Beacon Alley (to Godshill)

18.0 2nd rd ← (Bagwich Ln)

18.8 1st rd ↗ (Southview), at next T-jct visually ↑

19.8 At T-jct *dismount* and walk ← on grass verge, after 50m, cross rd → (🚗🚗!) (Merstone Ln)

21.2 1st rd → (to Sandown, **23**, becomes 🚲)

23.7 Ep ↗ via rd, at lhts ↑ via 🚲 (to Sandown, **23**)

25.6 Cross rd ↟ (🚲, **23**) *(for* 🛒 **Pedallers Cafe** ←*)*

27.6 Cross rd ↑ (🚲 to Sandown, **23**)

28.8 Crossing "Longwood Ln"; for Sandown route, see page 151, for route to Ryde, see page 152.

Sandown is worth the short detour to celebrate your North-South achievement. The esplanade, beach and pier provide a classic seaside feel; an easy-going landmark compared to the exposed Needles.

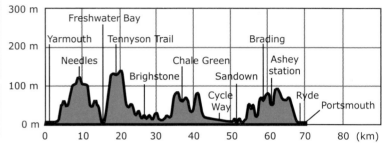

This is the route into Sandown, returning to the same location. For route to Ryde, see next page

0.0 *(28.8)* At crossing "Longwood Ln" ↑ (go east) via 🚲 (**23**)

0.6 Ep (🚻) → via rd (to Town Centre, Sunshine Trail)

1.2 At zebra crossing ← via 🚲 tunnel (Sunshine Trail)

1.3 After tunnel imm ← and join rd ↖ *(ignore signs* Sunshine Trail*!)*

1.4 1st rd → (Nunwell St)

1.7 At give way jct ↑ (Melville St, to Sandown Pier)

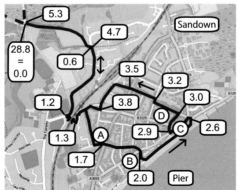

2.0 At give way jct ↑ (Pier St), keep ↖ onto esplanade 🚶🏊🏠🚻📷🍴 ℹ️ ***Sandown***

2.6 Follow bend ←, then 2x ← (High St) 🚗

2.9 2nd rd → (Albert Rd)

3.0 At T-jct ← (Victoria Rd)

3.2 At T-jct ↟ (Grove Rd)

3.5 At give-way jct ↑ (Grove Rd)

3.8 At give-way jct → (to ***Station***), 1st rd ←

4.0 ↗ onto 🚲, through tunnel, ep → via rd (Sunshine Trail, to Newport, **23**)

4.7 1st 🚲 ← (Sunshine Trail, to Newport, **23**)

5.3 Crossing "Longwood Ln"; *reset mileage for route to Ryde, see page 152*

Route 20: Isle of Wight & Portsmouth

The ride to Ryde provides a last pleasant dose of countryside cycling. At **Ashey station** you may see a train of the **Isle of Wight steam railway** passing. Its platform is a good place for a picnic. There is also a normal train service from Sandown to Ryde. In **Ryde** you should take the **Wightlink ferry** at the start of the pier for the direct connection to Portsmouth Harbour station and ferries to France (£13 pp, every 30 mins, last around 11 pm). Those cycling further east on the south coast are best to use the **Hovertravel** service for **Southsea**, linking onto National Route 2 to Hayling Island (£17 pp, every 30 mins, last around 8 pm).

0.0 *(5.3 & 28.8)* At crossing "Longwood Ln", go north via rd
0.4 At T-jct → (Lower Rd, to Brading)
1.9 At jct "Sheep Ln", follow bend ↗ (*ignore signs Wight &!*)
2.7 At T-jct ← via steep climb (The Mall)
3.5 At jct with lhts 🍴 **Brading** ↖ 🚗🚗 and imm ↖ again (in front of Town Hall, West St)
3.7 At sign "no motorised traffic" ↑
4.0 At end "Doctor's Ln" at T-jct ←
5.5 1st through rd ↖ ("Ashey")
6.5 At T-jct ← 🚗 and imm → via gravel path (Footpath R29 Ashey, dismount as needed)
7.2 Cross railway at 🚂 **Ashey station** (Footpath R97 to Great Upton, dismount as needed)
7.6 Ep ↑ via rd (Station Rd, later Gatehouse Rd)
8.9 At rndabt ↑ (Upton Rd, to Ryde)
10.6 Keep ↑, join one-way system 🚗
11.0 At jcts with lhts (2x) ↑ (West St) 🚗
11.4 On corner "Lind St" ↑ (West St)
11.5 At T-jct → (Spencer Rd), next T-jct ← (St Thomas St)
12.0 At rndabt 🚂 🍴 ⚓ **Ryde** ↑ 🚗, For **Portsmouth** 1st rd ←, for **Southsea** 2nd rd ←

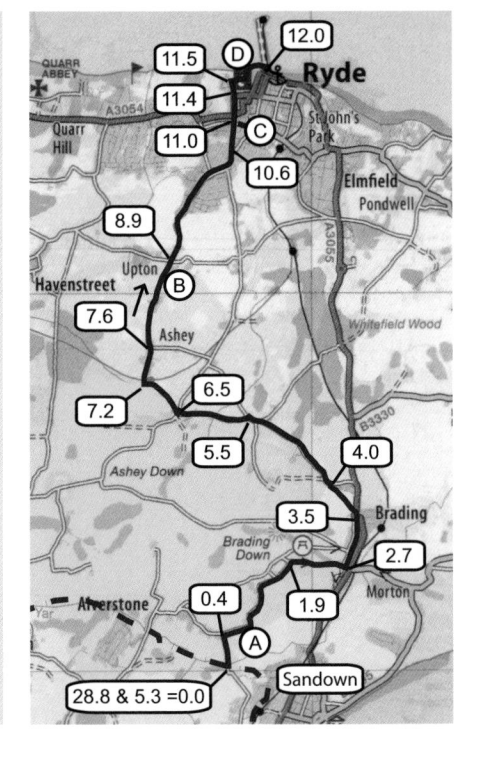

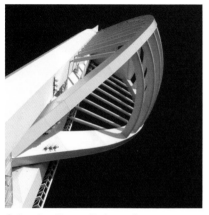
Spinnaker Tower, Portsmouth.

Route to ferry port (for Brittany Ferries to France):
0.0 After ferry, at end of square of railway & bus station ⃗ ♦ ⃗. ⃗ ⅋ 🛈 **Portsmouth Harbour**, ← via rd (to Historic Dockyard, **22**), follow bend to → 🚃
0.8 Move out of bus lane on left to bus lane on right (**!**), keep ↑ at lhts (to Ferry Port/"Out of city", **22**) 🚃
1.1 Before rndabt ← via 🚲 (to Ferry Port/"Out of city", **22**)
1.4 At end of 🚲 tunnel, make U-turn ↘ onto rd, before lhts ↖ onto pavement 🚲 (**22**)
1.9 1st rd ↖ (to Ferry Port/"Out of city", **22**), see ⃗. *super store on your right*
2.2 At jct with lhts ↑ cross main rd, then imm → via pavement 🚲 on left side of main rd (**22**)
2.8 Via 🚲 crossing ← to ferry terminal, end of route

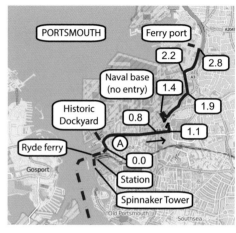

The city of **Portsmouth** has plenty to offer for those with time on their hands. The **Spinnaker Tower**, immediately on your right after leaving the ferry from Ryde, provides splendid views from its summit (£10 pp). There is a shopping mall next to the tower for those who'd like to take souvenirs overseas. The **Portsmouth Historic Dockyard** provides a full day out. The all-attraction ticket costs £38 pp, tickets per attraction also available.

Highlights are three particular war ships. The **Mary Rose** sank in 1545 just two miles out from Portsmouth Harbour. The ship wreck was lifted out of the mud of the Solent estuary in 1982 and is now on display in a purpose-built museum. The **HMS Victory** played a key role in the battle of Trafalgar (1805) and is on show in full glory in a dry dock. The **HMS Warrior** is a large iron war ship, the largest of its kind when built in 1861.

From busy **Portsmouth Harbour Station** direct trains head for Waterloo and Victoria (London), Winchester and Southampton (for change to Cross Country trains), Bristol and Brighton. For Dover, travel via Havant and Brighton. With limited space for bicycles and bike reservations only possible on some trains, it is best to avoid peak hours! **Brittany Ferries** can take you to Le Havre, Caen, Cherbourg and St Malo in France.

Rte	Km	Page	Ref	Town	Info	Name, address and postcode	Phone (+ 44)	Internet	Distance to route & extra directions
1	0.0	25	A	Berwick-upon-Tweed	⌂ 🍴	The Castle Hotel, 103 Castlegate, TD15 1LF	01289 307900	www.thecastleberwickupontweed.co.uk	-
1	0.2	25	B	Berwick-upon-Tweed	⌂	Cara House B&B, 44 Castlegate, TD15 1JT	01289 302749	www.carahouse.co.uk	-
1	0.5	25	C	Berwick-upon-Tweed	⌂ 🍴	The Elizabethan Town House B&B, 8 Sidey Crt, TD15 1TR	01289 304580	https://elizabethan-town-house.co.uk	-
1	0.8	25	D	Berwick-upon-Tweed	🚲	Berwick Cycles, 17a Bridge St, TD15 1ES	01289 331476	http://berwickcycles.co.uk	0.1 km (← just before bridge)
1	0.8	25	D	Berwick-upon-Tweed	🛏 🍴	YHA Berwick-upon-Tweed, Dewar's Ln, TD15 1HJ	0345 3719676	www.yha.org.uk	0.1 km (← just before bridge, then 1st rd →)
1	1.3	25	E	Tweedmouth	⌂ 🍴	Harrow Bank B&B, 41 Main St, TD15 2AD	01289 309415	www.harrowbank.com	0.1 km (keep ↑)
1	3.1	25	F	Spittal	⌂ 🍴	Eastwatch Guest House, 10 Sea Rd, TD15 1RN	07595 223387	https://eastwatch.co.uk	-
1	10.9	26	A	Cheswick	⌂ 🍴	Ladythorne House, TD15 2RW	01289 387382	www.ladythornehouse.co.uk	-
1	18.2	26	B	Holy Island Lindesfarne	⌂ 🍴	The Lindesfarne Hotel, TD15 2SQ	01289 389273	www.thelindisfarnehotel.co.uk	7.0 km (←, access via tidal causeway only!)
1	18.2	26	B	Holy Island Lindesfarne	⌂ 🍴	The Ship Inn, Marygate, TD15 2SJ	01289 389311	www.theshipinn-holyisland.co.uk	7.3 km (←, access via tidal causeway only!)
1	0.6	26	C	West Mains	⛺ 🍴	The Barn at Beal, Beal Farm, TD15 2PB	01289 540044	http://barnatbeal.com	-
1	2.2	26	D	West Mains	🛏 🍴	Eat & Sleep Lindesfarne Bunkhouse, TD15 2PD	01289 381827	https://eatandsleeplindisfarne.co.uk/	- (at the back of petrol station)
1	4.9	27	A	Fenwick	⌂ 🍴	Fenwick B&B, The Village, TD15 2PJ	07803 966544	https://fenwickbedandbreakfast.co.uk	-
1	13.4	27	B	Belford	⌂ 🍴	Belford Old Vicarage B&B, North Bank, NE70 7LY	01668 213025	www.belfordoldvicarage.co.uk	0.3 km (keep ↑)
1	20.3	27	C	Bamburgh	⛺ 🍴	Waren Caravan & Camping Park, NE70 7EE	01668 214366	www.meadowhead.co.uk	0.9 km (2nd rd ⤢)
1	23.9	27	D	Bamburgh	⌂ 🍴	Lord Crewe Hotel, Front St, NE69 7BL	01668 214243	www.lord-crewe.co.uk	-
1	7.1	28	A	Seahouses	⌂ 🍴	Horncliffe Guest House, 5 King St, NE68 7XN	07958 772401	www.horncliffeguesthouse.info	0.1 km (at 2nd rndabt ←)
1	23.0	29	A	Embleton	⌂ 🍴	Dunstanburgh Castle Hotel, NE66 3UN	01665 576111	www.dunstanburghcastlehotel.co.uk	-
1	23.5	29	B	Embleton	⛺ 🍴	Dunstan Hill C&CC, NE66 3TQ	01665 576310	www.campingandcaravanningclub.co.uk	1.0 km (keep ↑)
1	2.7	29	C	Howick	⌂ 🍴	Old Rectory Howick B&B, NE66 3LE	01665 577590	www.oldrectoryhowick.co.uk	0.3 km (via rd with sign 'Howick' →)
2	3.4	31	A	Alnwick	⌂ 🍴	Castle View Guest House, 1b Bailiffgate, NE66 1LZ	01665 605773	www.castleviewalnwick.com	-
2	3.5	31	B	Alnwick	⌂ 🍴	The Black Swan, 26 Narrowgate, NE66 1JG	01665 510683	www.theblackswan-alnwick.co.uk	0.1 km (keep ↑)
2	3.5	31	C	Alnwick	⌂ 🍴	The Market Tavern, 7 Fenkle St, NE66 1HW	01665 602759	www.thetavernalnwick.co.uk	0.1 km (keep ↑, 1st rd ⤢)
2	3.5	31	D	Alnwick	⌂ 🍴	The Georgian Guest House, 3/5 Hotspur St, NE66 1QE	01665 602398	www.georgianguesthouse.co.uk	0.6 km (keep ↑, at T-jct ↖, 1st rd →)
2	3.5	31	E	Alnwick	🛏 🍴	Alnwick Youth Hostel, 34-38 Green Batt, NE66 1TU	01665 660800	www.alnwickyouthhostel.co.uk	0.7 km (keep ↑, at T-jct ↖, 1st rd →, keep ⤢)
2	8.9	32	A	Shilbottle	⌂ 🍴	Deneview B&B, 12 North Side, NE66 2YE	01665 575475	www.deneviewbedandbreakfast.co.uk	0.2 km (keep ↑keep, so no right turn)
2	15.9	32	B	Warkworth	⌂ 🍴	Fairfield Guest House, 16 Station Rd, NE65 0XP	01665 714455	www.fairfield-guesthouse.com	-
2	16.6	32	C	Warkworth	⌂ 🍴	Warkworth House Hotel, 16 Bridge St, NE65 0XB	01665 711276	www.warkworthhousehotel.co.uk	0.1 km (via main rd to Town Centre)
2	16.6	32	C	Warkworth	⌂ 🍴	Bertram's B&B, 19 Bridge St, NE65 0XB	01665 798070	www.bertrams.co.uk	0.1 km (via main rd to Town Centre)
2	2.3	33	A	Amble	⌂ 🍴	Harbour Guest House, 26 Leazes St, NE65 0AA	01665 710381	http://harbour-guest-house.edan.io	-
2	2.3	33	A	Amble	⌂ 🍴	Number 16 B&B, 16 Leazes St, NE65 0AL	07814 096442	www.numbersixteenamble.co.uk	-
2	2.6	33	B	Amble	🚲 hire	Pedal Power Cycling, Unit 6, Coquet Enterpr Pk, NE65 0PE	01665 713448	https://pedal-power.co.uk	0.7 km (T-jct ↘, rndbt ↖, at Fontburn → path)
2	14.1	33	C	Creswell	🛏 ⛺ 🍴	Hemscot Hill Harm, Calico Barn, Widdrington, NE61 5EQ	01670 458118	www.tractorsandtents.com	-

Rte	Km	Page	Ref	Town	Info	Name, address and postcode	Phone (+ 44)	Internet	Distance to route & extra directions
2	25.8	34	A	Biggin by the sea	⌂ ⛛	The Old Ship, 63 Front St, NE64 6NJ	01670 817231	-	0.4 km (at T-jct ←)
2	0.9	35	A	Blyth	⌂ ⬞	Commissioner's Quay Inn, Quay Rd, NE24 3AF	0191 5803610	www.inncollectiongroup.com/commissioners-quay-inn/	-
2	7.0	36	A	Old Hartley	⌂ ⬞	Waterford Arms, Collywell Bay Rd, NE26, 4QZ	0191 2370450	https://waterford-arms.co.uk	-
2	12.2	37	A	Whitley Bay	⌂ ⬞	York House Hotel, 106-110 Park Av, NE26 1DN	0191 2528313	https://yorkhousehotel.com	0.2 km (after bath house bldng ↗, then ⬆)
2	12.2	37	A	Whitley Bay	⌂ ⬞	Sandsides Guest House, 122 Park Av, NE26 1AY	0191 2530399	www.sandsides.com	0.2 km (after bath house bldng ↗, then ⬆)
2	12.2	37	B	Whitley Bay	⌿	Dixons Cycles, 184 Park View, NE26 3QP	0191 2532035	-	0.5 km (after bath house bldng ↗, ⬆, ⬆, →)
2	15.3	37	C	Tynemouth	⌂ ⛛	Park Hotel Tynemouth, Grand Pde, NE30 4JQ	0191 2571406	https://parkhoteltynemouth.co.uk	-
2	16.0	37	D	Tynemouth	⌂ ⛛	Grand Hotel Tynemouth, 14 Grand Pde, NE30 4RE	0191 2936666	www.grandhoteltynemouth.co.uk	-
2	16.8	37	E	Tynemouth	⌂ ⛛	No 61 B&B, Front St, NE30 4BT	0191 2573687	https://no61.co.uk/	0.2 km (at clock tower → into High St)
2	19.6	37	F	North Shields	⌿	Tyne Cycles, 19-20 Rudyerd St, NE29 6RR	0191 2592266	-	0.5 km (1st rd →, → via Stanley St, T-jct ←)
3	10.0	39	A	Newcastle	⌂ ⬞	Hotel du Vin, Allan House, City Rd, NE1 2BE	0191 3898628	www.hotelduvin.com	0.2 km (↑ via rd, 1st rd → up the hill)
3	14.0	41	A	Newcastle	⌂ ⬞	Angel View Hotel, Low Eighton, Gateshead, NE9 7UB	0191 4103219	www.angelviewhotel.co.uk	0.2 km (at rndabt to ⚲ on right side of rd, →)
3	2.4	41	B	Newcastle	⌿	Low Fell Cycles, 644 Durham Rd, Gateshead, NE9 6JA	0191 4826131	www.lowfellcycles.com	0.7 km (at T-jct ←, at T-jct ←, at T-jct →)
3	0.0	43	A	Newcastle	⌿	Backyard Bike Shop, Hillgate Quay, NE8 2BH	07519 098963	www.backyardbikeshop.com	0.5 km (via Millennium Br, then → to Tyne Br)
3	0.9	43	B	Newcastle	⌂ ⛛	Royal Station Hotel, Neville St, NE1 5DH	0191 2320781	www.royalstationhotel.com	-
3	0.9	43	B	Newcastle	⌂ ⛛	The County Hotel, Neville St, NE1 5DF	0191 2322471	www.countyhotel.co.uk	-
3	1.2	43	C	Newcastle	🏨 ⛛	Heroes Bunkz, Grainger St, NE1 5JE	0191 2313131	www.heroeshotel.co.uk	-
3	1.6	43	D	Newcastle	🏨 ⛛	YHA Newcastle, 17 Carliol Sq, NE1 6UQ	0345 2602583	www.yha.org.uk	0.2 km (← via High Bridge, T-jct ←, 1st rd →)
3	1.8	43	E	Newcastle	⌂ ⛛	Grey Street Hotel, 2-12 Grey St, NE1 6EE	0191 2306777	www.greystreethotel.co.uk	-
3	2.2	43	F	Newcastle	⌂ ⛛	The Vermont Hotel, 10-15 Sandhill, NE1 3AF	0191 2331010	www.vermont-hotel.com	-
3	10.1	45	A	Newburn	⌂ ⬞	The Keelman's Lodge, Grange Rd, NE15 8NL	0191 2671689	https://keelmanslodge.co.uk	0.1 km (→ at riverside cafe)
4	0.2	47	A	Heddon on the Wall	⌂ ⬞	Heddon Lodge B&B, 38 Heddon Banks, NE15 0BU	01661 854042	https://heddonlodge.co.uk	0.6 km (↑ via rd, at T-jct ←, 2nd rd ↗)
4	5.8	48	A	Ryton	⌂ ⛛	Hotel Michelangelo's, Stella Rd, NE21 4LU	0191 4132921	www.michelangelorestaurants.co.uk	0.6 km (↑ via rd, at T-jct ←, at T-jct →)
4	5.8	48	A	Ryton	⌂ ⛛	Hedgefield House, Stella Rd, NE21 4LR	0191 4137373	https://hedgefieldhouse.co.uk	0.6 km (↑ via rd, at T-jct ←, at T-jct →)
4	20.4	50	A	Consett	⌿	Steel Town Cycles, Unit 4, 25-27 Derwent St, DH8 8RL	07883 803632	https://steeltowncycles.co.uk	0.2 km (at lhts →, ← via Derwent St)
4	4.3	51	A	Knitsley	⌂ ⬞	The Old Mill, DH8 9EL	01207 581642	www.theoldmillknitsley.co.uk	0.1 km (from cycle path →, ← via rd
4	9.0	51	B	Lanchester	⌂ ⬞	The Old Post Office B&B, 27 Front St, DH7 0LA	01207 528420	http://theoldpostofficelanchester.com	0.3 km (← via rd, at T-jct →)
5	1.9	53	A	Durham	⌂ ⬞	The Victorian Town House B&B, 2 Victoria Tc, DH1 4RW	0191 3709963	www.durhambedandbreakfast.com	0.2 km (↑, T-jct ←, ↖ via Albert St, 1st rd ↗)
5	1.9	53	B	Durham	⌂ ⛛	The Bridge Hotel, 40 North Rd, DH1 4SE	0191 3868090	www.bridgehoteldurham.com	0.1 km (↑, T-jct →)
5	2.3	53	C	Durham	⌿	Recyke Y'Bike, 17 North Rd, Dh1 4SQ	0191 4471770	https://recyke.bike	-
5	2.6	53	D	Durham	⌂ ⬞	The Georgian Town House B&B, 11 Crossgate, DH1 4PS	0191 3868070	www.thegeorgiantownhousedurham.co.uk	0.2 km (↗ via North Rd, 1st rd ↗, 1st rd ↙)
5	2.6	53	D	Durham	⌂ ⬞	Castle View Guest House B&B, 4 Crossgate, DH1 4PS	0191 3868852	www.castle-view.co.uk	0.2 km (↗ via North Rd, 1st rd ↗, 1st rd ↙)
5	3.1	53	E	Durham	⌂ ⛛	The Victoria Inn, 86 Hallgarth St, DH1 3AS	0191 3865269	www.victoriainn-durhamcity.co.uk	0.2 km (← via New Velvet, at split of rds ↖)

Rte	Km	Page	Ref	Town	Info	Name, address and postcode	Phone (+ 44)	Internet	Distance to route & extra directions
5	8.9	54	A	Littletown	♠ ⚲	York House B&B, Front St, DH6 1PZ	07904 875517	https://yorkhousedurham.co.uk	-
5	12.5	54	B	Haswell	▲ ⚲	Colliery Farm C&CC, Green Ln, DH6 2AA	07770 440257	www.campingandcaravanningclub.co.uk	2.8 km (← to Haswell, at T-jct ←, 2nd rd ←)
5	3.8	55	A	Hartlepool	♠ ⚲	The Cosmopolitan Hotel, Middlegate, TS24 0HY	01429 274347	www.thecosmopolitanhotel.co.uk	-
5	0.0	56	A	Hartlepool	⚵	Wetrocknride, 210a York Rd, TS26 9AB	01429 866777	https://wetrocknride.co.uk	1.8 km (via town centre route, see map)
5	3.5	57	A	Seaton Carew	♠ 〒	The Norton Hotel, 1 The Green, TS25 1AR	07486 393184	www.thenorton.co.uk	0.1 km (→ via main rd, 1st rd ←)
5	3.5	57	A	Seaton Carew	♠ 〒	Altonlea Guesthouse, 19 The Green, TS25 1AT	01429 271289	www.altonlea.co.uk	0.1 km (→ via main rd, 1st rd ←)
5	3.5	57	B	Seaton Carew	♠ 〒	The Marine Hotel, 5-7 The Front, TS25 1BS	01429 266244	www.marinehotel-hartlepool.com	-
5	3.9	57	C	Seaton Carew	♠ 〒	Aarondale Guest House, 46-48 Station Ln, TS25 1BG	01429 868868	www.aarondalehotel.co.uk	-
5	7.4	59	A	Middlesbrough	⚵	Blue Giraffe Bicycles, Cairn Ct Unit 4, Whorlton Rd, TS2 1QA	01642 241627	www.bluegiraffebicycles.co.uk	0.2 km (via Whorlton Rd from alt. route)
6	0.6	61	A	Middlesbrough	♠ 〒	The Grand Astoria Venue Hotel, 61 Wilson St, TS1 1SF	01642 247171	www.thegrandastoriavenue.co.uk	0.2 km (at 2nd traffic lhts →)
6	0.8	61	B	Middlesbrough	♠ 〒	Jurys Inn Hotel, Fry St, TS1 1JH	01642 232000	www.jurysinns.com	0.2 km (at lhts ←, 1st rd ←)
6	11.7	64	A	Great Ayton	⚵	NRG Cycles, 39 High St, TS9 6NH	01642 723527	www.nrgcycles.co.uk	-
6	12.2	64	A	Great Ayton	♠ 〒	Royal Oak Hotel, 123 High St, TS9 6BW	01642 722361	https://royaloakgreatayton.co.uk	-
6	17.7	64	B	Kildale	▲ ⛺ ⚲	Kildale Camping & Barn, Park Farm, YO21 2RN	01642 722847	https://kildalebarn.co.uk	0.4 km (after 2nd railway bridge → via gravel)
6	19.6	64	C	Kildale	♠ ⚲	The Old Rectory B&B, YO21 2RQ	01642 723993	www.theoldrectorykildale.com	-
6	0.0	65	A	Castleton	♠ 〒	The Downe Arms, High St, YO21 2EE	01287 660223	https://downearmscastleton.co.uk	0.1 km (at T-jct →)
6	2.4	65	B	Danby	♠ 〒	The Duke of Wellington Inn, YO21 2LY	01287 660351	https://dukeofwellingtondanby.co.uk	-
6	8.2	65	C	Glaisdale	▲ ⚲	Lawnsgate Farm, Shaw End, Lealholm, YO21 2AT	07887 401023	https://lawnsgatecamping.com	-
6	11.5	65	D	Glaisdale	♠ 〒	Greenhowe B&B, Hall Ln, YO21 2PR	01947 897217	http://greenhowe.co.uk	0.1 km (↗ at triangle green)
6	12.4	65	E	Glaisdale	♠ 〒	The Arncliffe Arms, 1 Arncliffe Tc, YO21 2Q	01947 897555	https://www.arncliffepubglaisdale.co.uk	-
6	12.8	65	F	Glaisdale	♠ ⚲	Beggars Bridge B&B, Station House, YO21 2QL	01947 897409	www.beggarsbridge.co.uk	- (after railway subway imm ←)
6	22.5	65	G	Aislaby	♠ 〒	The Forge, 22 Main Rd, YO21 1SW	01947 811522	https://theforgeaislaby.co.uk	0.2 km (↑)
6	24.1	65	H	Sleights & Briggswath	♠ ⚲	Gramarye B&B, 15 Coach Rd, YO22 5AA	01947 811656	www.gramaryesuites.co.uk	0,3 km (→ via pavement main rd, 1st rd ←)
6	26.7	65	I	Ruswarp	♠ ⚲	Glenview B&B, 1 The Avenue, YO21 1NG	01947 606094	www.glenviewbandbwhitby.co.uk	0.3 km (at T-jct ←, 1st rd →)
7	2.7	67	A	Whitby	♠ 〒	The Willows B&B, 35 Bagdale, YO21 1QL	01947 600288	www.thewillowsguesthouse.co.uk	-
7	3.8	67	B	Whitby	♠ 〒	White Horse & Griffin Hotel, 87 Church St, YO22 4BH	01947 604857	https://whitehorseandgriffin.com	-
7	3.9	67	B	Whitby	♠ ⚲	Sanders Yard, 95 Church St, YO22 4BH	01947 825010	www.sandersyard.co.uk	-
7	4.2	67	C	Whitby	⛺ ⚲	YHA Whitby, Abbey House, East Cliff, YO22 4JT	0345 3719049	www.yha.org.uk	-
7	4.8	67	D	Whitby	▲ ⚲	Folly Gardens, Green Ln, YO22 4EN	01947 601364	www.follygardens-whitby.co.uk	0.6 km (→ via Green Ln on alternative route)
7	8.9	68	A	Hawsker	⚲ hire	Trailways, The Old Railway Station, Station Rd, YO22 4LB	01947 820207	www.trailways.info	0.2 km (cross main rd via lhts ↘ onto trail)
7	3.8	69	A	Robin Hood's Bay	▲ 〒	Bayness Farm, Bayness, YO22 4PJ	-	https://baynessfarm.co.uk	0.2 km (access from trail via Off Road Centre)
7	5.1	69	B	Robin Hood's Bay	♠ ⚲	Grosvenor Hotel, 1 Station Rd, YO22 4RA	01947 880320	www.thegrosvenor.info	-
7	5.1	69	B	Robin Hood's Bay	♠ ⚲	Streonshalh B&B, Mount Pleasant South, YO22 4RQ	01947 881065	www.streonshalh.co.uk	- (after Grosvenor Hotel 1st rd ←)

Rte	Km	Page	Ref	Town	Info	Name, address and postcode	Phone (+ 44)	Internet	Distance to route & extra directions
7	6.4	69	C	Fylingthorpe	▲ ⚲	Middlewood Farm Holiday Park, Middlewood Ln, YO22 4UF	01947 880414	www.middlewoodfarm.com	- (direct access from trail)
7	8.6	69	D	Fylingthorpe	🏨 ▲ ⚲	YHA Boggle Hole, Mill Beck, YO22 4UQ	0345 3719504	www.yha.org.uk	1.5 km (↙ via rd, at T-jct ↖, at sharp bend ↑)
7	19.8	69	E	Hayburn Wyke	🏠 ▲ ⚲	Hayburn Wyke Inn, Newlands Rd, YO13 0AU	01723 870202	www.hayburnwykeinn.co.uk	0.2 km (↙ via gravel rd)
7	23.0	69	F	Cloughton	🏠 ⚲	Station House B&B, Station Ln, YO13 0AD	01723 870896	www.cloughtonstation.co.uk	-
7	23.0	69	G	Cloughton	🏠 🛜	Blacksmith's Arms Inn, High St, YO13 0AE	01723 870244	https://blacksmithsarmsinn.co.uk	0.4 km (↗ via rd, at T-jct → via right side rd)
7	26.9	71	A	Scarborough	▲ ⚲	Scarborough C&CC, Field Ln, Burniston Rd, YO13 0DA	01723 366212	www.campingandcaravanningclub.co.uk	1.1 km (at T-jct ←)
7	26.9	71	B	Scarborough	🏨 ⚲	YHA Scarborough, Burniston Rd, YO13 0DA	0345 2602896	www.yha.org.uk	1.7 km (at T-jct ←, at T-jct → via right side rd)
7	29.3	71	C	Scarborough	🏠 ⚲	The Headlands Hotel, 16 Weydale Av, YO12 6AX	01723 373717	https://theheadlandshotel.co.uk	0.1 km (keep ↑)
7	30.6	71	D	Scarborough	🏠 ⚲	Delmont Hotel, 18-19 Blenheim St, YO12 7HE	01723 364500	www.delmonthotel.co.uk	0.5 km (↗, T-jct ←, 1st ←)
7	30.6	71	E	Scarborough	🏠 🛜	The Albert, 58 North Marine Rd, YO12 7PE	01723 447260	www.thealbertscarborough.co.uk	0.5 km (↗, T-jct ←, 1st →, T-jct ←,)
7	30.6	71	F	Scarborough	🚲	Grip Cycles, 10 Lower Clark St, YO12 7PP	01723 351188	www.gripcycles.co.uk	0.7 km (↗, T-jct ←, 1st →, T-jct ←, 2nd →)
7	30.6	71	G	Scarborough	🚲	Richardson Cycles, 38-40 Castle Rd, YO11 1XE	01723 352682	http://richardsoncyclesscarborough.co.uk	0.8 km (↗, T-jct ←, 1st →, T-jct ←, 2nd →)
7	32.9	72	A	Scarborough	🏠 🛜	Barrington Guest House, 3 Palace Hill, YO11 1NL	01723 314864	www.thebarringtonguesthouse.co.uk	0.2 km (at lhts →)
7	0.0	72	B	Scarborough	🏠 🛜	The Central Hotel, The Crescent, YO11 2PW	01723 447570	http://thecentralhotelscarborough.co.uk	0.4 km (use station route, see map)
7	0.0	72	C	Scarborough	🏠 ⚲	Weston Hotel, 33/34 Esplanade, YO11 2AR	01723 373423	https://westonhotel.co.uk	- (use the alternative route or use cliff lift)
7	0.0	72	D	Scarborough	🏠 ⚲	Ambassador Hotel, 36/38 Esplanade, YO11 2AY	01723 362841	http://ambassadorhotelscarborough.co.uk	- (use the alternative route or use cliff lift)
7	13.7	73	A	Hunmanby	▲ ⚲	Orchard Farm Holiday Village, Stonegate, YO14 0PU	01723 891582	www.orchardfarmholidayvillage.co.uk	1.1 km (at rndabt ↑, 1st rd ↖ to Filey)
7	13.8	73	B	Hunmanby	🏠 ⚲	The Southgate B&B, 8 Bridlington St, YO14 0JR	01723 891521	http://thesouthgatebandb.com	-
8	13.2	75	A	Weaverthorpe	🏠 ⚲	The Star Inn, Main St, YO17 8EY	01944 738346	https://thestarinnweaverthorpe.com	-
8	13.5	75	A	Weaverthorpe	🏠 ⚲	The Blue Bell Inn, Main St, YO17 8EX	01944 738204	www.bluebellweaverthorpe.com	-
8	19.6	77	A	Acklam	🏨 🏠 ⚲	Acklam Farm Stays B&B, YO17 9RR	07846 269128	www.acklamfarmstays.com	2.0 km (←, 1st rd ↖)
8	29.8	77	B	Stamford Bridge	🏠 ⚲	Birkhouse B&B, Buttercrambe Rd, YO41 1AR	01759 529054	https://birkhousebandb.wixsite.com	-
8	32.6	77	C	Stamford Bridge	▲ ⚲	Weir Park, 4 Buttercrambe Rd, YO41 1AN	01759 371377	www.yorkshireholidayparks.co.uk	2.0 km (to town via 🚲, ep ←, T-jct ←, 1st →)
9	14.9	79	A	Bempton	🏠 ⚲	Akos B&B, Newsham Hill Ln, YO16 6XE	07740 172217	www.akosbandb.co.uk	1.0 km (→ via rd to station, ↑ beyond station)
9	18.5	79	B	Flamborough	▲ ⚲	World Farm Camping, Bempton Ln, YO15 1AT	01262 850536	www.woldfarmcampsite.co.uk	1.1 km (in bend to right ← into gravel rd)
9	19.4	79	C	Flamborough	🏠 ⚲	Crabpot Guest House, 10 High St, YO15 1JX	01262 850555	www.crabpotguesthouse.co.uk	0.2 km (← via old High St)
9	19.4	79	C	Flamborough	🏠 ⚲	Cameron Court B&B, North Marine Rd, YO15 1LF	01262 422133	www.cameroncourtbandb.co.uk	0.4 km (← via old High St, at T-jct ↗)
9	31.7	79	D	Bridlington	🏠 🛜	The Expanse Hotel, North Marine Dr, YO15 2LS	01262 675347	www.expanse.co.uk	-
9	32.1	79	E	Bridlington	🏠 🛜	Ransdale Hotel, 30 Flamborough Rd, YO15 2JQ	01262 674334	www.ransdalehotel.com	0.1 km (at T-jct ←)
9	32.1	79	F	Bridlington	🚲	Chaiin Cycles, 133 Hilderthorpe Rd, YO15 3EX	01262 677555	http://chaiincycles.co.uk	2.0 km (at T-jct ←, use station route)
9	38.0	79	G	Carnaby	🏠 🛜	Ferns Farm Hotel, 29 Main St, YO16 4UJ	01262 678961	http://fernsfarm.co.uk	2.3 km (← at cross rds, at T-jct ←)
9	8.1	80	A	Iarpham	🏠 ⚲	St Quintin Arms, Main St, YO25 4QY	01262 490329	www.stquintinarms.com	2.0 km (at T-jct ←, 1st rd →)
9	31.4	81	A	Hornsea	🏠 ⚲	The Ellesmere B&B, Back Westgate, HU18 1BL	07926 725766	www.hornseabandb.co.uk	-

Rte	Km	Page	Ref	Town	Info	Name, address and postcode	Phone (+ 44)	Internet	Distance to route & extra directions
9	32.3	81	B	Hornsea	⌂ ⚲	Ashburnam Guesthouse, 1 Victoria Av, HU18 1NH	01964 515033	www.ashburnamguesthouse.co.uk	-
9	32.3	81	B	Hornsea	⌂ ⚲	Admiralty Guesthouse, 7 Marine Dr, HU18 1NJ	01964 536414	www.admiraltyguesthouse.co.uk	-
9	1.0	82	A	Hornsea	⚲ ⚲ hire	Switchback Cycles, Freeport, Rolston Rd, HU18 1UT	01964 537231	www.switchbackcycles.co.uk	1.1 km (← via main rd, → into 'Freeport')
9	5.7	82	B	Great Hatfield	▲ ⚲	Woodlake Campsite, HU11 4UP (adults only)	01964 536869	www.woodlakecampsite.co.uk	1.4 km (←, T-jct ↖, 1st ↗, T-jct ←, 1st →)
9	9.7	82	C	New Ellerby	⌂ ⚲	The Railway Inn, Lambwath Ln, HU11 5AP	01964 563770	www.therailwayinnpub.co.uk	0.1 km (← via rd)
9	22.4	83	A	Hull	⌂ ⚲	Cornmill Hotel, Mount Pleasant, HU9 1NR	01482 589000	www.cornmillhotel.com	0.2 km (↑, at end ←, opposite large jct)
9	22.5	83	B	Hull	⚲	Jobes Cycles, 222 Holderness Rd, HU9 2AA	01482 589000	www.jobescyclesltd.co.uk	0.2 km (← via main rd, under railway viaduct)
9	23.7	83	C	Hull	⌂ ⚲	Trinity Hotel, 309-323 Hedon Rd, HU9 1NU	01482 222600	www.trinityhull.co.uk	-
9	24.0	83	D	Hull	⌂ ⚲	The Embassy Hotel, 367-371 Hedon Rd, HU9 1RA	01482 326416	http://theembassyhotelhull.co.uk	-
10	5.3	85	A	Hull	⌂⌂ ⚲	Hull Trinity Backpackers, 51-52 Market Pl, HU1 1RU	01482 223229	https://hulltrinitybackpackers.com	0.2 km (← via Liberty Lane, at T-jct ←)
10	5.8	85	B	Hull	⌂ ⚲	Burlington Hotel, 11a Manor St, HU1 1YP	01482 229031	www.burlingtonhotelhull.co.uk	-
10	0.6	85	C	Hull	⌂ ⚲	The Gilson Hotel, 11 Anlaby Rd, HU1 2PJ	01482 323299	www.gilsonhotel.co.uk	0.1 km (→ at lhts into Ferensway, 1st ←)
10	5.2	86	A	Hull	⚲	Jobes Cycles, Anlaby Rd, HU4 6DJ	01482 568398	www.jobescycles.co.uk	0.7 km (← via main rd, at rndabt ↗)
10	9.3	86	B	Cottingham	⚲	R-Evolution, Station Rd, HU16 4LL	01482 844422	www.r-evolution.org.uk	0.5 km (see map for station route)
10	10.5	86	C	Cottingham	⌂ ⚲	The Toll Cottage, 297 Northgate, HU16 5RL	01482 840263	https://thetollcottage.co.uk	0.2 km (at T-jct ←, keep ↑)
10	18.5	87	A	Beverley	⌂ ⚲	Minster Garth House, 2 Keldgate, HU17 8HY	01482 882402	www.beverleybedandbreakfast.com	0.1 km (at T-jct ←)
10	0.2	87	B	Beverley	⌂ ⚲	Newbegin House B&B, 10 Newbegin, HU17 8EG	01482 888880	www.newbeginhousebbbeverley.co.uk	0.1 km (← via Windmill Walk, →, 2nd ←)
10	0.3	87	C	Beverley	⌂ ⚲	The King's Head, 37-38 Saturday Market Place, HU17 9AH	01482 868103	https://kingsheadpubbeverley.com	-
10	0.3	87	C	Beverley	⌂ ⚲	Dock and Duck Coaching Inn, 33 Ladygate, HU17 8BH	01482 862419	www.bedandbreakfastbeverley.com	0.1 km (on Saturday Market Place ↗)
10	0.5	87	D	Beverley	⚲	Minster Cycles, 5-7 Norwood, HU17 9ET	01482 867950	www.minstercycles.co.uk	0.3 km (go in right lane for turn →, keep ↑)
10	0.6	87	E	Beverley	⌂ ⚲	The Beverley Arms, 25 North Bar Within, HU17 8DD	01482 296999	www.beverleyarms.co.uk	-
10	19.8	88	A	Market Weighton	⌂ ⚲	The Londesborough Arms, 44 High St, YO43 3AH	01430 872214	www.thelondesborougharms.com	0.2 km (at T-jct ←, at T-jct ←)
10	32.3	89	A	Pocklington	⚲	Cycle Lane Ltd, 6 Clarkes Ln, YO42 2AW	01759 306770	www.cyclelane-ltd.co.uk	- (at T-jct ↑ onto square, ← via alleyway)
10	32.3	89	A	Pocklington	⚲	The Feathers Hotel, 56 Market Pl, YO42 2AH	01759 303155	www.thefeatherspocklington.co.uk	- (at T-jct →)
10	4.4	89	B	Pocklington	▲⌂⌂ ⚲	Yapham Holds Farmhouse, Feoffee Ln, YO42 1PF	01759 305644	www.yaphamholdsfarmhouse.com	-
10	8.7	89	C	Fangfoss, Stamford Bridge	▲ ⚲	Fangfoss Park, YO41 5QB	01759 380491	https://fangfosspark.co.uk	0.1 km (at T-jct →)
10	13.6	89	D	Stamford Bridge	▲ ⚲	Weir Park, 4 Buttercrambe Rd, YO41 1AN	01759 371377	www.yorkshireholidayparks.co.uk	0.6 km (at T-jct ←, at T-jct ←, 1st rd →)
11	5.5	91	A	Dunnington	▲ ⚲	Ashfield Touring Caravan Park, Hagg Ln, YO19 5PE	01904 488631	www.ashfieldtouringcaravanpark.co.uk	1.1 km (at T-jct ←, 1st ←)
11	14.1	93	A	York	⌂ ⚲	The Black Swan, 23 Peasholme Green, YO1 7PR	01904 679131	www.blackswanyork.com	-
11	14.9	93	B	York	⌂ ⚲	Lamb & Lion Inn, 24 High Petergate, YO1 7EH	01904 612078	www.lambandlioninnyork.com	0.1 km (use Bootham Bar route)
11	14.9	93	C	York	⌂ ⚲	Guy Fawkes Inn, 25 High Petergate, YO1 7HP	01904 623716	www.guyfawkesinnyork.com	-
11	14.9	93	C	York	⌂ ⚲	Dean Court Hotel, Duncombe Pl, YO1 7EF	01904 625082	www.deancourt-york.co.uk	-
11	14.9	93	C	York	⌂ ⌂⌂ ⚲	The Fort Boutique Hostel, 1 Little Stonegate, YO1 8AX	01904 639573	www.thefortyork.co.uk	-

Rte	Km	Page	Ref	Town	Info	Name, address and postcode	Phone (+ 44)	Internet	Distance to route & extra directions
11	15.1	93	D	York		YHA York, Water End, Clifton, YO30 6LP	0345 3719051	www.yha.org.uk	1.9 km (use river route, see map)
11	0.0	93	E	York	hire	Cycle Heaven, Station Rd, YO24 1AY	01904 622701	www.cycle-heaven.co.uk	1.3 km (use station route, see map)
11	0.2	93	F	York		The Queens Hotel, Skeldergate, YO1 6DH	01904 611321	www.queenshotel-york.com	-
11	2.0	93	G	York		Gregory's Guest House, 160 Bishopsthorpe Rd, YO23 1LF	01904 627521	www.gregorysofyork.co.uk	0.2 km (after Millennium Bridge →)
11	2.0	93	H	York	hire	Cycle Heaven, 31 Hospital Fields, YO10 4FS	01904 636578	www.cycle-heaven.co.uk	0.2 km (before Millennium Bridge, ←)
11	6.7	94	A	Bishopthorpe		Twisted Cogs, Home Farm Buildings, Main St, YO23 2RA	01904 849180	www.twistedcogs.co.uk	0.8 km (← via Copmanthorpe Ln, T-jct ←)
11	6.7	94	B	Bishopthorpe		York Marine Services Camping, Ferry Ln, YO23 2SB	01904 704442	www.yorkmarine.co.uk	1.5 km (← via ", T-jct ←,→ Acaster Ln,1st ←)
11	8.8	94	C	Naburn		Millbridge Farm Camping Park, Howden Ln, YO19 4RW	01904 651142	-	- (↗ via ramp down, →)
11	17.1	94	D	Ricall		White Rose Villa B&B, 33 York Rd, YO19 6QG	01757 248115	www.whiterosevilla.info	-
11	17.6	94	E	Ricall		The Greyhound (pub), 82 Main St, YO19 6TE	01757 249101	www.thegreyhoundriccall.co.uk	-
11	25.1	95	A	Selby		Hazeldene B&B, 32-34 Brook St, YO8 4AR	01757 704809	www.hazeldene-selby.co.uk	1,4 km (via Abbey,New L,Massey St,Union L)
11	12.6	95	B	Hirst Courtney		8 West Bank, DN14 9PZ	07557 993074	www.appleblossomcaravanandcamping.com	-
11	16.1	96	A	Carlton		Selby Camping, Bridge Farm, DN14 9LN	07545 249964	https://selbycamping.weebly.com	-
11	0.0	96	B	Snaith		Downe Arms Hotel, 15 Market Pl, DN14 9HE	01405 860544	www.the-downe-arms.co.uk/	0.3 km (after railway crossing, 2nd →)
11	0.0	96	B	Snaith		The Brewers Arms, Pontefract Rd, DN14 9JS	01405 862404	www.thebrewersarms.co.uk	0.6 km (after railway crossing, 3rd →)
11	5.8	96	C	Pollington		Parkside Guesthouse, Main St, DN14 0DW	01405 869759	www.parkside-guesthouse.com	1.0 km (↑)
11	5.8	96	C	Pollington		Fir Tree Barn B&B, Main St, DN14 0DN	01405 862286	www.firtreebarn.com	1.1 km (↑)
11	12.4	96	D	Sykehouse		Oakside Camping, Oakside, Mawson Green, DN14 9AJ	01405 785408	www.oaksidecamping.com	0.7 km (after bridge ↖)
11	32.3	97	A	Bentley		The Bay Horse Inn, Chapel St, DN5 0DE	01302 874414	www.bayhorseinnpubbentley.co.uk	- (on corner left of T-jct)
12	3.5	99	A	Doncaster		Kellett Hotel, 87-89 Thorne Rd, DN1 2ES	01302 321248	www.kelletthotel.co.uk	0.7 km (↑, ← via Prince's St)
12	3.5	99	B	Doncaster		The Regent Hotel, Regent Sq, DN1 2DS	01302 364180	www.theregenthotel.co.uk	0.4 km (↑, ← via Regent Sq)
12	3.9	99	C	Doncaster		Pedal Power, 153 St Sepulchre Gt, DN1 3AW	01302 341575	-	-
12	5.1	100	A	Mexborough		Low Lock Riverside Retreat, Off Pastures Rd, S64 0JJ	07415 886672	www.lowlock.co.uk	2.1 km (← via rd at cycle bridge, 1st rd ↙)
12	13.5	101	A	Wombwell		Geared Up Cycles, 23 Barnsley Rd, S73 8HT	01226 756281	www.gearedupcycles.co.uk	0.1 km (→ via main rd)
12	13.5	101	B	Wombwell		Churchill's Hotel, 1 High St, S73 0DA	020 80998579	www.oyorooms.com	0.4 km (→ via main rd)
12	19.0	102	A	Worsbrough		Biketyke, 65 Park Rd, S70 5AD	01226 233432	https://biketyke.co.uk	0.4 km (→ via main rd)
12	30.7	102	B	Penistone	hire	Cycle Penistone, off St Mary's St, S36 6DT	01226 872310	www.cyclepenistonecic.com	2.5 km (→, after viaduct town centre ↙)
12	30.7	102	C	Penistone		Taylor's B&B, 40 Bridge St, S36 6AJ	07889 848015	http://taylorsbandb.com	2.8 km (→, after viaduct town centre ↙, ←)
12	30.7	102	D	Penistone		Lyndene B&B, 30 Ward St, S36 6EP	07495 629160	https://lyndenebedandbreakfast.com	2.8 km (→, after viaduct town centre ↙, →)
12	5.5	103	A	Worthley		Finkle Green B&B, Finkle Street Ln, S35 7DH	01142 881520	www.finklegreen.com	1.3 km (← via gravel path, ep →via rd)
13	9.9	105	A	Stannington		Loadbrook Farm B&B, Loadbrook, S6 6GT	01142 343679	www.loadbrookfarm.com	1.9 km (↑, follow tarmac rd, 1st rd →)
13	15.5	105	B	Fulwood		Fox Hagg Farm, Lodge Ln, S6 5SN	01142 305776	www.foxhaggfarm.com	3.5 km (← via rd, 1st rd ←, down steep hill)
13	21.3	106	A	Bamford		North Lees, Birley Ln, S32 1DY	01433 650838	www.peakdistrict.gov.uk	2.8 km (ep, at car pk ← via rd, at T-jct ←)

Rte	Km	Page	Ref	Town	Info	Name, address and postcode	Phone (+ 44)	Internet	Distance to route & extra directions
13	24.9	106	B	Bamford	⌂ ☰	Yorkshire Bridge Inn, Ashopton Rd, S33 0AZ	01433 651361	www.yorkshire-bridge.co.uk	-
13	29.4	106	C	Hope	⌂ ⚒	Round Meadow Barn B&B, Parsons Ln, S33 6RB	01433 621347	www.roundmeadowbarn.co.uk	0.5 km (← via Parsons Ln)
13	30.8	106	D	Hope	▲ ⚒	Laneside Caravan Park, S33 6RR	01433 620215	www.lanesidecaravanpark.co.uk	0.2 km (← via A6187)
13	31.1	106	E	Hope	⌂ ☰	The Old Hall Hotel, Market Pl, S33 6RH	01433 620160	www.oldhallhotelhope.co.uk	0.1 km (↑ via A6187)
13	31.1	106	E	Hope	⚲ ☍ hire	18 Bikes, Castleton Rd, S33 6RD	01433 621111	www.18bikes.co.uk	0.1 km (← via A6187)
13	0.0	107	A	Castleton	⌂▲ ⚒	YHA Castleton Losehill Hall, Squires Ln, S33 8WB	0345 3719628	www.yha.org.uk	1.5 km (↑ via A6187, ← via signed drive)
13	0.0	107	B	Castleton	⌂ ☰	The Peak Hotel, How Ln, S33 8WJ	01433 620247	www.thepeakhotel.co.uk	0.3 km (← via A6187)
13	0.0	107	C	Castleton	⌂ ⚒	B&B Ramblers Rest, Back St, Millbridge, S33 WR	01433 620125	https://ramblersrest-castleton.co.uk	0.2 km (↑ via A6187, in bend to right ↑)
13	0.0	107	D	Castleton	⌂ ☰	Ye Olde Nags Head, Cross St, S33 8WH	01433 620248	www.yeoldenagshead.co.uk	0.1 km (↑ via A6187)
13	0.0	107	E	Castleton	⌂ ☰	Bulls Head Hotel, Cross St, S33 8WH	01433 620256	http://bullsheadcastleton.co.uk	-
13	0.1	107	F	Castleton	⌂ ⚒	The George Hotel, Castle St, S33 8WG	01433 620238	www.georgehotelcastleton.co.uk	-
13	7.5	107	G	Peak Forest	⌂▲ ⚒	Bushey Heath Farm, Pittlemere Ln, SK17 8JE	01298 605022	https://busheyheathfarm.com	1.2 km (in bend to the right ↑ via gravel, →)
13	12.9	108	A	Tideswell	⌂ ⚒	Rockingham Lodge B&B, Market Sq, SK17 8LQ	01298 871684	www.rockinghamlodge.co.uk	1.6 km (↑, in Tideswell ↗, ← onto square)
13	19.1	108	B	Miller's Dale	⌂▲ ⚒	YHA Ravenstor, B6049, SK17 8SS	0345 3719655	www.yha.org.uk	1.7 km (↑ under viaduct, T-jct ← via B6049)
13	28.1	109	A	Hassop	⚲ ☍ hire	Monsal Trail Cycle Hire, Hassop Station, DE45 1NW	01629 810588	www.monsaltrail.co.uk	-
13	30.5	109	B	Bakewell	⚲	Peakland Cycles, Milford, DE45 1DX	01433 639853	https://peaklandcycles.co.uk	0.3 km (→, before private rd ←, ep →, →)
13	30.5	109	C	Bakewell	⌂ ☰	The Peacock Hotel, Old Market Hall, Bridge St, DE45 1DS	01629 813635	www.peacockbakewell.co.uk	0.1 km (↑ via main rd ↑)
13	30.7	109	C	Bakewell	⌂ ☰	The Red Lion, The Square, DE45 1BT	01629 812054	www.red-lion-bakewell.co.uk	0.1 km (← via Water St, ↖, at end →)
13	1.8	110	A	Over Haddon	⌂ ⚒	The Lathkil Hotel, School Ln, DE45 1JE	01629 812501	www.lathkil.co.uk	1.3 km (→, at T-jct ←, in Over Haddon ←)
13	1.8	110	B	Over Haddon	▲ ⚒	Mandale Farm, Haddon Grove, DE45 1JF	01629 812416	www.mandalecampsite.co.uk	3.1 km (→, at T-jct ←, 1st rd →, 2nd rd ↖)
13	3.7	110	C	Youlgrave	⌂ ⚒	Bull's Head, Fountain Sq, DE45 1UR	01629 636307	www.thebullsheadyoulgrave.co.uk	1.2 km (← to Youlgrave, in Youlgrave ↓→)
13	9.2	110	D	Youlgrave	⌂ ⚒	Arbor Low B&B, Upper Oldhams Farm, Monyash, DE45 1JS	01629 636337	http://arborlow.co.uk	0.2 km (← via Arbor Low driveway)
13	10.6	110	E	Parsley Hay	☍ hire	Parsley Hay Cycle Hire Centre, SK17 0DG	01298 84493	www.peakdistrict.gov.uk	-
13	16.4	110	F	Biggin	⌂ ⚒	Biggin Hall Hotel, SK17 0DH	01298 84451	www.bigginhall.co.uk	0.8 km (↖ via side path, ep → via rd)
13	19.4	111	A	Alsop	▲ ☰	Rivendale Holiday Caravan Park, Buxton Rd, DE6 1QU	01355 310441	www.rivendalecaravanpark.co.uk	0.3 km (↘ down ramp, →, at T-jct ↑ cross rd)
13	22.0	111	B	Alsop	⌂ ☰	Newton House Hotel, Buxton Rd, DE6 1NJ	01355 310391	www.newtonhousedovedale.co.uk	- direct access from Tissington Trail
13	27.6	111	C	Tissington	▲ ⚒	Ashbourne Heights Holiday Park, Buxton Rd, DE6 1LE	01355 350228	www.ashbourne-heights.co.uk	0.2 km (← via gap in hedge, → on rd)
13	28.5	111	D	Thorpe	⌂ ☰	Station House B&B Thorpe, Off Narlows Ln, DE6 2AT	01355 350764	www.stationhousebedandbreakfast.co.uk	- (at end station car pk)
13	31.8	111	E	Ashbourne	▲ ⚒	Callow Top Holiday Park, Buxton Rd, DE6 2EQ	01335 344020	www.callowtop.co.uk	0.3 km (→ down ramp, → on rd)
13	32.5	111	F	Ashbourne	☍ hire	Ashbourne Cycle Hire Centre, Mappleton Rd, DE6 2AA	01335 343156	www.peakdistrict.gov.uk	-
13	32.5	111	G	Ashbourne	⌂ ⚒	Orchard Dales B&B, North Av, DE6 1EZ	01335 300730	www.orcharddales.co.uk	0.6 km (↗ via car pk, ← via rd, T-jct ←)
13	33.0	111	H	Ashbourne	⌂ ☰	The George & Dragon, 43 Market Pl, DE6 1EU	01335 343199	www.georgeanddragonashbourne.co.uk	0.5 km (via town centre route from tunnel end)
13	33.0	111	I	Ashbourne	⚲ ☍ hire	The Bike Barn, The Stables, Wellington Yard, DE6 1GH	01335 300708	www.thebikebarnashbourne.co.uk	0.5 km (via town centre route from tunnel end)

Rte	Km	Page	Ref	Town	Info	Name, address and postcode	Phone (+ 44)	Internet	Distance to route & extra directions
13	33.0	111	J	Ashbourne	🏠⚒	Compton House B&B, 27-31 Compton, DE6 1BX	01335 343100	www.comptonhouse.co.uk	0.3 km (*minimum 2 nights*, via bus station)
14	20.5	113	A	Etwall	🏠⚑	Blenheim House Hotel, Main St, DE65 6LP	01283 732254	-	-
14	33.6	115	A	Burton-on-Trent	🏠⚑	Grail Court Hotel, 164b Station Rd, DE14 1BN	01283 741155	www.grailcourthotel.com	-
14	33.9	115	B	Burton-on-Trent	🏠⚑	The Tree Queens Hotel, 1 Bridge St, DE14 1SY	01283 523800	www.threequeenshotel.co.uk	0.3 km (← via High St)
14	8.6	116	A	Rosliston	⛺⚒	Beehive Woodland Lakes, Lullington Rd, DE12 8HZ	01283 763981	www.beehivefarm-woodlandlakes.co.uk	-
14	21.0	116	B	Measham	⚐	Pickering's Bikes, 39 High St, DE12 7HR	07845 267867	www.pickeringsbikes.co.uk	0.1 km (↑ in High St)
14	9.8	117	A	Ibstock	🏠⛺⚒	Pinewood Lodge, Overton Rd, LE67 6PD	01530 264477	www.pinewood-lodge.co.uk	-
14	10.8	117	B	Ibstock	🏠⚑	The Post House B&B, 120 High St, LE67 6LJ	01530 261610	www.posthousebandbibstock.co.uk	0.8 km (↑ to Ibstock, at T-jct →)
14	0.0	119	A	Leicester	🏠⚑	Abbey Hotel, 104 St Margarets Wy, LE4 0BT	01162 256599	www.trivelleshotels.com/abbey	0.6 km (via pavements around Abbey Park)
14	1.7	119	B	Leicester	🏠⚑	Hotel Campanile, St Matthews Wy,Bedford St North, LE1 3JE	01162 616600	www.campanile.com	0.1 km (→ via pavement along main rd)
14	2.9	119	C	Leicester	🏠⚒	Castle Park Hotel, 12 Millstone Ln, LE1 5JN	01162 511000	www.castleparkhotel.co.uk	0.1 km (← via Grey Friars)
14	3.4	119	D	Leicester	🏠⚑	Villare Hotel, 19-21 Nicholas Pl, LE1 4LD	01162 421330	www.thevillarehotel.co.uk	- (on corner of piazza)
15	0.4	120	A	Leicester	⚐	Billy's Bespoke Bikes, 9 Braunstone Gate, LE3 5LG	07543 730398	www.billys-bespoke-bike.co.uk	- (on corner of jct at right side of 🚲 crossing)
15	18.0	121	A	Ashby Magna	⛺⚑	Holly Farm Fishery Moby Park, Willoughby Rd, LE17 5NP	01455 202391	www.hollyfarmfishery.co.uk	-
15	25.6	121	B	Walcote	🏠⚑	Little Lodge B&B, 17 Lutterworth Rd, LE17 4JW	01455 550949	www.littlelodgewalcote.co.uk	0.1 km (↑ via main rd, on right side of rd)
15	26.8	121	C	Walcote	🏠⚒	Orchard Views B&B, 17 Lutterworth Rd, LE17 4JZ	07809 351101	www.hetwapenvanmiddelie.nl	-
15	41.5	122	A	Hillmorton	⚐	Paddox Cycles, 274a Hillmorton Rd, CV22 5BW	01788 576659	www.paddoxcycles.co.uk	-
15	43.0	122	B	Rugby	⚐	Rugby Cycle Repairs, 100-102 Cambridge St, CV21 3NH	01788 562299	https://rugbycyclerepairs.co.uk	3.0 km (via Ashlawn Cutting 🚲, see map)
15	43.0	122	C	Rugby	🏠⚒	Grosvenor Hotel, 81-97 Clifton Rd, CV21 3QQ	01788 535686	www.grosvenorhotelrugby.co.uk	4.0 km (via Ashlawn Cutting 🚲, see map)
15	43.0	122	D	Rugby	🏠⚑	Diamond House Hotel, 28-30 Hillmorton Rd, CV22 5AA	01788 572701	www.diamondhousehotel.co.uk	4.5 km (via Ashlawn Cutting 🚲, see map)
15	43.0	122	E	Rugby	🏠⚒	The Rugby Hotel, Sheep St, CV21 3BX	01788 573244	hwww.therugbyhotel.co.uk	5.0 km (via Ashlawn Cutting 🚲, see map)
15	30.1	124	A	Royal Leamington Spa	🏠⚒	Episode Hotel, 64 Upper Holly Walk, CV32 4JL	01926 883777	www.episodehotels.co.uk	0.2 km (→ at lhts, Willes Rd, 2nd rd →)
15	30.1	124	B	Royal Leamington Spa	⚐	Giant Bicycle Store, 75 Clerendon St, CV32 4PW	01926 460089	www.giant-leamington.co.uk	0.4 km (→ at lhts, Willes Rd, 4th rd →)
15	30.9	124	C	Royal Leamington Spa	🏠⚑	Headley Villa Guest House, 31 Russell Tce, CV31 1EZ	01926 424504	www.hedleyvillaguesthouse.co.uk	0,2 km (← via Regent Pl, keep ↑)
15	31.0	124	D	Royal Leamington Spa	🏠⚑	Thomas James Hotel, 45 Bath St, CV31 3AG	01926 312568	https://thomasjameshotel.tk	-
15	3.2	124	E	Warwick	🏠⚑	Cambridge Villa B&B, 20a-20b Emscote Rd, CV34 4PP	01926 491169	www.cambridge-villa-warwick.co.uk	0.1 km (ep →)
15	3.2	124	E	Warwick	🏠⚑	Parkhouse Guest House, 17 Emscote Rd, CV34 4PH	01926 494359	www.warwickparkhouse.co.uk	0.1 km (ep →)
15	4.5	124	F	Warwick	🏠⚒	The Punch Bowl, 1 The Butts, CV34 4SS	01926 403846	www.punchbowlwarwick.co.uk	- (at T-jct ←)
15	4.5	124	G	Warwick	🏠⚒	Blackhorse Inn, 62 Saltisford Rd, CV34 4TD	01926 659995	www.theblackhorseinnwarwick.co.uk	0.2 km (at T-jct →, 2x at rndabt ↗ to A425)
15	4.5	124	G	Warwick	🏠⚑	Kings Head Inn, 39 Saltisford Rd, CV34 4TD	01926 775177	www.thekingsheadwarwick.co.uk	0.2 km (at T-jct →, 2x at rndabt ↗ to A425)
15	0.6	124	H	Warwick	🏠⚒	Fourpenny Hotel, 27-29 Crompton St, CV34 6HJ	01926 491360	www.4pennyhotel.co.uk	0.1 km (→ via Compton St)
15	10.8	125	A	Charlecote	🏠⚒	The Charlecote Pheasant Hotel, Charlecote Rd, CV35 9EW	01789 279954	www.coastandcountryhotels.com	-
15	12.7	125	B	Wellesbourne	⛺🏨⚒	Twitey's Meadows, Low Farm, Hunscote Rd, CV35 9EX	07725 944204	http://twiteystipis.co.uk	0.7 km (1st rd →, to Hunscote)

Rte	Km	Page	Ref	Town	Info	Name, address and postcode	Phone (+ 44)	Internet	Distance to route & extra directions
15	18.6	125	C	Alveston	🏨 ⚒	YHA Stratford-upon-Avon, Wellesbourne Rd, CV37 7RG	0345 3719661	www.yha.org.uk	1.6 km (after school The Croft, 1st rd →)
16	2.3	126	A	Stratford-upon-Avon	🏠 ⚟	The Croft Guest House, 49 Shipston Rd, CV37 7LN	01789 293419	www.thecroftuk.co.uk	0.4 km (→ via rd, → via pavement)
16	2.3	126	B	Stratford-upon-Avon	🏠 ⚒	Swan's Nest Hotel, Banbury Rd, Bridge Foot, CV37 7LT	01789 266804	https://swansnesthotel.co.uk	0.1 km (→ via rd)
16	2.8	126	C	Stratford-upon-Avon	🏠 ⚟	Courtland Hotel, 12 Guild St, CV37 6RE	01789 292401	www.courtlandhotel.co.uk	0.5 km (via Sheep St & Henley St, see map)
16	2.8	126	D	Stratford-upon-Avon	🏠 ⚟	The Emsley B&B, 4 Arden St, CV37 6PA	01789 299557	www.theemsley.co.uk	1.0 km (via Sheep St & Henley St, see map)
16	2.8	126	E	Stratford-upon-Avon	🚲	Velo Fix, 26 Western Rd, CV37 0AH	01789 414466	www.velo-fix.co.uk	1.7 km (via Sheep St & Henley St, see map)
16	4.2	126	F	Stratford-upon-Avon	🏠 ⚟	Moss Cottage B&B, 61 Evesham Rd, CV37 9BA	01789 294770	http://mosscottage.org	1.0 km (→ via 🚲,ep → via rd,T-jct ← via 🚲)
16	4.3	127	A	Stratford-upon-Avon	⚠ ⚟	Dodwell Park, Evesham Rd, CV37 9SR	01789 204957	www.stratfordbikehire.com	-
16	0.2	127	B	Stratford-upon-Avon	🚲 hire	Stratford Bike Hire, Seven Meadows Rd, CV37 6GR	07711 776340	www.dodwellpark.co.uk	2.5 km (→ via 🚲,ep → via rd,T-jct ← via 🚲)
16	10.7	128	A	Lower Quinton	🏠 ⚒	Winton House B&B, Upper Quinton, CV37 8SX	01789 720500	http://wintonhouse.com	0.5 km (→ via Goose Ln)
16	19.7	128	B	Ebrington	🏠 ⚒	Holly House B&B, GL55 6NL	01386 593213	www.hollyhousebandb.co.uk	0.5 km (↖, 1st rd →)
16	22.2	128	C	Paxford	🏠 ⚟	The Churchill Arms, GL55 6XH	01386 593159	www.churchillarms.co	0.1 km (at triangle ↑ via country lane)
16	30.1	128	D	Moreton-in-Marsh	🏠 ⚒	Acacia B&B, 2 New Rd, GL56 0AS	01608 650130	www.acaciainthecotswolds.co.uk	0.1 km (← via New Rd)
16	30.2	128	D	Moreton-in-Marsh	🏠 ⚟	The Bell Inn, High St, GL56 0AF	01608 651887	http://thebellinnmoreton.co.uk	-
16	30.3	128	D	Moreton-in-Marsh	🏠 ⚒	White Hart Royal Hotel, High St, GL56 0BA	01608 650731	www.whitehartroyal.co.uk	0.1 km (↑via High St)
16	30.3	128	D	Moreton-in-Marsh	🏠 ⚒	Swan Inn, High St, GL56 0LL	01608 650711	www.swanmoreton.co.uk	0.2 km (↑via High St)
16	31.1	128	E	Moreton-in-Marsh	🚲	Cotswold Cycles, 3 Cotswolds Link, GL56 0JU	01608 650933	www.cotswoldcycles.co.uk	0.4 km (↑ via main rd, 1st rd →)
16	0.0	131	A	Long Hanborough	🏠 ⚒	Swan House Guesthouse, Millwood End, OX29 8BX	01993 883563	www.swanhouseguestrooms.co.uk	0.2 km (← via route to Combe Mill museum)
16	1.9	131	B	Long Hanborough	🏠 ⚟	Churchill Court Hotel, Main Rd, OX29 8LA	01993 881973	www.thechurchilcourt.co.uk	-
16	9.1	131	C	Woodstock	🏠 ⚒	The Blenheim Buttery, 7 Market Place, OX20 1SY	01865 811950	www.theblenheimbuttery.co.uk	6.3 km (Blenheim Palace route from Yarnton)
16	9.1	131	C	Woodstock	🏠 ⚒	The Star Inn Hotel, 22 Market Place, OX20 1TA	01993 811373	www.thestarinnwoodstock.co.uk	6.3 km (Blenheim Palace route from Yarnton)
16	0.0	133	A	Oxford	🏨 ⚟	YHA Oxford, 2a Botley Rd, OX2 0AB	0345 3719131	www.yha.org.uk	1.1 km (use station route, see map)
16	0.0	133	A	Oxford	🏠 ⚟	Westgate Hotel, 1 Botley Rd, OX2 0AA	01865 726721	www.westgatehoteloxford.co.uk	1.1 km (use station route, see map)
16	0.0	133	B	Oxford	🏠 ⚟	The Osney Arms Hotel, 45 Botley Rd, OX2 0BP	01865 243498	www.theosneyarms.com	1.5 km (use station route, see map)
16	0.0	133	C	Oxford	🏨 ⚟	Central Backpackers Oxford, 13 Park End St, OX1 1HH	01865 242288	www.centralbackpackers.co.uk	1.3 km (use station route, see map)
16	0.2	133	D	Oxford	🚲 hire	Bainton Bikes/Walton Street Cycles, 78 Walton St, OX2 6EA	01865 311610	www.baintonbikes.com	- (→ at jct)
16	2.3	133	E	Oxford	🏠 ⚟	Eurobar Hotel, 48 George St, OX1 2AQ	01865 725087	www.eurobar.co.uk	0.7 km (use Turl St & Ship St route, see map)
16	2.3	133	F	Oxford	🚲 hire	Bike Zone/Summertown Cycles, 28 St Michaels St, OX1 2EB	01865 728877	www.bike-zone.co.uk	0.4 km (use Turl St & Ship St route, see map)
16	2.3	133	G	Oxford	🏠 ⚒	Tower Guest House, 15 Ship St, OX1 3DA	01865 246828	www.towerhouseoxford.co.uk	0.2 km (use Turl St & Ship St route, see map)
16	4.0	133	H	Oxford	🏠 ⚒	Ethos Hotel, 59 Western Rd, OX1 4LF	01865 813580	www.ethoshotels.co.uk	0.5 km (via Thames path & Marlborough Rd)
16	4.0	133	I	Oxford	🏠 ⚒	White House View, 9 White House Rd, OX1 4PA	01865 721626	www.whitehouseviewguesthouse.co.uk	0.8 km (via Thames path & Marlborough Rd)
17	1.7	134	A	Oxford	⚠ ⚟	Oxford C&CC, 426 Abingdon Rd, OX1 4XG	01865 244088	www.campingandcaravanningclub.co.uk	-
17	0.0	135	A	Abingdon	🚲	Behind Bars Bikes, Coxeter House, 21-27 Ock St, OX14 5AJ	01235 533287	http://behindbarscycles.co.uk	0.3 km (↗ via High St, 2nd → Stratton W, ←)

Rte	Km	Page	Ref	Town	Info	Name, address and postcode	Phone (+ 44)	Internet	Distance to route & extra directions
17	0.1	135	B	Abingdon	♠ ⚲	S. Howard B&B, 22 East St Helen St, OX14 5EB	07811 293310	www.abingdonbedandbreakfast.com	-
17	0.1	135	B	Abingdon	♠ ⚲	St Ethelwold's House B&B, 30 East St Helen St, OX14 5EB	01235 555486	http://ethelwoldhouse.com	-
17	9.4	135	C	Didcot	♠ ≈	The Laurels B&B, 47 Wantage Rd, OX11 0BS	01235 812212	www.accommodationdidcot.co.uk	1.0 km (↑ at rndabt, 6th → Manor Cr, T-jct →)
17	9.4	135	C	Didcot	⚲	Mountain Mania Cycles, 62 Wantage Rd, OX11 0BY	01235 759366	www.mountainmaniacycles.co.uk	1.1 km (↑ at rndabt, 6th → Manor Cr, T-jct →)
17	4.6	136	A	Upton	♠ ⚲	Prospect House B&B, OX11 9HU	01235 850268	www.prospect-house.info	-
17	19.5	136	B	Wantage	♠ ⚲	Alfred's Lodge B&B, 23 Ormond Rd, OX12 8EG	01235 762409	www.alfredslodge.co.uk	-
17	20.2	136	C	Wantage	⚲	Ridgeway Cycles, 22 Newbury St, OX12 8DA	01235 764445	www.ridgewaycycles.com	0.1 km (at T-jct ←)
17	20.1	136	D	Wantage	♠ ≈	The Bear Hotel, 14 Market Pl, OX12 8AB	01235 766366	www.thebearwantage.co.uk	-
17	2.8	137	A	Letcombe Regis	▲ ♨ ⚲	The Courthill Centre, OX12 9NE	01235 760253	http://courthill.org.uk	2.2 km (in bend to the right ↑ to Marlborough)
17	3.0	137	B	Letcombe Regis	♠ ⚲	The Greyhound Inn, Main St, OX12 9JL	01235 771969	www.thegreyhoundletcombe.co.uk	-
17	15.0	137	C	Uffington White Horse	▲ ⚲	Britchcombe Farm, SN7 7QJ	01367 821022	www.britchcombefarm.co.uk	1.8 km (→ via gravel ⚡, 1st rd →, 1st rd →)
17	12.9	137	D	Chiseldon	♠ ⚲	Landmark Hotel, Station Rd, SN4 0PW	01793 740149	https://landmark-hotel-swindon.booked.net	0.4 km (end of gravel ⚡ ↑)
17	12.9	137	E	Chiseldon	♠ ⚲	Chiseldon House Hotel, New Rd, SN4 0NE	01793 741010	www.chiseldonhouse.com	0.3 km (end of gravel ⚡ ←)
17	0.0	139	A	Avebury	♠ ≈	Avebury Lodge B&B, High St, SN8 1RF	01672 539023	https://aveburylodge.co.uk	0.1 km (just before Keiller Museum, see map)
17	0.0	139	B	Avebury	♠ ⚲	Avebury Life, 5 Trusloe Cottages, Trusloe, SN8 1QZ	01672 539644	www.aveburylife.com	0.9 km (beyond Keiller Museum, see map)
17	3.1	139	C	East Kennett	♠ ⚲	The Old Forge B&B, SN8 4EY	01672 861456	http://theoldforge-avebury.co.uk	-
18	1.0	140	A	Alton Priors	♠ ⚲	Well Cottage, Honey St, SN9 5PS	01672 851655	https://well-cottage.net	-
18	7.2	140	B	North Newnton	▲ ⚲	Woodbridge Inn, SN9 6JZ	01980 630266	http://woodbridgeinnpewsey.com	-
18	9.3	140	C	Upavon	♠ ⚲	The Antilope Inn, 3 High St, SN9 6EA	01980 630025	https://antelopeupavon.com	-
18	22.8	141	A	Bulford	♠ ⚲	The Rose & Crown, 39 High St, SP4 9DS	01752 216391	www.theroseandcrown-bulford.co.uk	0.2 km (↗ via Orchard End, at T-jct ←)
18	26.3	141	B	Amesbury	♠ ⚲	Fairlawn House B&B, 42 High St, SP4 7DL	01980 622103	www.fairlawnhouse.co.uk	-
18	26.4	141	C	Amesbury	⚲	Hills Cycles, Smithfield St, SP4 7AL	01980 622705	-	0.2 km (← via Salisbury St, opposite rndabts)
18	26.5	141	C	Amesbury	♠ ⚲	Antrobus Arms Hotel, 15 Church St, SP4 7EU	01980 623163	http://antrobushotel.co.uk	-
18	27.0	141	D	Amesbury	♠ ⚲	Mandalay Guest House, 15 Stonehenge Rd, SP4 7BA	01980 623733	www.mandalayguesthouse.com	-
18	13.2	143	A	Salisbury	▲ ⚲	Salisbury C&CC, Hudson's Field, Castle Rd, SP11 3SA	01722 320713	www.campingandcaravanningclub.co.uk	-
18	1.2	143	B	Salisbury	♠ ≈	Victoria Lodge, 61 Castle Rd, SP1 3RH	01722 320586	www.victoria-guest-house.co.uk	0.3 km (→ via Ashley Rd, rndabt ↑, T-jct ←)
18	1.9	143	C	Salisbury	⚲	Stonehenge Cycles, 86 Fisherton St, SP2 7QY	01722 327851	www.stonehengecycles.com	0.4 km (ep → via bridge, keep ↑, T-jct →)
18	2.4	143	D	Salisbury	♠ ≈	Cathedral Hotel, 7-9 Milford St, SP1 2AJ	01722 343700	www.cathedralhotelsalisbury.com	-
18	2.4	143	D	Salisbury	♠ ≈	City Lodge, 33 Milford St, SP1 2AP	01722 326600	www.citylodge.co.uk	0.1 km (← via Milford St)
18	3.4	143	E	Salisbury	♠ ⚲	St. Ann's House, 32-34 St Ann St, SP1 2DP	01722 335657	www.stannshouse.co.uk	-
19	9.8	144	A	Downton	♠ ≈	The Bull Hotel, The Headlands, SP5 3HL	01725 510374	www.bullhoteldownton.com	1.2 km (at T-jct →, at lhts →)
19	21.7	145	A	Nomansland	▲ ⚲	Green Hill Farm, New Rd, Langford, SP5 2AZ	01794 324117	http://greenhillfarm.co.uk	1.3 km (at T-jct ← to Langford)
19	26.4	145	B	Fritham	▲ ≈	Forest Camping - Ocknell, Lyndhurst, SO43 7HH	02380 812740	www.campingintheforest.co.uk	1.6 km (↑ to Stoney Cross)

Rte	Km	Page	Ref	Town	Info	Name, address and postcode	Phone (+ 44)	Internet	Distance to route & extra directions
19	43.8	146	A	Brockenhurst	♠ ⚲	Meerut B&B, Fibbards Rd, SO42 7RD	01590 623129	www.meerut.co.uk	0.1 km (← opposite Tesco Express)
19	43.9	146	B	Brockenhurst	♠ ⚲	Cottage Lodge Hotel, Sway Rd, SO42 7SH	01590 622296	http://cottagelodge.co.uk	0.1 km (→ via Sway Rd)
19	0.0	147	A	Brockenhurst	⚲ hire	New Forest Cycle Hire, Station Car Park, SO42 7TW	01590 624808	www.newforestcyclehire.co.uk	0.5 km (station route, on south side of station)
19	0.0	147	A	Brockenhurst	♠ ☎	The Huntsman of Brockenhurst, Lyndhurst Rd, SO42 7RH	01590 622225	http://thehuntsmanofbrockenhurst.com	0.5 km (station route, on north side station)
19	1.1	147	B	Brockenhurst	▲ ☎	Forest Camping - Hollands Wood, Lyndhurst Rd, SO42 7QH	01590 622967	www.campingintheforest.co.uk	0.4 km (↑ via footpath next to main rd)
19	5.2	147	C	Brockenhurst	▲ ⚲	Forest Camping - Roundhill, Beaulieu Rd, SO42 7QL	01590 624344	www.campingintheforest.co.uk	2.2 km (↑, 1st gravel ⚲, 1st gravel ←)
19	11.8	147	D	East Boldre	♠ ☎	Turfcutters Arms, Main Rd, SO42 7WL	01590 612331	www.the-turfcutters-new-forest.co.uk	-
20	0.0	148	A	Yarmouth	♠ ☎	The Bugle Inn, The Square, PO41 0NS	01983 760272	www.thebugleinn.co.uk	0.2 km (walk ← via River Rd/Bridge Rd)
20	0.0	148	A	Yarmouth	♠ ⚲	Jireh House B&B, St James Square, PO41 0NP	01983 760513	www.jireh-house.com	0.1 km (walk ← via River Rd/Bridge Rd)
20	0.6	148	B	Yarmouth	⚲ hire	Wight Cycle Hire, Station Rd, Yarmouth Station, PO41 0QT	01983 761800	www.wightcyclehire.co.uk	0.2 km (at bridleway jct ↙ via ⚲)
20	3.8	148	C	Freshwater	⚲	Adrian's Bike Shop, 131a School Green Rd, PO40 9BB	01983 755007	www.adriansbikeshop.com	0.1 km (at rndabt →)
20	4.4	148	D	Freshwater	♠ ⚲	Buttercup House B&B, Camp Rd, PO40 9HL	01983 752772	http://buttercuphouse.co.uk	-
20	6.0	148	E	Totland	▲ ⚲	Stoats Farm Camping, Weston Ln, PO39 0HE	01983 755258	http://stoats-farm.co.uk	-
20	6.2	148	F	Totland	♠ ☎	Highdown Inn, Highdown Ln, PO39 0HY	01983 752450	www.highdowninn.com	0.3 km (at KP 76 →)
20	6.2	148	G	Totland	⚶ ⚲	YHA Totland, Hurst Hill, PO39 0HD	0845 3719348	www.yha.org.uk	0.5 km (at jct Highdown Inn → via Weston Ln)
20	1.4	149	A	Freshwater Bay	♠ ⚲	Albion Hotel, Gate Ln, PO40 9RA	01983 755755	www.albionhotel.co.uk	-
20	7.2	149	B	Brook	♠ ⚲	Clock House B&B, PO30 4EJ	01983 741212	www.clockhousebrook.co.uk	0.4 km (at jct ↗ into Brook, on the Alt. Route!)
20	2.7	149	C	Brighstone	♠ ⚲	Chilton Farm B&B, Chilton Ln, PO30 4DS	01983 740338	www.chiltonfarm.co.uk	-
20	4.5	150	A	Brighstone	⚶ ⚲	YHA Brighstone, North St, PO30 4HX	0845 3719348	www.yha.org.uk	0.1 km (← via North St)
20	4.5	150	A	Brighstone	♠ ⚲	Willses B&B, Upper Ln, PO30 4BA	01983 740438	www.willses.co.uk	0.3 km (← via North St, T-jct →)
20	5.1	150	B	Brighstone	▲ ⚶ ⚲	Grange Farm Brighstone Bay	01983 740296	http://grangefarmholidays.com	0.6 km (↑ via rd with 40 mph limit, at end ↑)
20	8.4	150	C	Brighstone	♠ ⚲	Island Fish Farm B&B, Punthouse Ln, Limerstone, PO30 4PL	01983 740941	www.islandfishfarm.co.uk	-
20	18.8	150	D	Godshill	♠ ☎	Chequers Inn, Rookley, PO38 3NZ	01983 840314	www.chequers-holidays.co.uk	0.3 km (↑ via rd, at T-jct → to rejoin route)
20	25.6	150	E	Newchurch	♠ ⚲	Rosemary Cottage B&B, Langbridge, PO36 0NP	01983 867735	www.rosemarycottagebreaks.co.uk	- (← via rd for 15m)
20	1.6	151	A	Sandown	♠ ⚲	Chadhill Hotel, 7 Hill St, PO36 9DD	01983 403231	www.chadhillhotel.co.uk	-
20	2.0	151	B	Sandown	♠ ☎	Royal Pier Hotel, 10 Pier St, PO36 8JP	01983 403187	www.royalpier.com	-
20	2.6	151	C	Sandown	♠ ☎	Sandringham Hotel, Esplanade, PO36 8AH	01983 406655	www.sandringhamhotel.co.uk	-
20	3.1	151	D	Sandown	♠ ⚲	The Denewood Hotel, 7 Victoria St, PO36 8AL	01983 402980	www.denewood-hotel.co.uk	-
20	0.6	152	A	Brading	▲ ⚲	Camping Club Adgestone, Lower Rd, PO36 0HL	01983 403432	www.campingandcaravanningclub.co.uk	-
20	8.8	152	B	Ryde	▲ ⚲	Roebeck Country Park, Gatehouse Rd, Upton, PO33 4BP	01983 562505	www.roebeckcountrypark.co.uk	-
20	11.0	152	C	Ryde	⚲ hire	TAV Cycles, 140-140a High St, PO33 2RE	01983 812989	http://tavcycles.co.uk	0.2 km (at 1st jct with lhts →, 2nd rd ←)
20	11.8	152	D	Ryde	♠ ⚲	Seahaven House B&B, 35-36 Thomas St, PO33 2DL	01983 563069	www.seahavenhouse.co.uk	-
20	0.2	153	A	Portsmouth	♠ ☎	The George Hotel, 84 Queen St, PO1 3HU	02392 753885	http://thegeorgehotel.org.uk	-